The
Academic
Imperative

The
Academic
Imperative

A Reassessment of Christian Education's Priorities

Richard A. Riesen

purposeful design.
p u b l i c a t i o n s

Colorado Springs, Colorado

Purposeful Design Publications is the publishing division of the Association of Christian Schools International (ACSI) and is committed to the ministry of Christian school education, to enable Christian educators and schools worldwide to effectively prepare students for life. As the publisher of textbooks, trade books, and other educational resources within ACSI, Purposeful Design Publications strives to produce biblically sound materials that reflect Christian scholarship and stewardship and that address the identified needs of Christian schools around the world.

The views expressed in this publication are those of the author, and they may not necessarily represent the position of the Association of Christian Schools International.

Unless otherwise identified, all Scripture quotations are taken from the New Revised Standard Version Bible © 1989 by the Division of Christian Education of the National Council of the Churches of Christ in the United States of America.

Printed in the United States of America
16 15 14 13 12 11 10   2 3 4 5 6 7

Riesen, Richard A.
The Academic Imperative
ISBN 978-1-58331-099-1   Catalog #6608

Designer: Julia Evans

Editorial team: John Conaway, Christina Nichols

Purposeful Design Publications
A Division of ACSI
PO Box 65130 • Colorado Springs, CO 80962-5130

Customer Service: 800-367-0798 • Website: www.acsi.org

Contents

FOREWORD

Richard Riesen is a giant; a giant thinker, questioner, and "reasoner." He does not think small. He is not afraid to raise questions that so many would rather not challenge—and then offer sound reasons for his conclusions. Several times while reading books by Dr. Riesen, I have said to myself, "Where was this guy when I first began life as an educator?"

Now, if you have a bit of a problem with challenging "conventional wisdom," whatever that is, or asking "why?" about some of the things in education that have somehow and someway become standard and accepted practice, then you might not get overly excited about *The Academic Imperative*. On the other hand—I assure you—if you believe that you might still have a bit to learn, you will be challenged and invigorated by Riesen's foray into reevaluating some of the ways we do Christian schooling.

As a matter of fact, you may find yourself more likely saying, "Why didn't I think of that?" In your reading it will very soon be discovered that Riesen is not one who simply creates ideas in his head then bounces them out there as some new and brilliant insight. Rather it becomes evident very quickly that he is a prolific reader who thoughtfully articulates discoveries and experiences of the past. He is not one to generalize and extrapolate a complex new conclusion based upon an isolated historical event or report. What he reads and responds to is not shallow stuff.

He takes the task and responsibility of Christian schooling seriously. He refuses to substitute intense academic fervor with spiritual platitudes (as some people might do because of a notion that Christian schooling ought to be about all things spiritual). Rather, he makes a powerful case for the role of academic excellence, high academic expectation, and hence high academic achievement in the life of one who is a follower of Jesus. He takes very seriously the distinctiveness of Christian schooling—of the integration of faith and learning. For him the result is not a recipe for hash stew—but rather a recipe for education cuisine that reflects the ability to identify the unique flavors of the ingredients that were included for an intended purpose.

He is a master at bringing to our attention how we in the Western world rather easily make synonymous things that are not. One issue addressed quite effectively is the generalization that implies that democracy and Christianity are the same thing. The point is not one of demeaning democracy; rather, it raises the standard of understanding about what Christianity truly is and alerts us to the tremendous danger of depicting Christianity as something not only greatly different but unbelievably less significant than it really is or less important to the development and maintenance of democracy. It is seriousness about both Christianity and democracy that he is after.

Riesen will very effectively challenge the notion that a utilitarian approach to teaching and learning is the most appropriate direction for education. And in this pursuit he offers a robust consideration of the critical role of leisure both from the aspect of how we ought to teach about it and at the same time how it ought to more effectively become a part of the greater education experience.

Examples of the effectiveness of his writing are the convincing cases he makes for the Socratic method of teaching and the importance of a liberal arts education. In the matter of the Socratic approach, he takes great pains to articulate both how and why he is convinced that it is a most effective strategy to nurture learning. He debunks erroneous concepts about Socratic methodology with explicit rationale and clarity. He simply does not take shortcuts on matters of importance.

My point in these introductory remarks about Richard Riesen and his latest work, *The Academic Imperative*, is clearly not to provide a review of the book but rather to extol his effectiveness in challenging educators—and in particular, those engaged in educating from a distinctively Christian perspective—that what we do and how we do it really is important. And I must add that when describing this author as a "giant"—in terms of thinking, questioning, and reasoning—I must add, he is a gentle one at that. His perspectives are not thrust upon the reader militaristically but rather with a gently persuasive reasonableness, always with room for challenge.

And so, it is with enthusiasm that I say with genuine conviction, "Read on!" It is highly possible that you, as a follower of Christ committed to effective teaching, just might become a better one tomorrow than you are today—and the Christian school movement as a whole just might have the opportunity to become even more effective tomorrow than it is today. And I am convinced that Richard Riesen will have played no small part in bringing our attention to matters of importance.

Ken Smitherman
Former President
Association of Christian Schools International

PREFACE

The first draft of this book I wrote well before the economic troubles of 2008 and 2009. When I asked (in the introduction), "What if, heaven forbid, the resources dried up—there were a major recession or depression—and we could not do all that we are currently doing?" it was therefore largely a rhetorical question. Like most of us, I had no idea how dire the situation might get. At the time I could see only continued prosperity, at least for the already prosperous. I could also see, as everyone could, the growing gap between the haves and have-nots, and it was that gap, especially apparent in the closing of so many Christian schools, chiefly in urban areas, that was primary among my reasons for writing.

It was not my only reason, however. With or without the widening gap, I thought, and still think, that the variety and sophistication of what some of us are accomplishing, and nearly all the rest of us want to accomplish, in the name of Christian education, is not in every case good. It may be bad. It may be distracting us from, or obscuring the importance of, first things, or simply rendering them less attractive as they compete with other things.

So while the financial crisis may require some of us to cut back on or eliminate what is no longer affordable, it may at the same time force all of us to focus on what is paramount, and to rethink what that is.

This book is a modest attempt to stimulate such rethinking. It is about one or two related issues as well—how we can do what we do simpler and better, as well as less expensively, for instance—but mostly about that.

Acknowledgments

I owe a very great deal to the encouragement of my friends at ACSI—Dr. Ken Smitherman, Dr. Derek Keenan, and Steve Babbitt. Their gracious reviews of the early drafts of this book are what made its publication a reality. Also Christina Nichols, editor at Purposeful Design, whose easy expertise and prompt, courteous responses to my (many) questions made negotiating the technical issues easy, even pleasant; and John Conaway, who read *Leisure, the Basis of Culture* long before I did (probably only he will appreciate the significance of that), and who likewise knows a thing or two about editing. The cover was designed by Julia Evans and is based on that for *School and Sports* and *Piety and Philosophy* (second edition) by Kristen Johnson. I am indebted to both ladies. My greatest debt, as always, is to my wife, Florence, and my son, Peter.

Introduction

Unless we change our direction, we are likely to end up where we are headed.

—Old Chinese Proverb

If there is one thing Christian educators will agree on it is that our enterprise is getting too expensive. Regardless of denomination or vision or mission—or even, often enough, location—a disquieting proportion of us are learning that our future could be in jeopardy. All across the country, Christian schools are closing. Even Roman Catholic schools, long reckoned inviolable, are unable in places to keep their doors open. Absent substantial endowments and generous donors there is not the wherewithal.

It is a vicious cycle. Less-well-off schools, typically serving lower-middle or lower-income families, can raise rates only at the risk of losing students for whom even a minimal increase may be too much; neither can they provide the kinds of facilities or extracurricular bells and whistles that would draw those capable of paying more. They are caught, unable to retain the students they want to help, and equally unable to compete with the wealthier school five miles down the road. In the opinion of those who know about these things, we may be headed for a future in which we will have a few excellent schools serving only the well-to-do.

Is there a solution? Are there ways to begin reordering the enterprise to make it less costly but also better? I think so. I do not subscribe to the view that in education big or high-priced is always superior, although admittedly it is difficult to resist the temptation to think that the affluent schools are the best schools—because they often are. In any case, a few excellent schools serving only the well-do-do cannot be healthy, not even, if you think about it, for the well-to-do, certainly not from a Christian perspective.

What if, heaven forbid, the resources dried up—there were a major recession or depression—and we could not do all that we are currently doing? Would some of us be forced to close shop? Or would we have already been considering ways to pare down, get leaner and also meaner?

In another book, *School and Sports: A Christian Critique* (2007), I tendered the judgment that for most of us athletics had become too important—taking up too much time and energy, too distracting, too expensive; threatening to undermine our essential, fundamentally academic purposes.

Here I want to suggest that other programs or practices might pose a similar threat. Not everywhere, of course, but in many places "school" has come to mean something like "an educational experience," consisting of a genuine emphasis on academic rigor, to be sure, but set against the background of a plethora of activities, some reinforcing intellect, some not, from Advanced Placement courses on one end to cheerleading tournaments on the other, with an almost limitless variety of classes, clubs, competitions, and "cocurriculars" in between. Way more is going on than reading, writing, and arithmetic. That is both positive and negative.

Positive in that all study all the time is not salutary either. The busyness may even be required, in the sense, as I said, that you cannot compete with Prep or St. Sebastian if you offer less. I understand that. But that fact too should give us pause.

And let us admit it, the increase in course offerings, music, art, and sports, along with the concomitant expansion of staff and plant, is very impressive, requiring enviable organizational and entre-preneurial skill, wisdom, and foresight. Would that all Christian schools enjoyed such resources!

I wonder, though (this is the negative part), whether we have come to the place where we could take time out for a little reassessment. Might it be helpful to ask ourselves whether we have become too successful? Is all this sophistication beneficial? By "beneficial" I mean, does it advance our purposes *as a school*? Does it make for the kind of careful, not to say creative, thinking we Christians ought to be expecting from those we teach? In a world threatened by ideological conflict abroad and political ignorance or indifference, not to mention culture wars, at home, can we afford to spread ourselves so thin? Do we not have an obligation to direct our energies to nurturing healthy intellects, as John Henry Newman put it, and, further, to producing citizens who can bring an educated Christian intelligence to bear on the issues that confront us? We may need to do less but do it better—simplify, prioritize, concentrate.

Thus the chapter "We've Got Too Much Going On," followed by "Education and Liberty." The point of that juxtaposition is that some things are simply and obviously more important than others. It is much more important, to name but one, to be training thinkers than it is to be training leaders, as so many Christian schools profess to do—unless we mean by "leaders" those who are also thinkers. A leader, after all, may be one who is merely adept at galvanizing the mass of opinion already held, figuring out what everyone is saying and saying it louder, or who is charismatic or popular. History, however, is evidence that those who make the most difference are those who perceive and comprehend, who get at the truth—and isn't that what schools are supposed to be about? Apart from a soul rightly ordered to and by God, clear thought is the one thing most needful, not only for our own sanity but for the sake of our nation's future. That is the case being made in chapters 3 and 4.

Chapter 5 argues for leisure, too little appreciated, but required, to my mind, if we are to produce the understanding vital for the maintenance of liberty, no less the intellectual salt and light we in Christian schools ought to aspire to. Chapter 5, in other words, provides part of the corrective to the problem raised in chapter 3.

In chapter 6 I give reasons for a style of teaching—what is sometimes called the Socratic method—that may encourage both the understanding and the leisure we want. It is not the whole answer, of course (no pedagogy is), and its success depends on multiple factors; but among its virtues is that it puts the responsibility for learning where it belongs—on the student. One of the activities we have too much of may be teaching.

Then there is the question of Jesus' teaching, which, some have claimed, was itself Socratic. Was it, and does His alleged use of the method confirm our use of it? If not, are we therefore justified in rejecting it, and how then to characterize how He taught? Jesus was preeminently a teacher. He is also our example. But for all the exhortation to "teach like Jesus," the subject is not as straightforward as it might appear. That's chapter 7.

"For Their Own Sakes" (chapter 8) is a defense of the liberal arts, disciplines long considered their own end, and a critique, in part, of the current obsession with "usefulness" in education, specifically that sort of usefulness that seeks to prepare students for vocation, but in the process fails to educate for healthy intellect, and so, truly, even for vocation.

Chapter 9 tries to sort out what "the liberal arts" are. It is a phrase often used but that seems to represent various things to various people. If we are going to have a meaningful conversation about "the importance of the liberal arts," as we should, it might be helpful to face some of the complexities of the subject.

The final chapter is where the rubber most troublesomely meets the road. A liberal and academic education for everyone may or may not be desirable, depending on one's convictions. But is it practicable? Or is it, as some would be happy to tell us, another perk enjoyed by the cognitively gifted or those privileged enough to attend "the better schools"?—an important question, especially in a democracy, but certainly not one that affords easy answers.

All of that must be preceded by some elaboration on the meaning of "education," its point and purpose, derived largely from classical and pagan sources (chapter 1), and, hence, how Christians should think about it (chapter 2).

Before we begin, though, an apologia, an assurance, and an admission. None may be required, but just in case. Also two notes.

The apologia. Throughout this book, notably in quotations from older writers, the pronoun of choice is "he" rather than "she," the reason being that for most of those writers education was largely a male privilege. That they wrote as they did is a reflection of cultural realities, as well as linguistic custom. The current preoccupation with political correctness on this issue is a recent phenomenon.

I have myself mixed up the pronouns from time to time, but with no very serious attempt to be "inclusive" or "gender neutral." No less do I dislike the awkwardness of "he/she," "his/her," "him/her," and similarly self-conscious constructions. (Have I used "she" as often as "he"? Did I say "women and men" as often as "men and women"?) Jacques Barzun, distinguished American historian of culture, has it, in my opinion, exactly right: "The truth is that any sex-conscious practice defeats itself by sidetracking the thought from the matter at hand to a social issue—an important one, without question. And on that issue, it is hardly plausible to think that tinkering with words will do anything to enhance respect for women among people who do not feel any, or increase women's authority and earnings in places where prejudice is entrenched" (2000, 83).

The word of assurance. This is a book about the importance of liberal learning. It is by no means, however, about the all-sufficiency of liberal or any other kind of learning, as no Christian could believe in the all-sufficiency of anything or anyone but Christ. We are within our rights, perhaps especially as teachers and school administrators, to extol the virtues of education. We are not within our rights as Christians to claim for it more than is its due. Intelligently managed it may have immense benefits, may in fact be indispensable for democratic institutions, but it cannot redeem men or make them good. There are too many evil men who are superbly educated and too many honest men who enjoy no education at all. Both stand as evidence against exalted claims for the power of knowing. Every day likewise brings fresh revelations that neither are the learned always wise. We will have gleaned as much from our Bibles. Men need primarily to be saved.

The admission. As I watch the news and read the papers; as I attempt to take in the enormity of the crisis of education in this country—inner-city youth largely, largely minority, who can hardly read or write or add when they ought to be explicating Shakespeare and negotiating logarithms—as I am weighed down, as we all are, by the seeming hopelessness of the situation and the tragedy of those individual lives, not to say the consequences for our country's future, I confess that I question the relevance, or rightness, of a book on liberty, leisure, and good learning. Is this not fiddling while Rome burns, the moral equivalent of discriminating between fine wines when our neighbors have nothing to eat? I'm not sure.

What I do know is that (a) there are private and Christian schools, (b) they were established for good reasons (and long before public schools), and (c) we who tend them are obligated before God to do our work to the best of our ability. We cannot serve everyone; and while it behooves us to take with utmost seriousness the plight of those less fortunate than ourselves, educationally no less than in other more obvious or pressing ways, it is equally our duty to think carefully and cogently about what it means to educate Christianly, and to carry out our task with the long, rich tradition of Christian scholarship, as well as the deepest spiritual concerns of Christ's kingdom, in view.

That entails, in my judgment, nothing less than the highest academic standards on the one hand, and a deep awareness of our own sin and weakness and humble dependence on the mercy of God on the other.

But neither of those priorities is incompatible with our responsibilities to the less fortunate. As I hope this book will demonstrate, the sharper our focus the simpler our task will be; also less expensive—or so it would seem. Thereby might we be in a better position to do something about what is becoming the foremost obstacle to Christian schooling in our day: its affordability.

I am aware that there is another solution—in the wealthier schools taking it upon themselves to provide financial aid to families to attend these same schools. It is a noble cause being nobly prosecuted by some of the best Christian (and nonsectarian) schools in the country, and may be the way out of our dilemma. It would be a blessed thing if the practice were extended, its great boon being that, apart from enlightening those who most need, in many (not all) cases, to appreciate and appropriate the benefits of an education, it provides the opportunity for those already so privileged to share the amplitude.

My worry is that it inclines in its own way to reinforce the belief that a good education takes lots of money. The requirements for teaching modern science have upped the ante, it is true, but for thousands of years some of the best minds were taught in remarkably modest, even reduced, circumstances—in one-room schoolhouses, or by pastor-fathers at home, or in a handful of famous cases with no teacher or school at all. Granted that this is not and never has been a scheme applicable to instructing large numbers of students, the principle remains: education need not be expensive.

But that is another book, and a topic about which I know too little. For this book we must begin at the beginning, with an elaboration, as I said, on what we intend by "education," its point and purpose.

The notes:

1. I am aware that there is a useful distinction to be made between "Christian education" and "Christian schooling," the former having to do usually with the more or less specifically academic aspect of the undertaking, the latter with its broader function, including the spiritual, moral, social, and physical welfare of students. In this book, however, I employ the two phrases pretty much interchangeably.

2. All quotations from the Bible are from the New Revised Standard Version, unless otherwise indicated or included in a citation from another work, in conformity with current practice.

One

The Point and Purpose of Education: The Western Tradition

On one occasion [Aristotle] was asked how much educated men were superior to those uneducated; "As much," said he, "as the living are to the dead."

—Diogenes Laertius, *The Lives and Opinions of Eminent Philosophers*

Of making many books there is no end, and much study is a weariness of the flesh.

—Ecclesiastes 12:12

The point and purpose of education? Establishing this is absolutely fundamental. Discussion of anything else—curriculum or extracurricular activities or whom to hire—is impossible without it.

The point of education is broadly and simply the three Rs in the form of the liberal arts, which the dictionary defines as "the studies (as language, philosophy, history, literature, abstract science) in a college or university intended to provide chiefly general knowledge and to develop the general intellectual capacities (as reason and judgment) as opposed to professional or vocational skills" (Merriam-Webster, Incorporated 2003, 716). General knowledge and general intellectual capacities, course content and the skills developed in coming to grips with that content. What else could be the aim of courses in English, history, math, science, and so on, and not one or some of them, but all of them together? And even though the dictionary says that the liberal arts belong to college or university, the increasing tendency of colleges and universities to emphasize training for career (according to a 2001 report from the Carnegie Institute [Ansary], 60 percent of all undergraduates are pursuing a technical or preprofessional degree) argues the necessity for elementary and secondary schools to bear the larger responsibility for such work.

An extended discussion of the liberal arts, what they are and what they are for, makes up chapter 9, but for the time being the dictionary definition is exactly the one we want, for two reasons. First, it aptly describes the curriculum of almost any school that calls itself one; it is in fact what I mean by "reading, writing, and arithmetic" or "what most schools do." Second, it gets it right about the purposes of curriculums of this kind. "General knowledge" and "general intellectual capacities" is the tidy and accurate way to express what are, one hopes, the direct results of being exercised by them: philosophy teaches both what has been thought and how to think philosophically; history teaches what has happened and the skills for analyzing why it happened; literature, what has been written and how to read it; science, scientific knowledge and how to proceed scientifically; and so on. These are purposes of a liberal arts education that grow naturally out of the liberal arts themselves. Nothing either complex or vague is required to explain how we get from courses taught to mission or vision statement, from means to stated end, or the other way around.

WHERE IT ALL CAME FROM

This scheme of education—general, academic, and varied—is a product of Western (Greco-Roman and Judeo-Christian) civilization. Its development began in ancient Greece and found its mature form in the fourth and third centuries BC, during that period in Greek history known as the Hellenistic, and was set up to teach the skills of reading, writing, and calculating in their most rudimentary and practical sense, but at its most expansive, to exercise and elevate the powers of the human intellect, even to nurture the individual soul. The Greeks referred to it as the *paideia*; but from its original definition of discipline, instruction, training (*paidion* is the Greek word for "child"; from it we get our words *pedagogue, pedagogy, pediatrics*, etc.), it came to denote the process by which Greek man was enabled "to realize ever more perfectly the human ideal" (Marrou 1956, 98). It signified "'culture'—not in the sense of something active and preparational like education, but in the sense that the word has for us today—of something perfected: a mind fully developed, the mind of a man who has become truly man" (99).

THE TRANSCENDENT AIMS OF EDUCATION

"A man who has become truly man." That brings us to what we might call the overarching or transcendent aims of education—because there has always been more to it than reading, writing, and arithmetic. "Education means," as Marrou reminds us, "essentially, moral training, character-training, a whole way of life" (1956, 147). Of education among the Athenians, another commentator says, "It is character rather than erudition at which the teacher must aim. It is what is just and unjust, honourable and dishonourable, holy and unholy that is instilled into the child from his very earliest years, even from his birth" (Barclay 1959, 104).

The precise goals of ancient Greek education are not easy to pin down, however. They are variously described as "culture," "character and taste," "the symmetrical development of body, mind, and imagination" (Freeman 1922, 43), or, in Marrou's estimate, "the achievement of the fullest and most perfect development of the personality," "a particular style of living—the style that distinguished man from the brutes, Greeks from barbarians," as well as "a mind fully developed, the mind of a man who has become truly man" (1956, 98–99).

It is possible of course that the goals of Greek education were all of those things, or were the same thing diversely interpreted or expressed, each a change on the theme of realizing "ever more perfectly the human ideal"; for, as Marrou suggests, this is "but the principle behind all education, pushed to its furthest limit and made absolute" (1956, 98). Education of whatever kind is always an attempt in some way to reform and refine the human being. That is what it should do—and all it can do. The Greek rhetorician and satirist Lucian of Samosata (AD c. 117–c. 180) summed it up like this: "We have not thought it sufficient for each man to be as he was born, either in body or in soul, but we want education and disciplines for them by which their good traits may be much improved and their bad altered for the better" (1961, 33). We might say that education's job, like the Army's, is to help us be all we can be.

PURPOSE VS. CURRICULUM

Whether all ancient Greeks agreed on the general purposes of education, not all agreed on the curriculum. The Athenian orator Isocrates (436–338 BC), for example, argued that education was essentially literary and practical; math was included, certainly, but the emphasis was on the arts of persuasion (rhetoric) and learning by "example" and "imitation," by "the study and criticism of first-class models," in the Homeric tradition (Marrou 1956, 84). Plato (427?–347 BC), on the other hand, advocated a more philosophic approach, building on "a fundamental belief in truth, and on the conquest of truth by rational knowledge" (66). Math, pure math, was indispensable in Plato's view, "necessitating as it clearly does the use of the pure intelligence in the attainment of pure truth" (*Republic* 526; Jowett 1952, 394).

Most interesting, Plato, contrary to Isocrates, eschewed Homer and Hesiod. The stories told to children, he urged, must be the right stories, especially those concerning the gods, more especially those concerning the gods' misbehavior, and may have to be censored. "The doings of Cronus, and the sufferings which in turn his son inflicted upon him, even if they were true, ought certainly not to be lightly told to young and thoughtless persons; if possible, they had better be buried in silence"—for if a young man should do to his father what Hesiod said Uranus did to Cronus, "he will only be following the example of the first and greatest among the gods," will have, in other words, honored sanction for his crimes. A Homer: "all the battles of the gods in Homer—these tales must not be admitted into our State, whether they are supposed to have an allegorical meaning or not. For a young person cannot judge what is allegorical and what is literal; anything that he receives into his mind at that age is likely to become indelible and unalterable; and therefore it is most important that the tales which the young first hear should be models of virtuous thoughts" (*Republic* 378; Jowett 1952, 321).

As we shall discover in chapter 9, there is scholarly debate in some quarters over whether Isocrates and Plato agreed on what I have called the transcendent aims of education—whether virtue was primary for both—but it does seem as if both, like Lucian, saw education as a means of making human beings better, no less morally than intellectually. At least it is pretty clear, in passages like the ones quoted, that whatever his disagreements with Isocrates over the shape of the curriculum, or however much he seemed to emphasize pure truth arrived at by pure thought, Plato was not indifferent to the character education of the young.

School vs. Education

What is highly significant, however, is that although the fundamental goal of education in the ancient world was in an important (if not always agreed upon) sense moral, the school was not the sole or primary source of that education. "The schoolmaster was only responsible for one small section of children's education—the mental side," says Marrou. Character training was the responsibility of the parents, or, often enough, the pedagogue; and despite the fact that the pedagogue was a (mere) slave, "through his daily contact with the child, and his example—whenever possible—and at any rate by his precepts and the careful watch he kept over him, he made a far greater contribution to his education, especially his moral education, than the purely technical lessons provided by the schoolmaster" (1956, 147).

The relevance of this for our own educating is obvious. Who should be responsible for the character as opposed to the academic training of our children? These days the responsibility for both is frequently left to the teacher, because "education," for us, often *means* "school." The reason is found in the history of Christian influences on early European culture. "The connection between elementary education and moral training," says Marrou, "which seems so natural to us today, is a heritage from the Middle Ages—to be more precise, from monastic schools, in which the same person found himself obliged to unite two quite distinct roles—that of the school-teacher and that of the spiritual father. In antiquity the schoolmaster was far too insignificant a person for any family to think of giving him the responsibility of educating its children, as it so often does today" (1956, 147).

The identification of "education" and "school" accordingly belongs to a later, medieval development in Christian ideas of learning. For the ancients the two rarely if ever were the same thing. Marrou cites as evidence one of the innumerable treatises "On the Education of Children" which the Greco-Roman age produced, wherein there are one or two comments on secondary schooling as a preparation for philosophy, or the value of a good memory, but "the rest is devoted entirely to the moral atmosphere which should surround education. And this is not so much a matter of instruction in the strict sense as of the formation of character, and for this the school was not recognized as being important" (1956, 147–48).

"Christian Education"

Interestingly, early Christians tended to hold similar views. The expression "Christian education," Marrou tells us, was first used in about AD 96 by St. Clement of Rome (fl. ca. 90–100), but it did not mean what we mean by it today.

> When we speak of "Christian education" today we usually mean that the child should be brought up in a Christian atmosphere—especially at school. We must remember that the Christians of the early Church meant something much more precise and much deeper by the phrase, something essentially religious. They meant, on the one hand, learning

the dogmas—the truths necessary for salvation; and, on the other, moral training—the laws of Christian behaviour.... Christian education, in the sacred, transcendent meaning of the word, could not be given at school like any other kind of education, but only in and through the Church on the one hand and the family on the other.

This Christian education of children, through which they learnt to share in the treasury of the faith, to submit to a healthy discipline in the matter of morals, was the parents' fundamental duty.... And this duty could not be delegated: the early Church would have had sharp words to say about "Christian" parents of today who think that they have done all that is required of them when they have passed their children over to a teacher or an institution. (1956, 314)

In the first Christian centuries, then, we have a scheme of education that could be seen as three-tiered: "school" was limited to academic instruction by a paid teacher, as in our own time; training in character or morality was the responsibility of the home; and inculcation in the things of the faith was done by the Church.

This scheme was very different from the one we have nowadays. For one thing, "never throughout the whole of antiquity, except for a few particular cases," according to Marrou, "did the Christians set up their own schools. They simply added their own specifically religious kind of training—which, as we have seen, came from the Church and the family—on to the classical teaching that they received along with their non-Christian fellows in the established schools" (1956, 317–18).

The reason Christians didn't set up their own schools, Marrou maintains—this is critical for an understanding of the subject—was that they had other priorities. Christianity, he says, "is first and foremost a religion, something that determines the relationship between God and man, not essentially, or primarily, a cultural ideal, a way of managing life on this earth.... The early generations of Christians had not worked out any specifically Christian form of education, any more than they had worked out a Christian system of politics. They put first things first, and they laid the rock-bottom foundations of any Christian civilization to come: a system of dogma, a system of morals, canonical discipline, and the liturgy" (1956, 318–19). Early Christianity, we could say, was busy about faith, not learning.

The fact that there obtained this working synthesis between Christianity and classical culture concerning education did not mean that there were no difficulties in the relationship overall. Indeed "there was a profound gulf between this culture and Christianity," claims Marrou (1956, 319). Many are the comments from Christians of the time condemning the classical "for being an independent ideal hostile to the Christian revelation" (320). Even, in particular cases, some well-known, with regard to learning. The famous question of Tertullian (c. 160/70–c. 215/20), "What indeed has Athens to do with Jerusalem? What concord is there between the Academy and the Church? What between heretics and Christians?" (with its implied answer unequivocally in the negative), suggests the intensity of the reaction (1980, 246). Although the object of Tertullian's scorn was not so much the conflict between faith and learning (as is sometimes mistakenly claimed) as it was attempts to mix pagan philosophy with true religion (thus his reference to "heretics") and thereby produce what he called "a mottled Christianity" (246), the conflict was all too real for some, Augustine (354–430) and Jerome (c. 345–c. 419) among them. Jerome's vivid accounting of his struggles over the issue makes the point: "Suddenly I was caught up in the spirit and dragged before the judgment seat of the Judge; and here the light was so bright, and those who stood around were so radiant, that I cast myself upon the ground and did not dare to look up. Asked who and what I was I replied: 'I am a Christian.' But He who presided said: 'Thou liest, thou art a follower of Cicero and not of Christ. For 'where thy treasure is, there will thy heart be also'" (1954, 35).

For all the agony of Jerome and the others, the practical solution for ordinary Christian parents to the problem of an education system sometimes inimical to Christian convictions was to allow their children to attend classical schools as a matter of necessity— "it being necessary to learn to read." Why necessary? In order for them to participate in religious studies; thus, ironically, "profane studies could not be given up without religious studies becoming impossible." The stipulation was that "the child must know what he was doing and not let himself be affected by the idolatry implicit in the teaching and even in the list of school events: he must behave like someone who knows he is being given poison and takes good care not to drink it." Inoculated against falsehood by the training he had received from his parents and the Church, he would make "the necessary discriminations and adjustments" (Marrou 1956, 321–22).

Tertullian distinguished, curiously, between Christian children being taught in classical schools and Christian teachers teaching in them, allowing the former but not the latter. The Church did not follow Tertullian in both judgments, however. Over the first several Christian centuries the number of Christian teachers in classical schools increased such that "in the fourth century Christians were to be found in all grades of teaching; there were Christians among the lowest schoolteachers and grammarians and Christians occupying the highest chairs of eloquence: in the course of his persecution in 362 Julian the Apostate found Prohaeresius holding the chair in Athens and Marius Victorinus the chair in Rome" (Marrou 1956, 323).

THE FIRST CHRISTIAN SCHOOLS

It was this very persecution under Julian in fact that was responsible for the establishment of history's first real, albeit short-lived, Christian schools. In a virulent official reaction against Christianity, Julian attempted to reestablish the old bond between paganism and classicism and turn Roman schools into an instrument for the return of pagan ideas, and so forbade Christians to teach in them. Could Christians in good conscience then continue to send their children to such schools? Moreover, without the advantage of a classical education, Christians were portrayed as barbarians. In this way did Julian force a counterreaction from the Christian community, heretofore quite comfortable with the educational status quo—and a rather remarkable reaction it was. "Having been ordered by the Emperor to be satisfied with 'going to their Galilean churches and reading Matthew and Luke,' they refused to allow themselves to be thus deprived of their literary inheritance and set to work to produce their own text-books as substitutes for the classics.... They set about rewriting the Pentateuch in the style of Homer, the historical books of the Old Testament in the style of the drama, and so on, using every kind of literary form and all manner of metres, from Menander's comedies to Pindaric odes. The New Testament became a series of Platonic dialogues" (Marrou 1956, 324).

This eminently creative project was transitory, though, as Julian's ban was lifted, on his death, in January 364, and "Christian teachers went back to their chairs, and everything went on as before, the Church accommodating herself to the classical education without any difficulty whatsoever" (Marrou 1956, 324).

That was the fourth century. The general situation did not change for a long time. That is, even when Christian teachers and students became the majority, the same classical-Christian balance seemed to hold; and although the fifth and sixth centuries saw an unprecedented interest in theology on the part of both clergy and laity, led by the likes of St. Basil (c. 329–79) in Caesarea, St. John Chrysostom (c. 344/54–407) in Constantinople, St. Ambrose (c. 339–97) in Milan, and St. Augustine in Hippo, "there is nothing to show that they ever created anything like a Christian school. They managed to reach a remarkable level of personal Christian culture, which they spread abroad by preaching and example, and, in the case of Augustine anyway, developed into a complete system of culture; they defined its ends, its methods, its limits. But they made no attempt to turn it into a real system of education. They themselves had been brought up in classical schools, they knew all about their dangers and deficiencies, and they found it natural to try to make the best of them" (Marrou 1956, 328–29).

The Christian response to classical education we might describe as "accommodationist" rather than "separatist." Christians made do with pagan schools, taking from them what was useful, and although keenly aware of the perils of such schools, they did not feel the need, apparently, to set up their own.

AFTER JULIAN

An anomaly in this tradition was the monastery school, developed, also in the fourth century, by the Desert Fathers in Egypt to educate the children (orphans?) they had adopted into their communities. The instruction offered in these schools was ascetic and moral, not intellectual and academic, with the one exception that it insisted on the importance of reading, so that the young could read the Bible. And although there were attempts to extend this type of learning (meant principally to prepare boys to be monks) beyond the monastery, the attempts largely failed. Even St. John Chrysostom, an early enthusiast for monastic education, eventually came to insist, "more emphatically than ever, on the parents' duty to bring up their children in a Christian manner, but he now added that it was the parents' mission, not the monks', to develop their children's religious consciousness" (Marrou 1956, 332).

In the monastic schools of the Christian West (as opposed to Egypt) the situation was different. In part because of the devastation wrought by barbarian invasions and the consequent decline of culture, the monasteries saw themselves as guardians of reading and the written word, as well as the required religious meditation on it. From Augustine on they imbibed a more academic atmosphere. "Books, writing-boards and pens are accepted as part of the monastery's general furniture and setting: even in Western Europe's darkest days the monastery remained a true home of culture" (Marrou 1956, 334).

With the final collapse of Roman civilization in the late fifth and early sixth centuries came the demise as well of the classical school, and the beginning of a second type of Christian school, the episcopal, or cathedral, school—designed, like the monastery school, for a special purpose. "The worse things got, the more difficult it became to find young men who had received the necessary minimum of secular knowledge that would enable them to be trained for the priesthood." It was as a result of the urgent need to train clergy that this type of education became, beyond the confines of the monastery, fairly general in the West (Marrou 1956, 334–35).

THE PARISH SCHOOL: A NEW KIND OF EDUCATION

With the organization of the parish system in the sixth century, along with the conversion of the masses, came the expansion of the episcopal schools into the villages, thus becoming parish schools, and this decision, says Marrou, "must be regarded as a memorable one, for it signified the birth of the modern school, the ordinary village school—which not even antiquity had known in any general, systematic form" (1956, 336). Even though they were, "so to speak, merely technical schools designed to produce monks and clerics," and limited typically to boys, "as soon as the secular schools that had carried on the classical tradition finally disappeared," they became "the only medium whereby culture could be acquired and handed on" (336–37). In truth it was in large part by means of the parish schools that classical culture was transmitted by the Church through that long stretch of early European history we used to refer to as the Dark Ages—no small contribution to Western Civilization! In his famous and once-popular *The Outline of History*, H. G. Wells titles his section on the monasteries and monastic schools "The salvation of learning by Christianity" (1961, viii).

And despite the fact that they were generally poor and obscurantist—"the schoolmasters in these Dark Ages did their best to keep their pupils away from all contact with a culture which they regarded as being far too sympathetic towards pagan traditions"—these schools were the beginnings of "a new kind of education, no mere offshoot of the education of classical antiquity" (Marrou 1956, 338). Devoted to the sacred text of Scripture and so more akin to the old rabbinical than the classical school, they were an attempt to make combined religious and academic instruction available to ordinary boys and (eventually) girls, with a veneration of the teacher, now both instructor and spiritual guide, unknown in pre-Christian Greece and Rome.

BUT WHY SCHOOLS AT ALL?

But surely the important question here, from a Christian point of view, is why schools at all; why anything but, say, catechism? For answer, there is a good deal in Marrou's comment that

"Christianity was an intellectual religion but it was a religion for the masses, and the humblest of the faithful, however elementary their intellectual development, received something equivalent to what the culture of antiquity had haughtily reserved for a philosophical elite—a doctrine about being and life, an inner life and spiritual direction.... This close association, even on the most elementary level, between literary learning and religious education, this synthesis of teacher and spiritual father in the person of the schoolteacher, seems to me [says Marrou] to be the very essence of the Christian school and mediaeval education as contrasted with the education of classical antiquity" (1956, 339). This double concern, that children be given the advantage of academic as well as religious instruction, be it ever so rudimentary (limited in some cases to reading and writing), and that that instruction be made available to the "least of these," regardless of class, has been singularly characteristic of Christian education down the ages, and behind the remarkable spread of Christian schools, the first schools of any kind in many places, throughout the world.

CONCLUSION

The point of education in the West, from its inception in Hellenistic Greece, has been fundamentally the inculcation of what we have called general knowledge and general intellectual capacities. It has been about training the mind—literacy, learning, scholarship—effected almost always by means of the liberal arts.

But not that alone. Even before the Christian conversion of the ancient world, there was a primary emphasis on "character" or "culture" or "a particular style of living." In the Christian era that emphasis was reinforced and, in conformity to the gospel, a spiritual stress added.

What we see in the first four or five Christian centuries is a kind of sampling, in embryo, of the varieties of Christian education that we have had with us ever since: first, the classical school providing liberal and humane studies, with Christian children getting their religious training entirely at home and church; second, the "real" but short-lived Christian schools, established during the persecutions of Julian, with their own textbooks and curriculums, but meant, still, to provide literacy as well as guidance in the faith; third, the exception, the monastic schools of Egypt, designed primarily to prepare boys to be monks; fourth, the monastery schools of the Western Church where there obtained, thanks to Augustine, a more academic atmosphere, which evolved into the village or parish school—this last the Christian invention, as it were, of schools reflecting the close association between literary and religious learning for ordinary people that persisted through the Middle Ages, and is "the very essence of the Christian school and mediaeval education as contrasted with the education of classical antiquity" (Marrou 1956, 339).

And while there was at first a tension between the Greco-Roman and Judeo-Christian ideals, expressed most famously by such Church Fathers as Tertullian, Augustine, and Jerome, the Church finally adopted the classical scheme of education "as all the education necessary for the study of higher truth in Scripture" (Kimball 1986, 41). This adoption was facilitated by the reality that "throughout the Middle Ages, fear of corruption by the liberal arts was to be matched by a reluctant or enthusiastic acceptance of their necessity for the literate Christian" (45). There was too the promise of the liberal arts to teach both truth and virtue, a promise the Church could inform or invigorate for its own uses. Furthermore, following the deposition of the last Roman emperor by barbarians in 476, "Christians tended to view classicism as a lesser threat than barbarism" (49). That is a nice way of putting it—and offers something to think about in the current cultural climate.

The Renaissance and Reformation impressed their own stamp on both Christian and public education (often the same thing), as did Christian humanism, in the fifteenth and sixteenth centuries; and they did so without altering the fundamental academic/religious character of European schools developed in the first six hundred years of the Christian era. That dual character, it might be argued, distinguished most schools, public and private, right up until—when, the 1960s? To our own day, what remains, after all the ups and downs, the to-ing and fro-ing and confrontation, between secular and sacred, is some combination of or balance between academic and, if not specifically religious, then character, training. For all the fuss about "the separation of church and state," the remnants of that same development may be seen (however diluted or disfigured) in programs such as "values clarification" in American government schools today.

That's the story in broad outline. When told like that it may beguile us into thinking that the melding of ancient *paideia* and Christian faith that became the modern school was an almost uninterrupted process, a natural evolution, not without its occasional twists and turns, but relatively unconstrained and probably inevitable.

While true in a general way, that is not all there is to it. From the beginning there has been opposition to secular learning from the faithful, often at the most erudite levels, as we have seen. The history of the modern Christian school movement is itself, in places, one of hesitation and ambivalence toward, if not thinly veiled opposition to, "intellectualism." Only recently have some Christian teachers and administrators begun to embrace the tradition of piety wedded to philosophy—no less respect for philosophy than for piety—that has distinguished Christian education for such a long time. So tenacious has been the anti-intellectual tendency in the Church down the ages that it may be well to look briefly at why it has had such a powerful and perennial appeal; also at why it did not come to dominate, and our response to what did.

T w o

Paideia and Faith: The Christian Response

For "what communion hath light with darkness? And what concord hath Christ with Belial?" How can Horace go with the psalter, Virgil with the gospels, Cicero with the apostle? Is not a brother made to stumble if he sees you sitting at meat in an idol's temple? Although "unto the pure all things are pure," and "nothing is to be refused if it be received with thanksgiving," still we ought not to drink the cup of Christ, and, at the same time, the cup of devils.

—Jerome, Letter XXII

And I confess that I both boast and with all my strength strive to be found a Christian; not because the teachings of Plato are different from those of Christ, but because they are not in all respects similar, as neither are those of the others, Stoics, and poets, and historians. For each man spoke well in proportion to the share he had of the spermatic word, seeing what was related to it…. Whatever things were rightly said among all men, are the property of us Christians.

—Justin Martyr, *The Second Apology*

It should be admitted at the outset that from a strictly biblical point of view it is easy enough to see how it might be thought that education of a genuinely Christian sort has nothing to do with the Hellenistic *paideia* or any of its offspring.

THE CLASSICAL MODEL VS. THE CHRISTIAN MODEL

First of all, the classical model was built on the pre- and non-Christian premise that man is "the centre and 'measure of all things'" and the aim of human existence, therefore, "the achievement of the fullest and most perfect development of the personality" (Marrou 1956, 98). Unlike the ancient Greeks, we Christians are not allowed to think that man is the measure of all things or that the goal of human existence is the fullest and most perfect development of the personality. For us, Christ is the measure of all things and the goal of human existence, man's "chief end" (as *The Westminster Shorter Catechism* has it), to "glorify God, and to enjoy him forever." Given the *paideia*'s humanistic premises, the Christian might argue, we cannot accept it as a model for our educating.

We might also argue, second, that truly biblical education should be committed to devotional or moral objectives. Its emphasis will not be reading, writing, and arithmetic, let alone anything as intellectual as "a mind fully developed." There is nothing about those things in the Bible, although there is plenty about worship, obedience, and righteousness. What the commentators tell us is that the instruction of children required by the Jewish Law was solely ethical and spiritual. It was about wisdom and understanding and conduct, never knowledge as such, certainly not about the mind in the sense of intellect, even less about anything like "culture." After reading the Old Testament we can only smile at the idea of the ancient Jews setting up secondary schools whose purpose was to teach world history or comparative religions or trigonometry, let alone "Women Writers" or "The History of Cinema." Theirs was an entirely different sort of education than the one we have inherited. The New Testament, for its part, has even less to say about either religious or secular education, in fact nothing at all.

Then there are those passages from Scripture itself that seem to be warning us off what is "merely academic." One thinks of Colossians 2:8 ("See to it that no one takes you captive through philosophy and empty deceit, according to human tradition") or 1 Corinthians 1:19–20 (about God's destroying the wisdom of the wise and thwarting the discernment of the discerning—ending with, "Has not God made foolish the wisdom of the world?"). Or Jesus' remarks about His Father having hidden truths from "the wise and intelligent" but revealed them to "infants" (Matthew 11:25–26), and the necessity of becoming "like children" in order to enter the kingdom of heaven (Matthew 18:3; similarly Mark 10:15). If Christian schooling is going to be biblical, therefore (we might contend), it cannot be essentially classical.

So there are reasons for Christians to respond negatively to any suggestion that they ought to be liberally educated, or that education is a Christian thing, if by education is meant what schools ordinarily do. And history will supply us with examples aplenty of Christians who did just that, who renounced education in practice or simply repudiated its pretensions. There is, for instance, the almost arrogant anti-intellectualism of certain Christian groups, ancient and modern, for whom the Bible was the only instruction they required or desired. There is the less arrogant but no less determined opposition of the present-day Christian school parent who piously declares that she is not really interested in academic training, thank you very much, only a caring environment, Christian nurture, and so on—so, please, let's not get too cerebral. There are also grades of resistance, from the louder fundamentalism regularly caricatured by the media to the quieter cynicism of the simple, practical saint whose antipathy to "book learning" can hardly be disguised. I do not mean to draw caricatures myself. These are simply examples that come to mind, taken from my own experience. I mean only to say that Christians down to our own day have, for various reasons and in varying degrees, found Christian grounds for disapproving education of an academic and intellectual kind, that is, of the usual kind; and some of the disapproval, it seems to me, when it is not merely recalcitrant, is arguably tenable from a strictly biblical point of view. The Bible is not, after all, about education.

THE CHRISTIAN ADOPTION OF THE CLASSICAL MODEL

Disapproval has not been, however, the majority Christian response to the classical model for education, as we saw in the previous chapter. The pragmatic reasons for Christianity's adoption of that model I outlined there, basically: Christian children needed to learn to read, as well as write and calculate, and the classical school taught those skills as well as they could be taught; also, the Church was interested primarily not in education but in putting first things first, "a system of dogma, a system of morals, canonical discipline, and the liturgy" (Marrou 1956, 319).

For present purposes Marrou's analysis, from what might be described as the spiritual perspective, is well worth our consideration. You should read it carefully.

> Precisely because they were living in a classical world, the Christians of the early centuries accepted the fundamental category of Hellenistic humanism as "natural" and self-evident—the view of man as an unconditioned source of value existing before any particular specification took place in him. It might be said that before one can be a Christian one must first be a man, mature enough on the purely human level to be able to perform an act of faith and acts of morality. It is a fact established by history and by ethnography that Christianity requires a minimum of civilization as a condition of its existence. So, if classical education had developed its own admirable technique for producing a perfectly developed type of human being, what point was there in looking elsewhere for some other kind of education? However that may be, the moment arrives when on to the fully human being it becomes necessary to graft the purely religious shoot of a supernatural Gift. In some way the unchanging technique of classical humanism made it marvellously apt for having the golden branch of the order of grace grafted on to it. A man educated according to classical standards could become an orator or a philosopher, whichever he liked; he could choose the life of action or the life of contemplation. He was now offered a further choice, with the announcement of Good Tidings: besides these things he could now lay himself open to grace, to faith, could receive the sacrament of baptism, could become a Christian. (1956, 319)

For the cause for which it was established—"to realize ever more perfectly the human ideal" (Marrou 1956, 98), beyond the abilities to read or add and subtract—the classical scheme of education was understood in its own way to be as good as there was, even by Christians. Even for certain Christian purposes. Although it could not bring new life, it might enhance the old. If Lucian was correct in his estimate of the underlying objective of education, to improve a man's good traits and alter his bad for the better, then classical schools did that, or attempted to.

Nor is such an objective contrary to Christian convictions about "using our gifts for the glory of God," "being all that we can be for His service," and the like. I assume that serving God to the best of our ability would not infrequently include a minimum of academic and intellectual refinement, and occasionally a good deal. As Marrou has pointed out and history demonstrated, it is by no means a bad thing if the Christian is, in addition to being God fearing and right living, a more fully formed, and informed, man or woman. We may therefore gladly make the classical education model our own, accepting it for what it is, grateful for the very considerable benefits it offers.

MAKING THE CLASSICAL MODEL OUR OWN

But what does it mean for a Christian to make the classical education model "his own," all the while accepting it "for what it is"?

To make it his own means to embrace it, to believe in its efficacy, to get all he can out of it, as a man might his gift of intellect by good reading or his physical health by regular exercise. It also means to understand that the classical model was developed in a philosophical or theological context that was not Christian, and that Christian presuppositions grounded in the biblical revelation—a "Christian worldview"—must therefore be determinative in his understanding of men and things, even as mediated by his liberal studies. As we learn literature, history, science, and math (for that is what a liberal arts curriculum is), and do so in an academic way (for that is what a liberal arts curriculum requires), we do not forget that Christian belief necessitates, besides faith, hope, and love, thinking Christianly (to use Harry Blamires' phrase), according to the Word as given in Christ and the Scriptures, summarized in the great creeds, and so on. Doctrines cannot be separated from ideas. They *are* ideas.

Even though our commitment to the liberal arts is a commitment to the academic disciplines for their own sakes, the metaphysics (as Gordon Clark calls it) that governs is "the metaphysics of the Being of the Triune God" (1946, 27). For Christians it is belief seeking understanding, not the other way around. Understanding is not thereby rendered unimportant—in education (as opposed, say, to worship) it is of utmost importance—but understanding is not a substitute for belief, as it might be for the secularist. Rather, understanding is informed by belief, as belief is often informed by understanding.

ACCEPTING IT FOR WHAT IT IS

By "accepting the classical model for what it is" I mean "for what it is and no more." I mean that Christians should not confuse the classical model with the biblical model. Whatever we teach—English or math or biology—we will teach "heartily, as to the Lord," as we are admonished to do (Colossians 3:23, KJV), but we should not think that in doing so we are fulfilling the demands of Deuteronomy 6 (requiring parents to instruct their children in the Law) or Proverbs 22:6 (about training children in the right way). Those verses, as any other verses in Scripture, are not about education of a liberal sort.

I am in no way implying that verses from Deuteronomy and Proverbs are not important in the rearing of our children. They are God's Word. If we are Christians we must heed them. I am saying only that such verses were never meant as proof texts for education based on a different model, the Greek model, which is nonetheless our model.

A corollary might be that you cannot squeeze lessons about character or faith out of literature or history by trying to make them teach what you want them, for Christian purposes, to teach. You must not force the text to provide support for your Christian views. If it is to provide such support (and of course it sometimes does), it must do so on its own. The only way that a Faulkner novel or a Shakespeare play can rightly yield instruction concerning how or how not to conduct ourselves in times of adversity or danger or temptation is if we approach the novel or play in as careful, informed, and scholarly a manner as possible, on its own terms and for its own sake. *Hamlet* cannot be used as a tract in a Christian case against the sins of ambition or revenge unless that is what the play itself requires, and what the play itself requires can be determined only by studying it properly. Careful exegesis is prerequisite to moral application. This is true of all reading, the Bible included.

CHRISTIAN WORLDVIEW

But is it not one of the principal objects of Christian education to learn to see the world, including *Hamlet*—and historiography and horticulture, and nearly every subject—"in a Christian way," "in terms of Christian categories," "according to a biblical worldview"? And doesn't what I've just said run counter to such an object?

I don't think so. Because what I intend by "learning to think in Christian categories" does not, or should not, violate the requirement for honest, objective, thorough scholarship. That is, "a Christian point of view" must not mean "sincerely held bias, but without rational or scholarly support."

It is entirely in order to ask whether William Cullen Bryant's "Thanatopsis" is in any sense a Christian poem, or *Lord of the Flies* or *The Scarlet Letter* a Christian novel, what it means for a work of art to be Christian, and the like. That kind of analysis is not only appropriate, it fairly cries out to be made, and is just the sort of exercise that can usefully effect "integration" in literature classes, or, *mutatis mutandis*, almost any class. In the first example we are asked to think in terms of the Christian doctrine of death, in the second the doctrine of sin, in the third the expression of true religion perhaps.

It is quite another thing, in the interests of a Protestant interpretation of history, to assert (as a history textbook from a

Christian publisher does) that "the Italian Renaissance [in contrast to the Reformation] was really a step backwards rather than a step forward." Such a comment fails to acknowledge what almost any history text will make clear: that the Reformation was in some sense a part of or an outgrowth of the Renaissance, that it is difficult to interpret one without the other—thus the coupling of the two in "Ren./Ref." courses. It would also seem a failure to recognize that God often uses "secular" movements to further His ends, as the Scriptures attest throughout.

No more can you say (as a Christian writer has said in a well-intentioned effort to provide biblical support for the pursuit of "extrabiblical" knowledge) that "knowledge is the fruit of study, and knowledge is necessary for wisdom," followed by the claim that even though wisdom begins with reverence for God (Proverbs 1:7), "such reverence alone will not bring wisdom."

It is true that "wisdom" in the Bible does not always refer to the wisdom of God, often to human skills or abilities; but there is no indication that I am aware of that study of an academic sort has anything to do with wisdom of a biblical sort.

The same writer goes on to quote a number of Old Testament passages (Job 28:1–11, Isaiah 19:11–13, Jeremiah 49:7, Zechariah 9:2–4) in support of the notion that the Bible values extrabiblical knowledge and acknowledges the wisdom of cultures outside Israel. In fact, every passage referenced says exactly the opposite. The point of all of them is the *un*wisdom of the nations referred to (or, in the case of the Zechariah passage, even though Tyre and Sidon are "very wise" ["very skillful" in the NIV], the Lord will "strip [Tyre] of its possessions").

What of those attempts, equally well-intentioned, to find Scripture verses legitimizing the various academic disciplines— Colossians 1:16–17, for instance, to justify the study of mathematics, as does a handbook on "integration" that I have seen. Colossians 1:16–17? Yes, for the reason that these verses say that Christ is the creator and upholder of all things, and mathematical concepts, space and number, are included in "all things." Sure—because *all things* are included in "all things"—but that fact suggests nothing about any subject in particular, let alone the study of it, certainly not algebra and geometry more than nouns and verbs, or apples and oranges, or ... There is no lack of examples, in that handbook as elsewhere in Christian education literature, of Scripture thus misused.

There is such a thing as thinking Christianly, and it is the Christian school's responsibility to make sure that students know what it means and how to do it. In a way, it is the Christian school's first responsibility. "A Christian education would primarily train people to be able to think in Christian categories," said T. S. Eliot (1949, 22); but doing so cannot mean intentionally skewed or inadequately considered. If the text doesn't say it you are not allowed to say that it says it, no matter how important you think your case is.

A Christian worldview structures—formats, we might say—the way we approach learning, and so is foundational. It incorporates a Christian epistemology or understanding of how we know things—revelation being one of the important ways—as well as how we see and understand what we know, through the prism, by means of, the Bible's governing ideas: creation, sin, redemption, incarnation, judgment, eternity, and so on. That is what *Christian* scholarship means. (See my *Piety and Philosophy: A Primer for Christian Schools*, chapter 6, for more on how a beginning in this might be made.)

But none of that will count for much unless attended, as I said, by honesty, objectivity, and thoroughness—because that's what Christian *scholarship* means. We want both a Christian worldview and the highest standards of academic integrity, neither to the exclusion of the other. Honesty, objectivity, and thoroughness are, after all, Christian as well as scholarly virtues.

The liberal arts are meant to cultivate other virtues as well, those necessary for the fullest realization of the curriculum's benefits: insight and empathy, literary and artistic sensibility, intuition and common sense, as well as a capacity for reasoning and analysis. I think we assume that.

The larger point is simply that such an education is what it is, a precious gift of Hellenistic culture, to be sure, impressed to some extent by what Marrou calls "the genuine Roman spirit" (1956, 97), and no less refined in its almost incalculable service to Christian civilization—but from a Christian point of view the best method of disciplining the mind, perhaps, but not of discovering the Truth or saving the soul, although by God's grace it sometimes can be, as almost anything can. To use it for training in "the discipline and instruction of the Lord" (Ephesians 6:4) is to ask it to do work it can very inadequately do at best. It is also to miss the blessings that it is intended to bestow. I wonder if in attempting to get biblical instruction by classical means we lose the rewards of both. Christian schools should make the liberal arts curriculum their own—love it, mine it, enjoy it—for what it is, likewise for what it is not. They should remember, in addition, that even though they are to see the results of their scholarship in the context of Christian conviction, that is a different thing from stretching the curriculum, for Christian purposes, into something other than what it is.

By all means teach the Law—and the Prophets and the Gospels and the Epistles—with all your heart, as God's Word. Also teach history, literature, and music, just as wholeheartedly. You may even proclaim that all of these things, and especially the ability to study them, are Heaven's good gifts. But you should not think that the Bible asks us to know history, literature, or music, or to be educated.

NATURE AND GRACE

That brings me to the most important consideration of this chapter, the distinction between Nature and Grace.* It is essential to any understanding of the gospel; and although I am sure that no informed believer will be unmindful of it, I am also pretty sure that it is sometimes forgotten in our zeal to prosecute the cause of Christian education.

---

*I use *nature* and *grace* in their broadest theological senses: *nature* to mean "human nature," as it is "naturally," prior to or otherwise without God's intervening act; and *grace* to mean a supernatural gift bestowed by God, especially, but not only, the gift of salvation in Christ. See, for example, among others, the *New Dictionary of Theology* (Ferguson, Wright, and Packer 1988) on either word.

The goal of all education, as Lucian reminded us, is to do something about what a man is inherently, not to allow him "to be as he was born, either in body or in soul" (1961, 33)—in a word, to improve him. I know there are those who urge that education's goal is to develop what is already there, latent, in the human being (they remind us that one of the meanings of *educo* is "to draw out"), not to improve in the sense of change or correct, but to nurture or nourish native interests or proclivities. But for all practical purposes I take that to be included in not leaving men "as they were born."

Valuable as such an effort at amelioration is, however, and necessary—no society could afford to neglect it—it can only improve the "old self," as the apostle Paul calls it (Colossians 3:9). It cannot make men new. That distinction is central to a Christian understanding of the world, education included. Even if our educating sometimes appears successful in improving men's good traits and altering their bad for the better, important as that is, they still need to be born again. This is as true of a purely religious education as it is of a purely academic one, and is the unbridgeable divide between education, of whatever kind, and the gospel. No matter how much you improve Nature you don't get Grace. Education, said Newman, makes the gentleman, not the Christian (5.9; 1982, 91); that is, education refines but it cannot transform.

Nor could a Christian be content with Plato's belief that knowing the right will be followed by doing the right.* Perhaps the most penetrating insight into moral psychology in all of literature is the apostle Paul's self-revelation, "I do not understand my own actions. For I do not do what I want, but I do the very thing I hate" (Romans 7:15), set as it is in what is itself one of the most remarkable passages in Scripture. It is questionable, therefore, how capable education is of even improving our good traits and altering our bad, because it is incapable of dealing with sin. The "keen and

---

*"Knowledge is a noble and commanding thing," says Socrates in *Protagoras*, "which cannot be overcome, and will not allow a man, if he only knows the difference of good and evil, to do anything which is contrary to knowledge, but that wisdom will have strength to help him" (352; Jowett 1952, 59). With this view Aristotle disagreed (*Nichomachean Ethics* 7.2; McKeon 1941, 1038).

delicate instruments" of human knowledge and human reason, as Newman called them, are hardly a match for "those giants, the passion and the pride of man" (5.9; 1982, 91).

I appreciate that there is, must be, some relationship between Christian instruction and Christian living—else why "train children in the right way" (Proverbs 22:6)? Or what to do, in the case of academic education, with Marrou's (undoubtedly accurate) judgment that Christianity is "an intellectual religion" (1956, 339)? But that relationship, how it works—how we get from learning to faith, or in this case from learning to "improvement" (if we do at all); how, if you will, Nature may work with Grace, or knowing is related to believing—is too big a subject for here. I mean only to remind us at this juncture of an important New Testament distinction.

Neither do I want to suggest that Nature is less important than Grace, or that because "what counts is a new creation" (Galatians 6:15, NIV), anything that does not tend toward that is unworthy of our attention. On the contrary, we are irrevocably, and absolutely rightly, committed to the academic training of our children, as we are to a very great deal in life that is much less exalted and neither particularly "religious" nor "spiritual." Ours is the faith of the Word made flesh, and our responsibilities, most of the time, have to do with what is ever so mundane—ever so important for all that. Grace should teach us to use the world well; and should not the most heavenly minded be of the most earthly use?

THE LIMITATIONS OF EDUCATION

Why is it important to be reminded of the limitations of education? The answer has to do with what I said a moment ago about embracing the classical model of education for what it is, as well as for what it is not. I am not entirely sure about the validity of what I will say next, and so may stand under correction, but my sense is that as Christian education gets better, more sophisticated, the more it will be tempted to be satisfied with itself. This may be especially true as it gets more "integrated," abler at articulating a Christian worldview or tendering its scholarly conclusions in Christian categories—because the more integrated it becomes the more difficult to remember that it is still only education, however important we believe that to be.

Such sophistication among Christian schools is of course an aspect of the increased academic sophistication of evangelical Christianity in general: denominations that a couple of generations back disdained secular education now touting advanced degrees from Oxford or offering them in graduate schools of their own, pastors for whom seminary or Bible school was once plenty of education (and for their congregations maybe too much!) feeling the pressure to acquire a doctorate of one sort or another, church administrators with MBAs, and so on. It is something of an irony that the wing of the Church that fifty or sixty years ago was generally regarded as anti-intellectual seems now so enamored of the very education it once shunned.

In many Christian circles the older antagonism to liberal learning has begun to give way to an understanding that if we are going to have schools we ought to have good ones; that if the battle in the culture wars is for the mind we cannot afford a scandal of the evangelical mind; that if we do our work poorly we dishonor the long, noble tradition of Christian scholarship; that if we have money for all manner of evangelical causes, from multimillion-dollar sanctuaries to religious amusement parks, we ought to have money to educate our children properly; that if we glory in the prominence of football players who witness for Christ we ought to take similar pleasure in training Christian geneticists; that, in any case, whatever we do, academic and intellectual work included, we ought to do it well, as unto the Lord. The list could go on, but you get the point: we are beginning to see the error of our ways, to change our minds about education and schools and what it means to think as well as act like Christians. All of that is welcome news.

There are dangers, though. The first I have already discussed: the danger of thinking that education of an essentially liberal sort can or should be enlisted to serve essentially biblical ends, or that the Bible can be quoted in support of calculus and world history, drama and art—the danger, that is, of conflating two sorts of education and missing the benefits of both.

The other danger I have only intimated, namely, that as we get increasingly sophisticated educationally—evangelicals are already frightfully affluent and culturally aware, not to mention politically savvy—we will forget that no matter how big or well-financed or well-known we are, no matter how esteemed our reputation in the community or how many of our graduates matriculate at name colleges and universities, we are still unprofitable servants, sinners saved by grace.

Of course I do not seriously think that any Christian school board member, administrator, or teacher would actually forget the meaning of the gospel, of grace working through faith (Ephesians 2:8). It is just that whereas I was once embarrassed by the seeming carelessness with which too many Christian schools treated their moral and professional responsibilities, especially with regard to students' intellects, I now feel an uneasiness in my soul when I see the impersonal superefficiency of their patently corporate style; the way the demands of their enormous budgets drive their admissions policies, even their curriculums; their unseemly emphasis, financially and otherwise, on athletics; their apparent need continually to get bigger and wealthier; their seeming inability to serve any but the better-off; and the like.

Conclusion

Education is a marvelous gift, not to be taken for granted or neglected, and the mind, it is said, is a terrible thing to waste, particularly, in our case, if it is a Christian mind. That means that some of us may need to pull up our socks, get better trained if need be, and, not mistaking for youth group the blessed educational arrangement bequeathed by the Greeks, start taking more seriously the intellectual welfare of the Christian young, fulfilling the role education was developed to perform, and not another.

Others of us may need to be reminded that no matter how rich and famous or influential and successful we become, the best school in the community or the best football team in the state, it remains true that "God chose what is foolish in the world to shame the wise; God chose what is weak in the world to shame the strong;

God chose what is low and despised in the world, things that are not, to reduce to nothing things that are, so that no one might boast in the presence of God" (1 Corinthians 1:27–29). "Unless the Lord builds the house," the psalm tells us, "those who build it labor in vain" (Psalm 127:1), and Jesus says that in the kingdom of God "many who are first will be last, and the last will be first" (Mark 10:31) and "apart from me you can do nothing" (John 15:5). An increasingly steadfast commitment to academic rigor (to the improvement of Nature) and an increasing sensitivity to our sin and inadequacy (to our continual need for Grace): both are required, at the same time and together.

Three

We've Got Too Much Going On

Do not say, the people must be educated, when, after all, you only mean, amused, refreshed, soothed, put into good spirits and good humour, or kept from vicious excesses.

—John Henry Newman, *The Idea of a University*

Having tried to make the case that we need to understand both the proper role and the limitations of liberal education within the Christian scheme of things, and at the same time having announced our intention, in agreement with the majority of Christians throughout the centuries, to prosecute such an education diligently and well, as many of us are doing, how should we proceed to assess the current situation? We might begin with a little introspection.

The question is, How serious are we about education? Do we really believe that what our young people need most—apart from their relationship to God, to their parents, their obedience to both, and the like—is to be educated, to be informed and articulate, able to think, to sort out the true from the false, the good from the bad, the beautiful from the ugly? Do we really believe not only that that is what they most need to be, but that that is what the Christian community, rather the whole of society, most needs them to be? Are we serious enough to concentrate on that one thing, to make it our focus, and to limit or eliminate other things that may be in the way of it? Because I am fairly certain that one of the problems in our Christian, as other, educating is that we are distracted—in two ways primarily.

WE ARE DISTRACTED

The first is the most straightforward way: we are going in too many directions at once; there are too many things to do to do any one of them well. I understand that young people are both energetic and capable. It is astounding how much some of them can pack into a week: varsity sports, the school musical, student body office, community service, Japanese and flute lessons, youth group at church (what else? karate or Cotillion?), in addition to a 4.3 grade point average—made possible by at least one, preferably two or three, Advanced Placement courses. It's all very impressive, and makes my own high school experience look like sloth itself.

Nor should I fail to admit that my own education at the secondary level was, by comparison, pretty weak. On the whole schools are much better now than they were then, and students probably a good deal sharper—although if I am not mistaken there is also a greater disparity between quality and other schools. This is by no means a censure of "modern education." As I have said, the sheer competence of some of today's young people, especially perhaps in fields like science, is almost breathtaking.

But is all the activity helpful? Forget for a moment, if you can, what is "simply required to get into Stanford," and consider what sort of young people we are after. Is it even possible for students, trying to keep up the schedule I have described, to produce what we might in our more thoughtful moments say we want? Good work requires opportunity to read carefully, to think, to reflect and muse. It requires time—and time is precisely what neither we nor our students have. They do a lot of things, admittedly a most extraordinary lot of things, but often it is not, because it cannot be, of the quality we should require or desire. You cannot be writing first-rate essays if you are knocking them out between three and six in the morning, just in time to make it to swim practice.

EXPERT OPINION

In *Schools That Do Too Much*, Etta Kralovec enlarges on the theme. Citing everything from the reduced number of class hours schools actually give to academics, to the inordinate emphasis on sports, to the impossibly broad missions mandated for public education, she concludes with the thesis of her title—and the question, "How do we rid our schools of the activities and programs that interfere with children's ability to make use of the school day for authentic and systematic learning?" (2003, 8).

"The school day in the United States," she argues, "is chaotic, truncated, and not designed to be conducive to real learning" (Kralovec 2003, 8). It's also too short: "the average instructional time in the United States for high school students is five hours and thirty minutes" (26). As for sports: "what school administrators are less willing to admit is that the schedule meets the needs of the competitive athletic program and always has" (24), and "the huge investment that some schools make in sports reflects a misplaced priority" (29). The other "extracurricular" activities? "School people believe that it is the community that wants sports programs, drug education in the schools, and Halloween parades during the school day. If this is true, perhaps it is time for our communities to begin conversations about the educational value of eighth-graders selling wrapping paper to pay for trips to Disneyland" (30).

In a politically incorrect chapter titled "Who Could Be against Dental Care?" Kralovec exposes "the tension between the academic program of the school and the 'social improvement' programs that litter the school day and disrupt its flow. How did it come to be that schools were responsible for the dental health of the young? When did we come to believe that the school day should be used to teach all manner of subjects beyond a core curriculum?" (2003, 36–37). In the margin of my copy of the book I wrote, "Amen!"

Carl Honoré, in *Under Pressure: Rescuing Our Children from the Culture of Hyper-Parenting*, takes a different, almost the opposite, tack. It's testing and homework and private tutoring—in a sense an *overemphasis* on studying—that are the targets of his ire, his investigation anyway. There is too much, in his view, of all three.

As the dean of admissions at MIT told him, "an obsession with academic achievement is squeezing the lifeblood out of schools—and the children who attend them." More important: "What happened to education for its own sake? When did our children's passion for learning, for finding a subject that really excites them, get pushed aside by the race to build the perfect résumé?" (2008, 114). I am not an expert on the history of education in America, and so do not know when, if ever, children had a passion for learning (I didn't), but I take the dean's point.

The issue here is personal ambition—parents' more often than their children's—as much as it is academic achievement, but the two are pretty much the same in the current order. You can't realize your personal ambitions unless you achieve academically. A lot more is involved in school than learning for its own sake—and that reality has bred a host of evils.

Cheating, for one, which is on the rise worldwide, according to surveys (Honoré 2008, 117); and academic cheating is born of intense academic competition, wherein "the classroom becomes a winner-take-all battlefield" (118).

Success, moreover, is figured largely by testing, exams of every possible sort. But "scores of studies have shown that the more people are encouraged to chase results and rewards—an A+ on the report card, say—the less interest they take in the task itself" (Honoré 2008, 121). One of the reasons for what Honoré sees as "the worldwide trend toward homeschooling" is parents' desire to escape "the tyranny of tests, timetables, and targets" (135). In Finland, a country with one of the highest per capita rates of graduation from university in the world, children face no standardized tests at all (122). "This presents a delicious irony: the nation that puts the least stress on competition and testing, that shows the least appetite for cram schools and private tutoring, routinely tops the world in PISA's [Programme for International Student Assessment's] competitive exams" (123).

Likewise the emphasis on homework. According to Honoré, some studies suggest that homework "has little or no effect on academic performance," at least among under-elevens (2008, 149).

Not that homework doesn't have its uses, especially after the elementary years. "But there are also limits. Homework works best when it is assigned in reasonable amounts to avoid crowding out time for rest, play, and socializing. It also needs a clear purpose beyond keeping kids busy and making teachers and parents feel good about themselves" (155).

In the scramble for the top, private tutoring has also become an expedient of choice for parents wanting to guarantee their children's success and feel good about themselves. Says an expert in education business interviewed by Honoré, "It's part of the repertoire of what a good parent does now: you sign them up for piano, tennis, and soccer, and you sign them up with a tutor" (2008, 156).

As with homework, the results for tutoring are mixed. Certainly it may help in certain circumstances. Just as often, though, it can "rob kids of the challenge—and the joy—of mastering a new piece of knowledge on their own. It can also mask weaknesses in the school system and create an uneven playing field among pupils" (Honoré 2008, 158). That is my response: should not any school worth its salt, confident of the quality of its teachers and teaching, be saying to parents, "You don't need a tutor for your child. We're taking care of his education"? In the end, according to a study conducted in the academic pressure cooker that is South Korea, "having a passion for learning is a more reliable indicator of academic success than is having a tutor" (157). In the margin next to that comment I wrote, "Duh!"

We might mention too the "Anything But Knowledge doctrine" (as Heather Mac Donald calls it) of the influential schools of education, wherein self-reflection or multiculturalism or "constructing knowledge," or whatever, has hijacked the curriculum (1998); but that subject, important as it is, is a book by itself, and has been addressed (Mac Donald 1998; Sowell 1993).

Even when we do turn our attention to academics, our interest or intensity becomes all about grades or test scores or amount of homework or extra tutoring. Is there not another way of doing things?

Admittedly, the studies adduced have mostly to do with public schools. But not entirely. (Honoré spent considerable time interviewing several highly successful private schools.) In any case, if as a Christian school board member, administrator, teacher, or parent you do not see something of your own institution reflected in the comments quoted—if you have managed to avoid the pitfalls of modern education philosophy and practice—you are to be commended, and have no need for proposals to address nonexistent problems. For the rest of us the question remains: Is there not another way of doing things?

A DIFFERENT SORT OF SCHEDULE

In his autobiographical *Surprised by Joy: The Shape of My Early Life*, C. S. Lewis provides a description of the "normal" day at Great Bookham in Surrey, the home of William T. Kirkpatrick, "The Great Knock," where Lewis received his education from his sixteenth to his eighteenth year; and that routine, he says, has served as his archetype ever since:

> If I could please myself I would always live as I lived there. I would choose always to breakfast at exactly eight and to be at my desk by nine, there to read or write till one.... At one precisely lunch should be on the table; and by two at the latest I would be on the road. Not, except at rare intervals, with a friend. Walking and talking are two very great pleasures, but it is a mistake to combine them.... The return from the walk, and the arrival of tea, should be exactly coincident, and not later than a quarter past four.... At five a man should be at work again, and at it till seven. Then, at the evening meal and after, comes the time for talk, or, failing that, for lighter reading; and unless you are making a night of it with your cronies (and at Bookham I had none) there is no reason why you should ever be in bed later than eleven. (1955, 141–43)

Now please listen carefully, because there is much room here for misunderstanding. I am not for a moment recommending that we in Christian schools be trying to reproduce in twenty-first-century urban or suburban America the kind of education Lewis enjoyed in the rural England of his boyhood prior to World War I. That would be wildly idealistic (no, impossible) at best, ridiculous or silly at worst. What Lewis was taught and the way he was taught it, even in his own day, was peculiar, the luxury of a very few, often as not the obviously gifted whose parents could afford it. It would hardly be described as "school" at all, as we of the modern factory model understand it. And as anyone who has read *Surprised by Joy* knows, Lewis' childhood was no ordinary childhood. Academically speaking it was remarkable by any standard. It was not what the vast majority of children, even then, would have been capable of or would have wanted. I am therefore in no sense saying, "See what Lewis did; we should do that." Nor am I implying that our business is to produce a lot of little C. S. Lewises. Heaven forbid. The kingdom of God requires an infinitely greater variety of gifts and tempers than that. Lewis himself would heartily agree.

But I do think there may be something to be learned from that wonderfully idyllic schooldays routine nonetheless. Not its specific content—not at what time Lewis ate his breakfast or took his tea—but rather the thing that most sticks out about it, its apparent leisureliness, its seeming lack of busyness, even lack of organization. Of course the whole point in a way was its organization—certain times every day for certain things—but what a marvelously simple, uncluttered routine it was. Besides eating and sleeping, he worked and walked. How different from the round of activities that occupies the successful student of today—the exact opposite in fact. The modern student is overwhelmingly busy. That is what we marvel at, or worry about. Lewis seemed remarkably unbusy (at least as a student; later it was different). Not a bad physical regimen either, a daily two-hour walk—refreshing mind as well as body, affording opportunity to muse, or not.

Irving Babbitt commented as early as 1908 that "we live so fast, as the saying is, that we have no time to think. The task of organizing and operating a huge and complex educational machinery has left us scant leisure for calm reflection" (72). Even when the educational machinery is not vast, it is often in its own way complex. All too rarely, in my experience, is there time to think or leisure for calm reflection, for any of us.

LESS IS MORE

Then there is the variety of courses. Prior to going to Great Bookham, Lewis attended Malvern College, a university preparatory school. His description of Malvern ("Wyvern" in *Surprised by Joy*) is on the whole critical in the extreme, but of its curriculum he says this: "In those days a boy on the classical side officially did almost nothing but classics. I think this was wise; the greatest service we can do to education today is to teach fewer subjects. No one has time to do more than a very few things well before he is twenty, and when we force a boy to be a mediocrity in a dozen subjects we destroy his standards, perhaps for life" (1955, 112–13).

That was written in 1955. It may be more relevant today. I know that there are college/university entrance requirements to deal with—so many years of prescribed courses to matriculate at most places (seven for the University of California, my state)—but is there not something important in Lewis' comment still? Come to think of it, seven was the number of studies in the combined trivium and quadrivium of the medieval university. What if our courses were limited to seven, with the insistence that they be done well? Less here may be more.

Again: we are not Lewises; his genius, his times and circumstances, are not our genius, times, and circumstances—nor should we wish them to be. All the same, I can't help but think that the difference between the quality of his Christian thought and our students' (and ours) may have something to do with his being undistracted in a way that we are not, that whatever else stands between us and him (and plenty of others like him) as regards special gifts or opportunities (about which we can do absolutely nothing), the one thing we could do something about is how we organize our schedules and curriculums, the preference we give to some things and not to others, the number and type of courses we require.

The great John Henry Newman in the nineteenth century

warned against "distracting and enfeebling the mind by an unmeaning profusion of subjects" (6.8; 1982, 107). Further, he said, "a thorough knowledge of one science and a superficial acquaintance with many, are not the same thing; a smattering of a hundred things or a memory for detail, is not a philosophical or comprehensive view" (109). To illustrate he pointed to "those earnest but ill-used persons, who are forced to load their minds with a score of subjects against an examination, who have too much on their hands to indulge themselves in thinking or investigation" (6.10; 112). We are distracted, first of all, by doing too much, even academically.

DISTRACTION OF ANOTHER SORT

The second way we are distracted is more psychological, but related to the first. Because our students' lives are so packed with things other than academic study, academic study too, many if not most of those things sponsored by the school itself, students naturally get the idea that that is what school is supposed to be. It may be mainly about books, but by no means only that; and in practice (whatever we say) the main thing is often lost sight of almost completely. Two or three times a week, student athletes miss class because of games; during play rehearsals homework gets done, if at all, between scenes, sometimes very late at night; days at a time are taken from school for choir tour; unending hours are devoted (let us be fair) to preparing for the Academic Decathlon or debate finals, or the missions trip—and on it goes. Invariably what is first is the extracurricular activity and what is second the academic work, certainly as regards emotional energy invested. The result, as I said, is that students think that that way of doing things is the norm or ideal, that the importance of their employments is about equal to the time given to them. What else could they think? That's the way school is set up—and the priority of trained intellect is lost in the shuffle.

Now, many of the things just mentioned I believe in—usually. I am not advocating that we abandon them in favor of an all-study-all-the-time diet. In fact I have argued elsewhere (in *School and Sports: A Christian Critique*) that some of us are in danger of putting too much academic pressure on young people. SAT/ACT scores, grade point averages, AP exams, college admissions applications are the evidence. The mind cannot work nonstop forever, any more than the body can. Our students, like us, need breaks, maybe more rather than fewer, and some of the activities I've mentioned may be the means by which breaks are made possible. Several, moreover, are "educational" in a way none of us would deny. (I could get my hands slapped for referring to them as "extracurricular" rather than "cocurricular.") That much I understand.

There is a difference, though, between a fundamentally and rigorously academic program of learning that makes a place for art or music or sports or play, and the kind of frenetic, competition- and pressure-packed schedule I have been talking about. What I am advocating is the possibility of doing things in a way that is both more rigorous and more relaxed, so that students are under less pressure but do better, by which I mean learn more of the sort, and in the way, we want them to learn.

"TECHNOLUST"

One wonders too about technological overkill. A revealing look at the effects of classroom electronics on student learning is offered in a washingtonpost.com article for February 10, 2008 ("A School That's Too High on Gizmos"). At a very high-tech high school in Alexandria, Virginia, according to the piece (written by English teacher Patrick Welsh), "faculty morale is the lowest and cynicism the highest I've seen in years"—because of what he calls administrative "technolust." "Principals and other administrators may live off headlines," he says, "but teachers live off whether their students learn." Not, apparently, at this school. As one social stud-ies teacher puts it: "Our students want to push a button or click a mouse for a quick A, B or C answer. Fewer and fewer of them want to think anymore because good thinking takes time." A math teacher says: "Math grows out of the end of a pencil. You don't want the quick answer; you want students to be able to develop the answer, to discover the why of it." Then the crowning indignity: "I see the same thing in my classes," complains the author, "especially when it comes to writing essays. Many students send their papers in over the Internet, and while the margins are correct and the fonts attractive, the writing is worse than ever. It's as if the rule is: Write one draft, run spell check, hit 'send' and pray." Thinking takes time; so does developing answers and worrying over essays. Some educators are beginning to doubt whether technology has helped us much here; available too is evidence that it may have made matters worse.

A LITTLE BACKPEDALING

True, the responses to the article were not all in agreement with it, and some were pretty hostile. Neither, apparently, is the matter of students' doing too much, like that of the baleful effects of technology on learning, as uncomplicated as I have made it sound.

As regards the first, there is reason to think that for all the concern about the amount of pressure being put on students, a good deal of it academic, today's young are studying less than they ever have. As for technology, several are the voices wanting us to believe that not only is e-learning not bad, it is positively good, in fact is begetting a generation of uniquely tuned-in, savvy young people who are, among other things, more intelligent than the generations who proceeded them.

What, then, of scholars under pressure? While there are a number of surveys, two alluded to earlier in this chapter, providing us with a portrait of the American student as overworked, "the actual habits of most teenagers and young adults in most schools and colleges in this country display a wholly contrasting problem, but one no less disturbing," at least according to Mark Bauerlein, an English professor at Emory University, in *The Dumbest Generation*. Bauerlein cites study after study showing that "their in-class and out-of-class punch cards amount to fewer hours than a part-time job" (2008, 6). The 2006 *High School Survey of Student Engagement*, for instance: in responding to the question regarding how many hours per week they spent "reading/studying for class," 90 percent "came in at a ridiculously low five hours or less, 55 percent at one hour or less." That in contrast to 31 percent who admitted watching television or playing video games at least six hours per week and 25 percent putting in six hours minimum surfing and chatting online (5). In a similar survey for college students (the 2006 *National Survey of Student Engagement*), almost one out of five (18 percent) registered one to five hours per week "preparing for class" and 26 percent six to ten hours per week; and while college professors estimate that a successful semester requires about 25 hours out-of-class study per week, only 11 percent reached that many (5–6).

Bauerlein points to other studies, all of which indicate the same thing: in contradistinction to the literature sympathetic to the plight of the overpressured young adult, these, "while they lack the human drama, they impart more reliable assessments, providing a better baseline for understanding the realities of the young American mentality and forcing us to stop upgrading the adolescent condition beyond its due" (2008, 6).

But Bauerlein's book is not primarily about whether American students are doing their homework, even though his reading of the data suggests that they aren't. It is mainly about the problem we touched on in the section on "Technolust": the impact of technology on student learning, and thus the readiness of the next generation to fulfill its responsibilities to society. That's the second issue we said we'd take up.

Bauerlein's subtitle sums up his thesis: *How the Digital Age Stupefies Young Americans and Jeopardizes Our Future*. The book is an analysis of a paradox, and it is this:

> We have entered the Information Age, traveled the Information Superhighway, spawned a Knowledge Economy, undergone the Digital Revolution, converted manual workers into knowledge workers, and promoted a Creative Class, and we anticipate a Conceptual Age to be....
>
> And yet, while teens and young adults have absorbed digital tools into their daily lives like no other age group, while they have grown up with more knowledge and information

readily at hand, taken more classes, built their own Web sites, enjoyed more libraries, bookstores, and museums in their towns and cities ... in sum, while the world has provided them extraordinary chances to gain knowledge and improve their reading/writing skills, not to mention offering financial incentives to do so, young Americans today are no more learned or skillful than their predecessors, no more knowledgeable, fluent, up-to-date, or inquisitive, except in the materials of youth culture. (2008, 8–9)

Perhaps worse, "they don't know any more history or civics, economics or science, literature or current events." They read less on their own; they write less, and less well. Most interestingly, "their technology skills fall well short of the common claim, too, especially when they must apply them to research and workplace tasks" (Bauerlein 2008, 9). The result: "The fonts of knowledge are everywhere, but the rising generation is camped in the desert, passing stories, pictures, tunes, and texts back and forth, living off the thrill of peer attention. Meanwhile, their intellects refuse the cultural and civic inheritance that has made us what we are up to now" (10).

The societal impact of what Bauerlein calls "a consistent and perilous momentum downward" (2008, 7) we will get to shortly. What, though, of the assertion that what he and others are claiming is no more than old-fogy alarmism, the all-too-familiar fears (and perhaps jealousies) that the passing generation has forever had with regard to the one succeeding it. Surely advances in technology, in the availability of knowledge and information, in incentives to creativity—surely all this, contra folk like Bauerlein, constitutes something important and good for the generation to whose present and future it so much seems to belong.

THE BENEFITS OF THE DIGITAL REVOLUTION

It does constitute something important and good, according to some. The claims are that the digital revolution is responsible for not only new leisure habits and lifestyle choices, but new intelligences, certainly new skills, even the ability to "construct knowledge."

"New technologies induce new aptitudes, and bundled together in the bedroom they push consciousness to diversify its attention and multiply its communications," as Bauerlein summarizes the case in defense of e-learning. "Through blogs and Listservs, young Americans join virtual communities, cultivating interests and voicing opinions. Video games quicken their spatial intelligence. Group endeavors such as *Wikipedia* and reality gaming nurture collaborative problem-solving skills. Individuals who've grown up surrounded by technology develop different hard-wiring, their minds adapted to information and entertainment practices and speeds that minds maturing in pre-digital habitats can barely comprehend, much less assimilate" (2008, 84). That is what is being asserted in books and articles and white papers anyway. "Screen time is cerebral, and it generates a breakthrough intelligence. E-literacy isn't just knowing how to download music, program an iPod, create a virtual profile, and comment on a blog. It's a general deployment capacity, a particular mental flexibility. E-literacy accommodates hypermedia because e-literates possess hyperalertness. Multitasking entails a special cognitive attitude toward the world, not the orientation that enables slow concentration on one thing—a sonnet, a theorem—but a lightsome, itinerant awareness of numerous and dissimilar inputs" (84).

In other words, all this uploading, downloading, blogging, inputting, posting, and viewing is not bad; it's downright good, better for the young mind, in some people's opinion, than a traditional education. As Jonathan Fanton, president of the MacArthur Foundation, put it, "Might it be that, for many, the richest environment for learning is no longer in the classroom, it is outside the classroom—online and after school?" (2007).

To begin with, says Steven Johnson in *Everything Bad Is Good for You*, games teach you to make decisions. "Novels may activate our imagination, and music may conjure up powerful emotions, but games force you to decide, to choose, to prioritize. All the intellectual benefits of gaming derive from this fundamental virtue, because learning how to think is ultimately about learning to make the right decisions: weighing evidence, analyzing situations, consulting your long-term goals, and then deciding" (2005, 41).

For all that, Johnson does not tell us what makes right decisions right; nonetheless these are substantial claims for what most of us would probably regard as mere games.

That's not all: "When gamers interact with these [virtual] environments, they are learning the basic procedure of the scientific method" (2005, 45).

Not even the much-maligned boob tube is totally evil. In fact it improves our minds. "So if we're going to start tracking swear words and wardrobe malfunctions," Johnson advises, "we ought to at least include another line in the graph: one that charts the cognitive demands that televised narratives place on their viewers. That line, too, is trending upward at a dramatic rate." How so? "Part of that cognitive work comes from following multiple threads, keeping often densely interwoven plotlines distinct in your head as you watch.... To follow the narrative, you aren't just asked to remember. You're asked to analyze" (2005, 63–64). And so on.

The Internet? It has challenged our intellects in three fundamental and related ways: "by virtue of being participatory, by forcing users to learn new interfaces, and by creating new channels for social interaction" (Johnson 2005, 118).

As a result, we are told, our IQs are improving—because our environment is becoming increasingly complex (Johnson 2005, 139ff., especially 147ff.). And in contrast to what we have heard, our moral behavior has likewise improved. Even though television violence and sex have verifiably increased in the last ten years, statistics indicate that actual violence has decreased (190–92).

The case for the positive impact of digitalization has been made by a number of writers, and in a variety of ways, but the gist of it, again, could be stated in the subtitle, this time, of Johnson's (2005) book: *How Today's Popular Culture Is Actually Making Us Smarter*.

Is It So?

That popular culture is making us smarter, let alone more moral, is hardly what most of us have learned to believe. In fairness, however (and so as not to appear too much an old fogy!), the case needs to be presented.

What are we to make of it? It does not fit, I must say, my own perceptions (preconceptions?) of what is happening.

Here in brief is Bauerlein's critique: "Even if we grant that visual media cultivate a type of spatial intelligence, they still minimize verbal intelligence, providing too little stimulation for it, and intense, long-term immersion in it stultifies the verbal skills of viewers and disqualifies them from most every academic and professional labor. Enthusiasts such as Steven Johnson praise the decision-making value of games, but they say nothing about games implanting the verbal tools to make real decisions in real worlds" (2008, 130). Nine out of ten adolescent Web postings and game sessions and messages reflect the reality of adolescent Web practices: they are "the adolescent expressions and adolescent recreations of adolescents" (131). Adult observers who marvel at the depth and pace of teen immersion in technology therefore give adolescents just what they want: "a rationale for closing their books, hanging out online, and jockeying with one another. Teenagers don't want to spend Tuesday night on science tasks or *1984*. With the screen luring them all the time with the prospect of a new contact in the last hour, the payoff for homework looks too distant, the effort too dull" (132–33).

Lest all of this sound like so much mere supposing, grounded in nothing more than personal grievance or envy (or perhaps in Bauerlein's case, one too many badly written essays), it should be noted that his critique of the technophiles is supported by page after page of studies indicating a decline in teen vocabulary and reading and writing skills. As interesting as anything are the studies done by public school districts, as well as independent organizations, showing (in the case of the Heritage Foundation's analysis of National Assessment of Educational Progress data in 2000) that among fourth graders and eighth graders, "Students with at least weekly computer instruction by well-prepared teachers do not perform any better on the NAEP reading test than do students who have less or no computer instruction" (K. Johnson 2000); or a study of 15-year-olds from 31 countries indicating that "once other features of student, family and school background are held constant, computer availability at home shows a strong statistically negative relationship to math and reading performance, and computer availability at school is unrelated to performance" (Fuchs and Woessman 2004). In May 2007, the *New York Times* reported a story from the Liverpool Central School District, just outside Syracuse, New York, according to which the district had decided to phase out laptops starting in the fall, thereby "joining a handful of other schools around the country that adopted one-to-one computing programs and are now abandoning them as educationally empty—and worse" (Hu 2007).

Well before computers in the classroom became ubiquitous, Jacques Barzun wrote that "the computer ... does not teach, does not show a human being thinking and meeting intellectual difficulties; it does not impart knowledge but turns up information pre-arranged and pre-cooked.... Wonderful for creating the cliché-ridden mind" (1991, 31). And if the computer does "think," in some sense, what then?

There is plenty more, from a variety of perspectives. But you get the point:

> Techno-pushers hail digital learning, and they like to talk of screen time as a heightened "experience," but while they expound the features of the latest games and software in detail, they tend to flatten and overlook the basic features of the most important element in their process, the young persons having the experiences. Digital natives are a restless group, and like all teens and young adults they are self-assertive and insecure, living in the moment but worrying over the future, crafting elaborate e-profiles but stumbling through class assignments, absorbing the minutiae of youth culture and ignoring works of high culture, heeding this season's movie and game releases as monumental events while blinking at the mention of the Holocaust, the Cold War, or the War on Terror. (Bauerlein 2008, 126)

All this is bad enough, but the deeper problems, as Bauerlein sees it, are not the failures simply to learn or know.

The first is what we might call a spiritual as well as an intellectual problem, the loss in this generation of adolescents of what Bauerlein calls "self-criticism in the light of tradition" (2008, 198). Confident of their technical superiority and the irrelevance of boring schoolwork (*boring*, not surprisingly, is the word of choice in this context), they become increasingly estranged from their culture's past and turned in on themselves. "They don't know much about history and literature, but they have feelings and needs, and casualty figures from Shiloh and lines from Donne don't help." Psychological assessments, moreover, show "rising currents of narcissism among Americans who haven't yet joined the workforce," and the rise can be traced "directly to self-esteem orientations in the schoolroom" (192). The result is that

> digital technology has fostered a segregated social reality, peer pressure gone wild, distributing youth content in an instant, across continents, 24/7.... What passes through them locks young Americans ever more firmly into themselves and one another, and whatever doesn't pass through them appears irrelevant and profitless. Inside the classroom, they learn a little about the historical past and civic affairs, but once the lesson ends they swerve back to the youth-full, peer-bound present. Cell phones, personal pages, and the rest unleash persistent and simmering forces of adolescence, the volatile mix of cliques and loners, rebelliousness and conformity, ambition and self-destruction, idolatry and irreverence, know-nothing-ness and know-it-all-ness, all of which tradition and knowledge had helped to contain. (200)

This is especially the case when the young have the uncritical sympathy of their mentors. The young don't require the endorsement of their preferences, but the stabilizing and corrective influence of wise teachers who will make sure their charges can read and write and think, who will acquit themselves of their responsibility to teach, not merely engage students, parroting student patois, about student priorities. Not about what is "relevant" either. "What young Americans need isn't more relevance in the classroom, but less.... Young people need mentors not to go with the youth flow, but to stand staunchly against it, to represent something smarter and finer than the cacophony of social life. They don't need more pop culture and youth perspectives in the classroom. They get enough of those on their own. Young Americans need someone somewhere in their lives to reveal to them bigger and better human stories than the sagas of summer parties and dormitory diversions and Facebook sites" (Bauerlein 2008, 199).

Where do those bigger and better—and correcting and inspiring—human stories come from? From the tradition, given shape and articulation in liberal learning, found primarily in books. "To replace the book with the screen is to remove a 2,500-year-old cornerstone of civilization and insert an altogether dissimilar building block" (Bauerlein 2008, 101).

That leads to the second of Bauerlein's deeper concerns regarding technology, what we might call societal: the impact of the breakdown of the Dumbest Generation's intellect on the future of American governance and liberty.

Reminding us of "the essential connection of knowledge and democracy" (2008, 212), Bauerlein goes on to say that knowledge "draws people out of themselves and beyond the present, sets their needs in a wider setting than private circumstances and instant gratification. Tradition raises conviction over consumption, civic duty over personal gain.... Citizens need a yardstick reaching back in time measuring actions and policies not only by their immediate effects, but also by their relation to founding principles and to divergences from them through history" (214–15). Not that this is the first generation to reject the past, says Bauerlein, but what was once informed rejection of the past has become uninformed rejection of the past. Either way, "if you ignore the traditions that ground and ennoble our society, you are an incomplete person and a negligent citizen" (233).

Bauerlein's final pages are a warning. "As of 2008, the intellectual future of the United States looks dim. Not the economic future, or the technological, medical, or media future, but the future of civic understanding and liberal education" (2008, 233). "The Dumbest Generation cares little for history books, civic principles, foreign affairs, comparative religions, and serious media and art, and it knows less. Careening through their formative years, they don't catch the knowledge bug, and *tradition* might as well be a foreign word." He concludes, "The ramifications for the United States are grave" (234; italics in original). "The Dumbest Generation will cease being dumb only when it regards adolescence as an inferior realm of petty strivings and adulthood as a realm of civic, historical, and cultural awareness that puts them in touch with the perennial ideas and struggles." And if this generation does not thus mature? "They may even be recalled as the generation that lost that great American heritage, forever" (236).

This is no blanket condemnation of a particular age group. Even Bauerlein acknowledges what would seem obvious, that young Americans' wits "are just as keen as ever," their ambitions "may even exceed their forebears'," and their experience of alienation from the adult world is typical (2008, 201).

There can be no doubt that the baptism, almost from the cradle, of this generation of adolescents and young adults into an electronic world has nurtured aptitudes and a way of looking at things, even certain "intelligences," different from those of their parents and grandparents. How could it not? And no doubt these aptitudes and intelligences are in their own way valuable, perhaps enviable.

My own experience suggests that many of the current crop of youth are very sharp indeed, and deeply committed to the betterment of their world. Where there is a question, it is not about their capabilities or potentialities. It is about their intellectual health and well-being, and that has to do with their education. Or as Bauerlein has it, the tragedy is that their keen wits are being wasted on "screen diversions," their ambitions merged on "career and consumer goals, not higher learning," and their alienation is one that "doesn't stem from countercultural ideas and radical mentors ... but from an enveloping immersion in peer stuff" (2008, 201).

The issue for us therefore is their learning; and unless we

agree that an education of the traditional sort, the sort most of us are engaged in, is simply passé, we have our work cut out for us.

Nor, in my view, do we have to agree that those like Bauerlein have it exactly or entirely right. Even if he has it largely, or partly, right, as I am inclined to think he has, we still have our work cut out for us.

It should also be remarked that Bauerlein's concern in this book is solely with "the intellectual condition of young Americans" (2008, 7) and the effects of the digital revolution on it. There are also profound moral and spiritual concerns, as comprehensively explicated in books like Candice Kelsey's (2007) superbly written and richly documented *Generation MySpace*. But that discussion, important as it is, would, in this context, take us off the main track. (I am told that "MySpace" is now old hat. But then any allusion of that sort is bound to be, at almost any time, old hat. Probably "old hat" is old hat.)

CONCLUSION

I would suggest that the overall picture is mixed, that while a large percentage of American young people may find school easy or boring or irrelevant, there is nonetheless a sizeable number who take their studies with commendable seriousness. These we should encourage and be thankful for. It does not necessarily follow, though, that our school programs are properly ordered or our curriculums wisely configured.

I have argued that in our educating many of us are doing too much. Admittedly a lot of it is impressive and not all bad. But it's not quantity of work we're after; it's quality of work—thorough, disciplined, Christian, requiring more time than we are allowing for.

Nowhere have I said that the other things—athletics or arts or social and service activities—are bad or undesirable. They are often both good and desirable, possibly necessary. It is their relative importance, the time and energy and money we give to them in relation to the main thing, that merits our consideration.

It may be that what I have described as an overbusy, distracting, too-diverse and diffuse educational agenda is exactly what you want; that is, you disagree with me about the purposes of education. Education in your view is in fact meant to be more or other than training the mind by means of the academic disciplines. And if you do disagree with me on this crucial issue, we will disagree throughout, because everything depends on that. Even the cost of education, the thing that provoked much of my thinking on these matters in the first place, even that will be a source of disagreement, for the reason that I want to maintain that as Christian education gets simpler it gets more focused—also less expensive. But if Christian education at its heart means more in your view—more activities, more to do to include everyone or meet everybody's needs or desires, or whatever the reasons—then it will get neither simpler nor less expensive. It will get more complex as it gets more costly.

As for the impact of the Digital Age: I will most certainly be accused (with some justification on both counts) of being a Luddite and a curmudgeon, and nearly everyone will likely interpret the data in terms of his own experience. In the interests of honesty I should confess that I am not really a Luddite—a curmudgeon maybe. I think computers are wonderful and like most everyone have come to depend on them. I am certainly not advocating their abandonment in the classroom. Neither of course is Bauerlein. To do so would be an exercise in futility. That clock is not going to be turned back; nor would anyone that I know want it to be.

This discussion is not about a particular electronic device, or even "technology." It is about their role in education, whether we may be "too high on gizmos," or, at the extreme, whether "the richest environment for learning is no longer in the classroom, it is outside the classroom—online and after school." It would seem unlikely, in any case, that there is simply nothing to what people like Bauerlein are saying, and the anecdotal evidence could easily enough be construed as solidly in his support.

We may not be in a position yet to make any definitive assessment of the impact of technology on learning, but every good teacher and administrator will have to, probably already has, come to some conclusions on the points being raised.

And, yes, all of us may be analyzing these things way too much. We often do. That's the thing about books. But you will decide on that as well.

An awful lot rests, as it always has, on the education of the young; but if Bauerlein and others are correct, the present situation affords no abundance of hope. "From their ranks," Bauerlein says, "will emerge few minds knowledgeable and interested enough to study, explain, and dispute the place and meaning of our nation. Adolescence is always going to be more or less anti-intellectual, of course, and learning has ever struggled against immaturity, but the battle has never proven so uphill" (2008, 234). Are there not reasons then to think that some simplifying, some prioritizing and concentrating, may be in order, if not for our own then for our democracy's sake?

That democracy, and education's role in it, is what we want to take up next.

Four

Education and Liberty

When the taste for physical pleasures has grown more rapidly than either education or experience of free institutions, the time comes when men are carried away and lose control of themselves at sight of the new good things they are ready to snatch. Intent only on getting rich, they do not notice the close connection between private fortunes and general prosperity. There is no need to drag their rights away from citizens of this type; they themselves voluntarily let them go. They find it a tiresome inconvenience to exercise political rights which distract them from industry. When required to elect representatives, to support authority by personal service, or to discuss public business together, they find they have no time.... Such things are all right for idlers to play at, but they do not become men of weight occupied with the serious business of life. Such folk think they are following the doctrine of self-interest, but they have a very crude idea thereof, and the better to guard their interests, they neglect the chief of them, that is, to remain their own masters.

—Alexis de Tocqueville, *Democracy in America*

In a letter to Colonel Charles Yancey dated January 6, 1816, Thomas Jefferson set out these often-quoted lines: "If a nation expects to be ignorant and free, in a state of civilization, it expects what never was and never will be" (1904, 14:384). Thirty-two years later, in his twelfth Annual Report of the Massachusetts School Board, Horace Mann, architect of public schooling in America, echoed Jefferson's sentiments almost exactly, only more dogmatically: "The establishment of a republican government, without well-appointed and efficient means for the universal education of the people, is the most rash and fool-hardy experiment ever tried by man" (Antioch University 2002–03).

If Jefferson and Mann were correct, a crisis of education is nothing less than a crisis of democracy: a government dependent on its citizenry for its maintenance will flourish only to the extent that its citizens are capable of maintaining it, and that in turn depends on their being educated to maintain it.

But unless the surveys are misleading us (or simply reveling in our shortcomings), we are in general a people woefully ignorant—of even the most rudimentary facts of geography and history. There is the well-publicized inability of high school students, for instance, to locate Chicago on a map or to place the Civil War in the correct century, or the professional football player with two years of university who recently told a reporter, "I couldn't find London on a map if they didn't have the names of the countries. I swear to God. I don't know what nothing is." If these are the kinds of questions that stump or intimidate us, what of the more substantive issues of the rule of law or the purpose of government or the meaning of justice?

How we got to the present state of affairs no doubt admits of several explanations, but Benjamin Barber's can't be too far off: "As it became professionalized and vocationalized in the years following World War II, education was increasingly decoupled from the life and practice of democracy. Today, education is widely discussed, but with a focus on performance, standards, global competition, and outcomes that has largely eclipsed its link to citizenship" (Barber 1999, 134).

The role of education in the maintenance of a free society is—need it be said?—fundamental. Our entire way of life, in an obvious sense, depends on it. Yet here we are, some of us, spending our time haggling with students and parents about why education is important, or whether it will help young people earn a living, or why we don't have a winning football team, or more proms and other "social activities." It's priorities we should be worrying about.

THE JEFFERSONIAN VISION

"Civic pedagogy and public schooling have always been crucial to those who advocate democratic forms of governance," says Barber. "Nowhere is this more evident than in the thought of Thomas Jefferson, in whose account of democratic practices the nurturing of education often seems more crucial than the nurturing of politics" (1999, 134). We could do worse than listen to the Master of Monticello.

In his early *Notes on the State of Virginia* (1781) Jefferson wrote that "of the views of this law [proposing the establishment of public schools] none is more important, none more legitimate, than that of rendering the people the safe, as they are the ultimate, guardians of their own liberty" (Padover 1943, Query XIV, 668). The object of the bill, he said, was "to diffuse knowledge more generally through the mass of the people." To do this he wanted to "lay off every county into small districts of five or six miles square, called hundreds, and in each of them to establish a school for teaching, reading, writing, and arithmetic" (667).

Six years later, writing to James Madison (December 20, 1787), Jefferson again expressed his confidence in the will and ability of ordinary citizens, when properly educated, to preserve their own rights: "And say, finally, whether peace is best preserved by giving energy to the government, or information to the people. This last is the most certain, and the most legitimate engine of government. Educate and inform the whole mass of the people. Enable them to see that it is their interest to preserve peace and order, and they will preserve them. And it requires no very high degree of education to convince them of this. They are the only sure reliance for the preservation of our liberty" (1904, 6:392).

The critical importance he gave to the role of education is reflected in comments he made in a letter to John Adams, October 28, 1813. Although his Virginia *Bill for the More General Diffusion of Knowledge* (1779) "has not yet been acted on but in a small and inefficient degree," he says, still "I have great hope that some patriotic spirit will, at a favorable moment, call it up, and make it the keystone of the arch of our government" (Jefferson 1904, 13:401).

Similarly to Monsieur Coray in France (October 31, 1823): "And true it is that the people, especially when moderately instructed, are the only safe, because the only honest, depositories of the public rights, and should therefore be introduced into the administration of them in every function to which they are sufficient...." It is not a perfect system, Jefferson admits, but it has important and built-in safeguards. The people, he says, "will err sometimes and accidentally, but never designedly, and with a systematic and persevering purpose of overthrowing the free principles of government" (Jefferson 1904, 15:483).

There is no need to multiply quotations. Evidence of Jefferson's "radical faith in the ability of ordinary citizens to arrive at responsible decisions, political as well as moral," derived in part from "his belief in the transforming power of reading and the written word" (D. Wilson 1999, 79)—"the necessary connection between literacy and self-government" (84)—can be found throughout both his official writing and his personal correspondence, and is summed up in Barber's remark that "education makes citizens; citizens make bills of rights; rights make democracy. There is no democracy without citizens, no citizens without public education" (1999, 142).

WHAT SORT OF EDUCATION AND FOR WHOM?

There remains the question of what Jefferson meant by "the mass of the people," and the further question, what sort of knowledge it was that he wanted more generally diffused among them.

By "the mass of the people" it seems pretty clear that he really did mean everyone, all sorts and conditions of men (and women), with an education for all, at least at the elementary level. It is also true that he distinguished between what he called "a natural aristocracy" and "an artificial aristocracy." The grounds of the first, he said in that same letter to John Adams of October 28, 1813, "are virtue and talents"; and the natural aristocracy "I consider as the most precious gift of nature, for the instruction, the trusts, and government of society." The artificial aristocracy, on the other hand, "founded on wealth and birth, without either virtue or talents ... is a mischievous ingredient in government, and provision should be made to prevent its ascendancy" (Jefferson 1904, 13:396).

It was this natural aristocracy, Jefferson judged, "those persons, whom nature hath endowed with genius and virtue," who "should be rendered by liberal education worthy to receive, and able to guard the sacred deposit of the rights and liberties of their fellow citizens, and that they should be called to that charge without regard to wealth, birth or other accidental condition or circumstance." Further, "it is better that such should be sought for and educated at the common expence of all, than that the happiness of all should be confined to the weak or wicked" (*A Bill for the More General Diffusion of Knowledge*, Section I; Padover 1943, 1048).

This educational vision might be described as "both democratic and meritocratic," as Jennings Wagoner has it. "Equality of opportunity for all at the foundation of the system was to be converted into the advancement of the talented few as the most able students progressed toward the top of the educational pyramid" (1999, 126). Or as Jefferson famously put it himself in his *Notes on the State of Virginia*, "the best geniuses [in Virginia's proposed public schools] will be raked from the rubbish annually"—eventually to matriculate at William and Mary College. Thus the general objects of that law were "to provide an education adapted to the years, to the capacity, and the condition of everyone, and directed to their freedom and happiness" (Padover 1943, Query XIV, 667).

This "differentiated system of education," not entirely egalitarian, as it may appear to us, and which "might be said to represent a modest compromise between private and public education," was nonetheless "a radical departure from the conventions of the day," says Wagoner (1999, 126). Certainly it was as remarkably democratic and unprivileged as perhaps it could have been for the time, and the basis for the universal education in America that was to come.

What then was the nature of this education; of what did it consist? Both a superb manager of details and a skilled organizer of masses of information—in addition to being a widely read and extraordinary thinker of independent mind regarding an encyclopedic range of topics, nor hardly diffident about offering his opinions!—Jefferson wrote almost as decidedly about the content of public education as he did about the necessity of it.

For the most part, his curriculum was what we would call liberal arts, beginning in the elementary schools (as we saw) with "reading, writing, and common arithmetick." In addition, students should be made acquainted with "Graecian, Roman, English, and American history" (*A Bill for the More General Diffusion of Knowledge*, Section VI; Padover 1943, 1049). Such grammar schools would also teach "the Latin and Greek languages, English Grammar, geography, and the higher part of numerical arithmetick, to wit, vulgar and decimal fractions, and the extraction of the square and cube roots" (Section XIII, 1052).

At the college level Jefferson advised (in a letter from Paris to John Bannister, October 15, 1785, objecting to sending American students to Europe for an education): "Classical knowledge, modern languages, chiefly French, Spanish, and Italian; Mathematics, Natural Philosophy, Natural history, Civil history, and Ethics. In Natural philosophy, I mean to include Chemistry and Agriculture, and in Natural history, to include Botany, as well as the other branches of those departments." He conceded that "the habit of speaking the modern languages cannot be so well acquired in America," but reckoned that "every other article can be as well acquired at William and Mary College, as at any place in Europe" (Padover 1943, 1055).

Jefferson recognized as well the importance of learning to reason. On being informed of the institution of a debating society named in his honor, he wrote Mr. David Harding, its founding president, on April 20, 1824: "In a republican nation, whose citizens are to be led by reason and persuasion, and not by force, the art of reasoning becomes of first importance" (1904, 16:30).

Thoroughgoing Enlightenment man that he was, Jefferson was particularly enthusiastic about the uses of science. Besides his proposals for including the various sciences in the curriculum of the University of Virginia, he advanced (in a September 28, 1821 letter urging a repeal of a duty on imported books) his conviction that "science is important to the preservation of our republican government, and that it is also essential to its protection against foreign power" (1904, 15:340).

The subject Jefferson mentioned more than any other, however, was history—because in learning it, citizens, "possessed thereby of the experience of other ages and countries, they may be enabled to know ambition under all its shapes, and prompt to exert their natural powers to defeat its purposes" (*A Bill for the More General Diffusion of Knowledge*, Section I; Padover 1943, 1048). These views were reiterated in his *Notes on the State of Virginia*. For the purpose of "rendering the people the safe, as they are the ultimate, guardians of their own liberty," he wrote there, "the reading in the first stage, where *they* will receive their whole education, is proposed, as has been said, to be chiefly historical. History, by apprizing them of the past, will enable them to judge the future; it will avail them of the experience of other times and other nations; it will qualify them as judges of the actions and designs of men; it will enable them to know ambition under every disguise it may assume; and knowing it, to defeat its views" (Padover 1943, Query XIV, 668; italics in original). Thus "History was to play a special role in the basic education of republican citizens.... In a society in which the governed were to be the guardians of their own liberties, no other study could be of comparable importance" (Wagoner 1999, 119).

A USEFUL EDUCATION

In case this emphasis on history, ancient languages, moral philosophy, reasoning, and the like tempt us to imagine that Jefferson was a champion of liberal arts for their own sakes, we should remind ourselves that what made any knowledge important for him was that it was useful.

What he meant by *useful* was preparation for republican citizenship. The study of history had a practical end; so did the other disciplines, as he made explicit in his list of the aims of the University of Virginia: "to give to every citizen the information he needs for the transaction of his own business"; "to enable him to calculate for himself, and to express and preserve his ideas, his contracts and accounts, in writing"; "to know his rights"; "to form the statesmen, legislators and judges, on whom public prosperity and individual happiness are so much to depend"; "to harmonize and promote the interests of agriculture, manufactures and commerce." He also included "to develop the reasoning faculties of our youth, enlarge their minds, cultivate their morals, and instill into them the precepts of virtue and order," and, "generally, to form them to habits of reflection and correct action, rendering them examples of virtue to others, and of happiness within themselves" (*The University of Virginia: Aim and Curriculum*; Padover 1943, 1097–98), but on the whole the list is expressive of his modern and Enlightenment belief that the virtue of education was its utility. Some have even argued that "Jefferson and others in his enlightened circle, dedicated to utilitarian ends as they were, promoted the push toward 'vocationalism' in American education" (Wagoner 1999, 132).

Another way to look at it is to see in Jefferson's own life an intellectual curiosity and (as he confessed in a letter to John Adams, May 17, 1818) "a canine appetite for reading" (Jefferson 1904, 15:169) that was in and of itself an edifying and joyful thing. As Wagoner says:

> Jefferson's insistence that education that is valuable must also be useful invites a definition of utility that transcends the moment and the mundane. To "pursue happiness" in the grandest meaning of that concept, Jefferson would have us understand, requires attention to the moral, civic, and aesthetic dimensions of life as well as to the immediately useful. In ways that Jefferson himself may not have wholly appreciated and never fully articulated, his own life underscored the fact that education is more than a *means*; it can also properly be an *end* in itself. Although Jefferson tended to measure the value of all his studies and activities on the basis of functional utility, his intellectually active mind, aesthetic sensibilities, and notions of virtue, service, and the progress of mankind all provide a remarkable example of a life that was both useful and beautiful. (1999, 133; italics in original)

Others of the Founders shared Jefferson's views on education, certainly, Madison notably. I have relied on Jefferson because he wrote so passionately and extensively about it; also because his work in this regard was the basis of so much actual practice, at the University of Virginia eminently, but not only there. We have as well his own wonderfully candid testimony, with which no one, presumably, would quibble. To General James Breckinridge he wrote (February 15, 1821): "Nobody can doubt my zeal for the general instruction of the people. Who first started that idea? I may surely say, myself" (Jefferson 1904, 15:315). Not for Jefferson alone, but preeminently: the people, properly educated, would be the "guardians of their own liberty."

A Christian would no doubt protest that there is more to it than that, that not even education, by itself, is capable of preserving a country's freedom—but further on that in a moment. At this point I think we can agree on Jefferson's essential point. Even if in our view universal education is not a sufficient condition for the maintenance of democracy, it is a necessary condition all the same.

We might also agree that if Jefferson and company had not made the point with such insistence, the truth of it is plain enough. A nation's governance is neither simple nor easy nor uncomplicated. It requires careful attention and not a little wisdom. It likewise requires a certain understanding of the issues, sometimes abstract and abstruse—and that requires education of at least a minimal sort: an education in history, as Jefferson said (often one of the least favorite subjects among students, if my experience is any gauge); in the skill of reasoning; and the more literature and philosophy and pure math and science and foreign language (for a wider, general appreciation of the nature of men and things) the better. Ignorance, we have been often reminded, is the soil in which tyrannies grow.

A SPECIAL ROLE FOR CHRISTIAN SCHOOLS?

But Jefferson and Mann were talking about public schools. Their role in the maintenance of democratic institutions might seem obvious. And it can be mandated. Public schools are, after all, a function of government; in them government has a vested interest—for good or ill. They can, and in some places in the world do, encourage mediocrity and enforce despotism. My purpose is not to defend public schooling, or to criticize it, but to lay out the case for education's role in a free society, not least in keeping it free.

What, then, of *Christian* schools, independent of government as they are? Is there anything special about their place in a self-ordered republic, by virtue of their being Christian? I think there is—because of the unique standing Christianity has had in the development of modern democracy, the topic we want to take up next.

I assume that what we mean by *democracy*, for purposes of the most general discussion, is "government of the people by the people for the people," as Lincoln put it in his Gettysburg address in 1863. There are of course fundamental questions and fundamental disagreements about what is meant, for instance, by the sovereignty of the people; about the differences between direct, participatory democracy and representative democracy; between republicanism and democratic socialism; and so on. There is also the important distinction between "the democratic *system* and the democratic *vision*," the former referring, according to John De Gruchy, to "those constitutional principles and procedures, symbols and convictions, which have developed over the centuries and which have become an essential part of any genuine democracy whatever its precise historical form," the latter to "that hope for a society in which all people are truly equal and yet where difference is respected; a society in which all people are truly free, yet where social responsibility rather than individual self-interest prevails; and a society which is truly just, and therefore one in which the vast gulf between rich and poor has been overcome" (1995, 7; italics in original). But both system and vision, says De Gruchy, are the products of, at least were nurtured by, Christianity: "Western Christendom undoubtedly provided the womb within which the democratic *system*, as we now know it, gestated, and it also contributed decisively to the shaping of the democratic *vision* through its witness, albeit ambiguous and severely compromised, to the message of the Hebrew prophets" (8; italics in original).

CHRISTIANITY AND DEMOCRACY

Indeed Christianity's indispensable contribution to democracy begins, in De Gruchy's view, with the Old Testament's prophetic vision of justice and *shalom* (1995, 44); from there it can be traced through Jesus, who liberated people from "the bondage of dehumanizing powers, and enabled them to discover their God-given dignity" (47); through the early Church (which in Augustine's view was "profoundly democratic" [62]);* through the Reformation and Luther's "advocacy of the 'religious sovereignty of the common man'" (71) and the Anabaptist or Radical Reformation ("the religious wing of the dispossessed" [74]); through the English Puritans and Nonconformists for whom (quoting Robert Dahl) "all men were not only equal in the eyes of God but equally qualified to understand the word of God, to participate in church government, and by extension to govern the Commonwealth" (Dahl 1989, 32); through the doctrine of the covenant, "which was the unique contribution which New England Puritanism made to the evolution of democracy, and especially federalism, in the United States" (De Gruchy 1995, 91). So it was that "in New England, Athens, and Jerusalem, Aristotle, Calvin, Locke, and Rousseau combined to shape American democracy" (92).

As for the relative significance of modern liberal views and Christian thought intimated in that catalogue of names and places: "Secular humanists and Christians have found each other, and discovered the extent to which the emancipatory values of truth, freedom, and justice are as, if not more, deeply rooted in biblical prophetic faith than the Enlightenment" (De Gruchy 1995, 125). This is what De Gruchy calls "the Christian matrix" in which democracy evolved in the Western world (57).

---

*In *City of God* 19.17, Augustine speaks of how the heavenly city, wayfaring on earth, "invites citizens from all nations and all tongues, and unites them into a single pilgrim band."

AMERICAN DEMOCRACY

If we focus on the exceptional case of American democracy, we must begin at the very beginning. "Well over a hundred years before the Revolution of 1776 or the Constitution of 1787," argues Hugh Heclo, "New England's Puritans had become the founding fathers of American democratic self-government." Then quoting Alexis de Tocqueville's celebrated *Democracy in America*: "Puritanism was not just a religious doctrine; in many respects it shared the most absolute democratic and republican theories" (Heclo 2007, 10; Tocqueville 1966, 30). "Anglo-American civilization ... is the product [wrote Tocqueville, demonstrating that amazing perspicacity for which he is so famous] ... of two perfectly distinct elements which elsewhere have often been at war with one another but which in America it was somehow possible to incorporate into each other, forming a marvelous combination. I mean the *spirit of religion* and the *spirit of freedom*" (Tocqueville 1966, 39–40; italics in original). (Tocqueville, by the way, is must reading for all high school civics or U. S. government classes.)

This spirit of freedom was undergirded by two things primarily: laws—regarding local independence, broad citizen suffrage with elected officials, free voting of taxes, trial by jury, government responsiveness to social needs—and compulsory public schooling, for promoting "a knowledge of the Bible in its true sense and original meaning" (Heclo 2007, 11; see Tocqueville 1966, 36–37). To the sneers of France's Enlightenment *philosophes* Tocqueville responded: "In America it is religion which leads to enlightenment and the observance of divine laws which leads men to liberty" (1966, 38). It could hardly have been better put by the most ardent Christian preacher.

The relationship between Christianity and democracy in this country, first lent concrete expression by the Puritans, is what Heclo describes as "this twisting helix of reciprocal influences" by which "in the years after Tocqueville returned to Europe, Christianity helped make a certain kind of democracy and democracy helped make a certain kind of Christianity in America" (2007, 35). But whatever we make of the way in which democracy has influenced Christianity (more on that shortly), "there have been few doubts about a larger bond that has grown over the centuries. It is the bond uniting Christianity and the democratic faith in the political society that is America" (76).

This is a remarkable story, and suggests why there may be for some an inducement to imbue American democracy itself with religious significance. Qualifications may therefore be in order.

QUALIFICATIONS

First, Christianity and democracy are not the same thing. Given the greatness of the American experiment and the intimate connection between the two in "this twisting helix of reciprocal influences," we may be tempted to forget that wonderful as this combination is, "the first political task of the Church is to be the Church," and "every earthly sovereignty is subordinate to the sovereignty of Jesus Christ," as Richard John Neuhaus reminds us (1981, 1). Though "Christians do not withdraw from participation in other communities," Neuhaus argues; though "we are called to be leaven and light in movements of cultural, political, and economic change"; and though "history is the arena in which Christians exercise their discipleship"—still, "the fulfillment of history's travail is the promised Rule of God, not the establishment of our human programs and designs" (1–2), not even the program and design of democracy, American or otherwise. Jesus' kingdom, as He Himself said, is not of this world (John 18:36). Here is the way Jacques Maritain put it in his influential *Christianity and Democracy*: "Christianity and Christian faith cannot be made subservient to democracy as a philosophy of human and political life or to any political form whatsoever" (1980, 24). That should not lessen our responsibility for, or our interest in, the prosecution of liberty by properly democratic means, but it is a hedge against the temptation to think that Christianity and democracy can be conflated.

Second, and related, just as Christianity and democracy are not the same thing, neither is democracy a religion substitute, as it can sometimes become, not only among those enthusiasts for American freedoms who have no great interest in obedience to

Christ, but also among certain Christians whose loyalty to the United States or the American way of life seems indistinguishable from their loyalty to the One whose kingdom is not of this world. This of course is no criticism of patriotism. The summons of this entire chapter is to an increased Christian patriotism in the shape of a more informed understanding of both democracy's connection to Christianity and America's unique expression of the combination of the two. The point is simply that belief in one's country or its "program and design" is not an alternative to submission to Christ.

The truth of this is seen in that the Christian faith can express itself and has expressed itself in a variety of political forms. This is the third of the four qualifications I want to make. "One can be a Christian and achieve one's salvation while militating in favour of any political regime whatsoever," says Maritain, "always on condition that it does not trespass against natural law and the law of God. One can be a Christian and achieve one's salvation while defending a political philosophy other than the democratic philosophy, just as one was able to be a Christian, in the days of the Roman Empire, while accepting the social regime of slavery, or in the seventeenth century while holding to the political regime of absolute monarchy" (1980, 24). The important thing, he says, is "by no means to pretend that Christianity is linked to democracy and that Christian faith compels every believer to be a democrat; it is to affirm that democracy is linked to Christianity and that the democratic impulse has arisen in human history as a temporal manifestation of the inspiration of the Gospel" (24–25).

My fourth and last point by way of qualification or clarification is that if, as Maritain has it, "the democratic state of mind proceed[s] from the inspiration of the Gospel," it stands to reason that "it cannot exist without it" (1980, 39). Here is his case:

> To keep faith in the forward march of humanity despite all the temptations to despair of man that are furnished by history, and particularly contemporary history; to have faith in the dignity of the person and of common humanity, in human rights and in justice—that is, in essentially spiritual values; to

have, not in formulas but in reality, the sense of and respect for the dignity of the people, which is a spiritual dignity and is revealed to whoever knows how to love it; to sustain and revive the sense of equality without sinking into a levelling equalitarianism; to respect authority, knowing that its wielders are only men, like those they rule, and derive their trust from the consent or the will of the people whose vicars or representatives they are; to believe in the sanctity of law and in the efficacious virtue—efficacious at long range—of political justice in face of the scandalous triumphs of falsehood and violence; to have faith in liberty and in fraternity, an heroical inspiration and an heroical belief are needed which fortify and vivify reason, and which none other than Jesus of Nazareth brought forth in the world. (39–40)

That's about as eloquent a summing up of the brief for Christianity's influence on democracy as one needs to galvanize heart and mind in the interests of an informed, no less than a biblically informed, patriotism.

DEMOCRACY'S INFLUENCE ON CHRISTIANITY

But democracy has also influenced Christianity, sometimes profoundly, and not always for good, perhaps especially in America. The prostitution of the doctrine of the worth and therefore the rights of the person into a license for unbridled individualism (which Heclo maintains is a legacy of the 1960s) has, in a number of commentators' view, shaped evangelical lifestyles as much as anyone else's. According to James Montgomery Boice, evangelical preacher and theologian, "The sad truth is that they [evangelicals] perhaps even more than others have sold out to individualism, relativism, materialism and emotionalism, all of which are the norm for the majority of evangelical church services today. Evangelicals may be the most worldly people in America" (Heclo 2007, 139–40). But no less Roman Catholics: "The old hostilities between Protestants and Catholics have indeed diminished in modern America," says Heclo, "inasmuch as most people in both Christian congregations now seem to regard individual choice as their *de facto* religious creed and commitment" (140). Others are just as critical. "To survive in America's highly emotional, exquisitely individualistic, and depressingly anti-intellectual culture," claims Alan Wolfe, "American evangelical Christianity all too often absorbs, rather than confronts, the culture of narcissism.... The focus—in evangelical forms, the relentless focus—is on what God can do for you, not what you can do for God" (Wolfe 2007, 202).

The implications for American democracy are obvious. If Christians, whose faith has uniquely inspired modern democratic theory and practice, have themselves become willing victims of corrupted notions of what democracy means, how can they constitute the core of those needed to defend that democracy in the future? And to the extent that notions of individual rights, freedom, liberty, and so on become detached from their theological moorings, to that extent will we face "a condition of devout, serious Christians alienated from the quest for democracy, and of devout serious democrats hostile to Christianity" (Wolfe 2007, 205).

PERSUASION AND PRODDING FOR THE FUTURE

But to avoid painting our prospects in overly somber tones, we should allow Heclo to persuade us, and prod us, to "encourage more serious attention to the vital relationship between Christianity and our American democracy." By "serious attention," he says, "I mean thinking with care, like grown-ups, and not succumbing to the emotional sloganeering that dominates our public shouting matches on this subject" (2007, 211). It is a word in season for us all.

Nor can Christians afford to withdraw into "internal exile in this country" (Heclo 2007, 235), even in the face of what might be "a growing disengagement between American democracy and traditional Christianity" (234). For their own sakes as well as the country's they need to remain faithful to their charge—because "from the beginning of our nation, a conditional, non-idolatrous attachment to America has offered Christians committed to their first love an ongoing opportunity to turn their words into deeds.... Without idolatry toward either, Christians can love their country as they love their neighbor" (235).

In four crucial ways, argues Heclo, "traditional Christianity is one important force that can help teach 'the art of being free'" (2007, 236). These are important practical considerations.

First, "traditional Christianity comes with an elemental moral code that helps stabilize and order an otherwise chaotic democratic society" (Heclo 2007, 236). Second, "the packet of moral imperatives that comes with traditional Christianity includes obligations that regularly lead [Christians] to do good works for others"; and although Christians know that good works don't get them into heaven, "good works are likely to come from people who believe there is a heaven and that it is their real home" (237). Third is "the reforming impulse that traditional Christianity carries into society.... Of the many types of groups making up civil society, the church of Christ is one dedicated—again by the content of its creed—to pursuing a moral vision of the larger society" (237). Fourth, "once we disabuse ourselves of the heresy of fideism—that is, confining religion to the realm of irrational blind faith—it is clear that Christianity can help preserve the role of reason in democratic discourse about humankind's most fundamental issues" (238); for even though "non-believers may not believe the Christians' answers ... a democratic society is surely better off for having to confront the Big Questions rather than pretending they do not exist" (239).

What all of this adds up to, says Heclo, is that "traditionalist Christians who sincerely try to live out their faith are not people we should want to see retreat from active citizenship. In fact, they make for the kind of companions we should all like to have on board a wandering ship of state as it navigates dark seas.... One could do much worse by way of fellow passengers" (2007, 240).

What all this all adds up to for Christian education should be equally plain. If we are to be the sort of fellow passengers Heclo describes—intelligent, thoughtful, and informed, as well as sincere—we have work to do. But it is a good and noble work to be sure. Jefferson would agree, would he not?

THREE DISCLAIMERS

Finally, three disclaimers.

1. What I have been saying in this chapter is in no way meant to imply that non-Christians do not or cannot contribute moral stability to American democracy, or that they are in any sense less patriotic. Such a notion is condemned by those like Franklin and Jefferson or Montesquieu and Paine, none of them a Christian but all profoundly influential in the cause of American liberty. That is not to mention the great company of patriots past and present—presidents, statesmen, soldiers, intellectuals, as well as countless ordinary citizens—of other religions or none at all.

2. What I have been saying does not mean that in the development of American democracy there were no influences other than Christianity. This too is obvious, and related to (1). The influence of the Enlightenment, often anticlerical at best, anti-Christian in its later manifestations, was of course foundational. So were the thinking and habits of ancient Greece and Rome.

3. Nor does any of it mean that Christian theology or devotion and political philosophy or patriotism can be conflated, as we said earlier. "The first political task of the Church," it is well to keep in mind, "is to be the Church," as Neuhaus reminded us, and "every earthly sovereignty is subordinate to the sovereignty of Jesus Christ."

To be awakened to these things is, one hopes, to avoid misunderstanding about the Christian's, and the Christian school's, role in American democracy. It is not to suggest that it is in any way thereby diminished.

CONCLUSION

That the chapter on "Education and Liberty" follows the chapter on "We've Got Too Much Going On" is not arbitrary. I mean by that juxtaposition to point up the contrast between the plethora of activities that occupy the time and attention of many Christian schools, not all of which activities (we would be forced to admit) are of real import—between those activities and the gravity of our responsibilities as educators of informed citizens, especially perhaps in a time like the present when we are being pulled in a thousand directions, not only by cultural forces, broadly speaking, but by educational fads and fancies as well.

With both the intimate bond between education and democracy and that between Christianity and democracy, who better than Christian schools to challenge and inspire to responsible citizenship? We have the profoundest reasons for doing so. The highest obligation and deepest privilege as well.

Five

"Leisure, the Basis of Culture"

For thus saith the Lord God, the Holy One of Israel; In returning and rest shall ye be saved; in quietness and in confidence shall be your strength: and ye would not.

—Isaiah 30:15, KJV

I want now to take up a related and no less important topic. I confess at the outset that so little is this talked about—I have never seen it addressed in a discussion of Christian education—so little is it appreciated and so countercultural are its implications, that I wonder if I can make myself understood. I mean the topic of leisure.

"The First Principle of All Action Is Leisure"

As unfamiliar as many of us may be with leisure, its importance was not missed by earlier ages. In company with so much that has shaped our thinking about most things, not least education, it had a singular significance for the Greeks. Aristotle argued in his *Politics* that "nature herself, as has been often said, requires that we should be able, not only to work well, but to use leisure well; for, as I must repeat once again, the first principle of all action is leisure. Both are required, but leisure is better than occupation and is its end; and therefore the question must be asked, what ought we to do when at leisure?" He adds: "It is clear then that there are branches of learning and education which we must study merely with a view to leisure spent in intellectual activity, and these are to be valued for their own sake" (*Politics* VII.3; McKeon 1970, 1306–7).

James Schall comments: "It seems odd that such great thinkers as Plato and Aristotle would associate leisure with the end of all we do, that they would hold that leisure is that for which we do everything else. But this is what they in fact claim" (2001, 102).

Precious few Americans will have given anything like that sort of priority to leisure, either in theory or practice. We are both busy and bored. We need to be entertained. "Millions long for immortality," someone has wryly remarked, "who don't know what to do on a rainy Sunday afternoon."

By contrast, Schall reminds us, "Cicero began the third part of his famous *De Officiis* ('On Duties') with these memorable words: 'Publius Cornelius Scipio, the first of the family to be called Africanus, used to remark that he was never less idle than when he had nothing to do, and never less lonely than when he was by himself'" (2006, 39). Boredom is a form of the sin of sloth, *acedia*, one of the Seven Deadly Sins. We Christians ought to be vigilant therefore against the seemingly constant protestations of the young that they are bored. The world is too interesting a place, the young too full of God-given life and health, for anyone to be bored, not to be thankful, by enjoying it and using it, for all that they have around them and in them.

LEISURE: THE NECESSARY CONDITION FOR EDUCATION

As leisure was considered the end for which we work, so is it the condition of a proper education. The Greek word for *leisure* is *skole*, from which we get our English word *school*. Likewise in Latin, where *skole* is translated *otium*, which means ease, or, again, leisure. The Latin for *business*, on the other hand, is *neg-otium* or no-*otium*, no-leisure, from which we get our word *negotiate* (Schall 2001, 102–3).

This is fascinating stuff. It is also, as I said, decidedly unmodern. Who among today's students would think of school as leisure?

For many it's drudgery, something to get through—to get through, in the case of college students, often enough, so that they can get on with their vocation, their work. More interesting from a history of language perspective is that according to surveys, the work that the largest number of college students are seeking by means of their education, if we can judge by their majors, is business (Ansary): *neg-otium*. On two counts, then, it will be difficult to convince most students that education has anything to do with leisure: (1) school doesn't seem much like leisure and (2) school in their view is meant to prepare them for work, the opposite of leisure.

THE AMERICAN OBSESSION WITH WORK

Behind the statistics regarding college majors is a culture-wide phenomenon, the American obsession with work, what one writer calls "the frenzied need to work." Nowhere is the need more frenzied than in the United States, unless it is in Japan or China. But then modern China presents us with a problem of its own special interest, I mean its rootedness in the Marxist exaltation of the worker over the intellectual (combined now, of course, with a thoroughly capitalist appetite for prosperity)—which was chiefly what the disastrous and tragic Cultural Revolution was about.

But America is especially famous for its work ethic, which no one could doubt is largely a good thing, the source of a very great deal that is salutary in the world. Anyone who has traveled even a little knows how central that ethic is to the abundance in which we live. Famously it has been called the Protestant work ethic, but for the moment I am not concerned whether or not it is a peculiarly Protestant phenomenon, only to remark on its prominence in Western, especially American, life and thought, and the way in which its prominence, not to say hegemony, has made it almost impossible for leisure to get a hearing. Leisure in some places is reckoned the luxury of the very wealthy, the idle rich, not of ordinary working people. It is therefore undemocratic, and in that way too perhaps un-American. Maybe even un-Christian, related to those two other L words, *lethargy* and *laziness*.

A Bit of Background

But we should pause here for a bit of background.

The reason leisure was so valued in the ancient world is that it was seen to be required for the preservation of society. There needed to be someone, unencumbered by the daily grind of making a living, even of running the state, who had time to think about things, including but not limited to how best to run the state. As Schall puts it, "A city needed someone to preserve its soul, someone free from the cares and concerns of political and economic life. Leisure implied that there must be space and time for what was beyond politics, for neither business nor politics seemed to exhaust what we sought." We humans are creatures whose special capacity is to know, who want and need to know. But "work and business prevent us from leisure, from contemplation and theory, from consideration of the highest things. Slaves and businessmen were not considered part of the polis because the things they did took so much of their time, energy, and effort that they did not have the opportunity to reflect, to consider in any deep fashion" (2001, 103).

Modern America and Ancient Greece

What is conspicuous in any attempt to apply the lesson of ancient Greece to our own situation is that in American democracy it is precisely the workers—doctors and lawyers and businessmen, but also butchers, bakers, and candlestick makers—who are expected to do the thinking, about politics in any case, often in a fairly theoretical and sophisticated kind of way. We do this indirectly, through our representatives, it is true, but we do it nonetheless. There is no leisured class in the ancient sense on which that responsibility rests. It rests on all of us. We are the polis. Consequently (thanks to the Founders) everyone in the United States, whatever his economic or social status, is required by law to attend school between the ages of six and sixteen. Everyone, in addition, has the opportunity to extend that education beyond the required ten years to include a BA, an MA, or a PhD. That much we have going for us, and it is a very great deal to be sure. It is an arrangement that the slave or businessman in ancient Greece could never have dreamed of.

Granted, it is more complex than that. First, such an education in America is neither everywhere equally accessible, nor equally cherished, nor of equal quality. Second, to say that such an education should be the privilege (or the responsibility) of all members of a democracy may be to forget that any society needs trained workers just as much as it needs trained thinkers. Both issues I take up in chapter 10. Here I want simply to establish the basic point that in the most general way democracies, as Jefferson and Mann have instructed us, require educated citizens, that their education be of a certain sort, and that in this country that education is available to, even mandated for, everyone, in a rudimentary way at least.

It is this sound general education, as it is called, done properly, that requires leisure. Notice that I said "done properly." Time and incentives for "just thinking about things" are too few and far between, perhaps especially in school, where they are needed most. That was the complaint of chapter 3. This may be part of an answer. Is it time we began considering ways by which leisure can become more a part of the way we live and think? Should we begin talking, if nothing more, about its importance?

LEISURE DEFINED

I come finally to where it might be thought I should have started, with what I mean by leisure. I have left the definition to last on purpose, for a reason which I think you will concede.

We could do worse for our definition than begin with G. K. Chesterton's essay "On Leisure": "I think the name of leisure has come to cover three totally different things," he says. "The first is being allowed to do something. The second is being allowed to do anything. And the third (and perhaps most rare and precious) is being allowed to do nothing" (1953, 215). As we shall see, leisure here does not mean mere idleness or indolence, but I do not entirely disagree with Chesterton: leisure of any meaningful sort must begin, or so it seems to me, with at least the possibility of being allowed to do precisely nothing. How could it be leisure of a kind that is fruitful of cogitation or rumination if at the back of the mind is some guilt about the need to *do* something?

Yet, according to Josef Pieper, whose book is the seminal work on this subject, "leisure" is something other than idleness. In fact he argues that "idleness in the old sense ... has so little in common with leisure, that it is the very inner disposition to non-leisure, that it is really 'lack of leisure'" (1998, 30). Leisure is "a condition of the soul ... not necessarily present in all the external things like 'breaks,' 'time off,' 'weekend,' 'vacation,' and so on." "Against the exclusiveness of the paradigm of work as *activity*," he says, "there is leisure as 'non-activity'—an inner absence of preoccupation, a calm, an ability to let things go, to be quiet" (30–31; italics in original). "Leisure is a form of that stillness that is the necessary preparation for accepting reality; only the person who is still can hear, and whoever is not still, cannot hear." Lastly, "leisure is the disposition of receptive understanding, of contemplative beholding, and immersion—in the real" (31).

"BE STILL AND KNOW THAT I AM GOD"

If all of this sounds "mystical" or "spiritual" of a kind that has no connection to Christian faith, let me bring us back to Pieper's primary argument. The epigraph for his book includes "Be at leisure—and know that I am God," the Septuagint's Greek rendering (we are told [Index, 157]) of the familiar "Be still, and know that I am God!" (Psalm 46:10 in most English translations; 45:11 in the Catholic Douai version).* It is leisure as stillness of the biblical sort that Pieper is after: "The deepest root, then, from which leisure draws its sustenance—and leisure implies the realm of everything that, without being useful, nevertheless belongs to a complete

---

*The Septuagint is the earliest translation of the Old Testament into Greek, finished sometime, it is thought, in the third century BC. Its name derives from the (apparently apocryphal) account of how the work was done by seventy-two Jewish scholars, sent from Jerusalem to Alexandria at the behest of Ptolemy II (309–246 BC), for his library there.

human existence—the deepest root of all this lies in worshipful celebration" (1998, 55). In Pieper's conception leisure and worship belong together. "When separated from worship, leisure becomes toilsome, and work becomes inhuman" (54).

Whatever we make of Pieper's understanding of leisure, the minimum we can take from it is an acknowledgement of not only the value of leisure as opposed to "useful work," but the relationship of leisure to the stillness that knows that God is God, even to the worship of God as God. For Pieper—it is another of his Christian insights—leisure is a means of grace. In leisure, in the absence of our working, as we listen or pray or worship, we are sometimes *given* insights—and that, it seems to me, is a profoundly pertinent notion for those of us in Christian education, that enterprise that is, as we regularly tell ourselves, the integration of faith and learning. Here is Pieper's way of putting it:

> The surge of new life that flows out to us when we give ourselves to the contemplation of a blossoming rose, a sleeping child, or of a divine mystery—is this not like the surge of life that comes from deep, dreamless sleep? And as it is written in the Book of Job: "God gives us songs in the middle of the night" (35, 10), and as wise people know, God gives His blessings to his own, and what rejoices them, in sleep—in just the same way, do the greatest, most blessed insights, the kind that could never be tracked down, come to us above all in the time of leisure. In such silent openness of the soul, it may be granted to man for only an instant to know "what the world/ holds in its innermost," so that afterwards the insights of that happy moment have to be re-discovered through the effort of "labor." (1998, 32–33)

Or as Schall tells us, "Mankind's story is more a drama of his receptivity than it is of his creativity, though it is that too" (2006, 42)—although receptivity and creativity are related, are they not? The biblical admonition "Be still" is entirely relevant to the academic and intellectual life, as it is elsewhere in the Christian life.

Two Final Things

There are two concluding remarks.

First, in attempting to say something about the importance of leisure I am not saying that work is unimportant. In another context I would say that many students need to work harder; they aren't working hard enough. (I haven't forgotten the surveys of student study habits cited in chapter 3.) Laziness is the temptation of nearly everyone, perhaps especially children or adolescents confronted with parabolas or *Paradise Lost*. There is much academic exercise that can be done properly only by diligent effort, concentration, keeping at it until you get it—by memorizing, or starting the problem over, or rewriting (then rewriting again). That is the case in the bulk of what we do in school. You can't "just think about things" unless you have something to think about, and that is gained, for most of us, by toil.

There is at the same time a need to emphasize the importance of "doing nothing" in the sense of stopping and smelling the roses, or standing and staring, or, as Pieper would have it, "a celebratory, approving, lingering gaze of the inner eye on the reality of creation" (1998, 33). Nor does it take too great an effort of imagination to see that "working hard" at homework assignments is not necessarily antagonistic to leisure of the type we're describing here. It stands to reason, does it not, that labor, of an intellectual sort, and leisure, also of an intellectual sort, cannot be mutually exclusive. If they were, what of the lives of so many, maybe all, of the greatest writers, philosophers, artists, poets, scientists, and mathematicians? And if it is true, as has been said, that "there can be no high civilization where there is not ample leisure" (as surely it is), it is also true (we would be happy to admit) that there can be no high civilization where there is not also plenty of sweat. But you will not miss my point. It is simply that in an American culture that has no lack of emphasis on work, there is need to be reminded of the essentiality of leisure, especially of that kind without which the most important things never get done, in school not least.

Second, I must address the question whether what I am suggesting is easy to do. Obviously not. I confessed at the outset that I wondered whether it would even be understood. It could therefore be no easier to put into practice—in which case that might be the place to begin: by simply trying to understand what is meant by "Leisure, the Basis of Culture," then how we might encourage ourselves and our students to both work hard and appreciate—better, appropriate—the wise and biblical admonition "Be still."

CONCLUSION

This book may introduce what to some are unusual notions, or those enough out of sync with the typical rhythm of educational life to be impractical or impossible to implement. The importance of leisure, I suspect, may be one of the most unusual and most impractical. Everywhere, it seems, we are being pressured to increase, not decrease, the pace of student activity, to do more not less; and it often appears that the pressure is coming as much from ourselves—administrators, teachers, parents, and students—as it is from forces over which we may think we have no control, college admission offices, for instance, or the need to compete, as I said, with St. Sebastian or Prep down the road.

So it is on this topic that we might find ourselves at odds with the system more than anywhere else; and frankly I am not sure what can be done about it, or if anyone really wants to do anything about it. There is an undeniable attraction about doing things, and in the present educational climate, who could dispute that more—more courses, more activities, more opportunities—is what sells? That it might be in everyone's interests to step back, slow down, do less, may be an idea that will get no hearing. I have even had parents tell me they *wanted* to be asked to organize candy sales. They felt more involved, more needed, when they were. And here I thought I was doing them a huge favor by suggesting that we should not be occupying their own and their children's time with such things! But that, like a hundred other activities now reckoned part of normal American life, was for them what schools were supposed to do.

If I have been less than clear or convincing in my presentation of leisure as Pieper has articulated it, or if that is not what suits us, I hope I have gotten us as far as the need to pause for a moment over ideas that bear the stamp of ages, if for no other reason than to whet our thinking. In an era when "the problems of American education" figure so large in our national conversation, it couldn't hurt. Not even in Christian schools can everyone be satisfied with the tempo or quality of student life and work as it is.

The Socratic Method

The Master said: To study without thinking is futile. To think without studying is dangerous.

—Confucius, *Analects*

It is about time, I suppose, that I attempted to say something "practical," give a suggestion or two about how actually to do something. For a book on education, how to teach, or some aspect of teaching, might be an appropriate topic. I claim no expertise here—my years in the classroom don't amount to much compared with most of my colleagues'—but let me give it my best effort.

In response to the claim (I had actually heard it made) that "the Socratic method is the pedagogy of the Son of God," I once wrote an essay titled "Jesus and the Socratic Method," wherein I argued that the Socratic method was certainly not the teaching style of Jesus, and tried to say in what ways Jesus' teaching differed from that of Socrates. In the same essay I also said that though I did not think that Jesus' method was the Socratic method, I should not be understood to mean that the Socratic method was a bad method. In fact, I said, I preferred it. It may be the best method.

At the beginning of this book I urged that one of the things we might have too much of, complicating our educating, was teaching, for the reason that more responsibility should be placed on the student and less on the teacher—as long, of course, as we understand what is meant by "responsibility." Here I want to try to say what I think, not only about that, but about why I think the Socratic method also means less is more, as well as how it might contribute to nurturing that ability, the subject of the last chapter, to work hard and "be at leisure" at the same time.

A Definition

I should begin by stating what I mean by the Socratic method, because I have often heard the phrase used to describe something other than what it truly is (or originally was), as I ordinarily use it myself.

Socratic method refers to the pedagogical style of Socrates, the famous fifth century BC (470–399) Greek philosopher, Plato's mentor and the protagonist in the Dialogues, which are Plato's rendering of Socrates' conversations with an interesting variety of interlocutors on an equally interesting variety of philosophical issues: ethical, political, aesthetic, and so on. All one has to do is read one of the Dialogues to understand how Socrates' "method" works: Socrates asks a question that, when answered, is followed by another question based on the answer to the previous question, then another and another, until a conclusion is reached. Along the way Socrates points out where the answerer is off the mark, and by this series of questions leads him, pulled along by the answerer's own logic, as it were, down a certain path. Whether Socrates himself is also pulled down this path is not clear. Does Socrates know ahead of time where the "answer" lies and so design his questions to lead to it, or is he merely the master logician whose conclusions are nothing more than the result of his having himself followed where the logic took both him and his interlocutor? Either way it is the logic that keeps the dialogue going. The subject matter (if we can call it that) is in a sense the dialogue itself, the verbal interplay between Socrates and the other—because unlike modern styles of teaching, Socrates neither lectures on a topic nor explicates a text. He simply inquires, probes, and provokes, in the abstract as it were. Here is a short sample taken from *Meno*. The discussion is about virtue.

> *Soc.* By the gods, Meno, be generous, and tell me what you say that virtue is; for I shall be truly delighted to find that I have

been mistaken, and that you and Gorgias do really have this knowledge; although I have been just saying that I have never found anybody who had.

Men. There will be no difficulty, Socrates, in answering your question. Let us take first the virtue of a man—he should know how to administer the state, and in the administration of it to benefit his friends and harm his enemies; and he must also be careful not to suffer harm himself. A woman's virtue, if you wish to know about that, may also be easily described: her duty is to order her house, and keep what is indoors, and obey her husband. Every age, every condition of life, young or old, male or female, bond or free, has a different virtue: there are virtues numberless, and no lack of definitions of them; for virtue is relative to the actions and ages of each of us in all that we do. And the same may be said of vice, Socrates.

Soc. How fortunate I am, Meno! When I ask you for one virtue, you present me with a swarm of them, which are in your keeping. Suppose that I carry on the figure of the swarm, and ask of you, What is the nature of the bee? and you answer that there are many kinds of bees, and I reply: But do bees differ as bees, because there are many and different kinds of them; or are they not rather to be distinguished by some other quality, as for example beauty, size, or shape? How would you answer me?

Men. I should answer that bees do not differ from one another, as bees.

Soc. And if I went on to say: That is what I desire to know, Meno; tell me what is the quality in which they do not differ, but are all alike;—would you be able to answer?

Men. I should.

Soc. And so of the virtues, however many and different they may be, they have all a common nature which makes them virtues; and on this he who would answer the question, "What is virtue?" would do well to have his eye fixed: Do you understand?

Men. I am beginning to understand; but I do not as yet take hold of the question as I could wish.

Soc. When you say, Meno, that there is one virtue of a man, another of a woman, another of a child, and so on, does this apply only to virtue, or would you say the same of health, and size, and strength? Or is the nature of health always the same, whether in man or woman? (*Meno* 71–72; Jowett 1952, 174–75)

And on it goes in what the *Oxford Dictionary of Philosophy* describes as "the method of teaching in which the master imparts no information, but asks a sequence of questions, through answering which the pupil eventually comes to the desired knowledge" (Blackburn 1994, 356). *Random House Webster's Unabridged Dictionary* adds that the use of questions, as employed by Socrates, is meant to "develop a latent idea, as in the mind of a pupil" (1997, 1812).

VARIATIONS ON THE THEME

Modern versions of the Socratic method are usually variations on this rather spare, strictly interrogative arrangement. They are based on some form of questioning, all right, but questioning about something already there, a book or problem assigned, mathematical, scientific, historical, or literary, often enough the Dialogues themselves. The "lesson" or "class" is not simply the unadorned dialectic between master and pupil; rather it is a discussion, stimulated and directed by queries and comments, usually from a teacher, among a number of students, typically sitting around a table, about a "subject."

This variation I would describe as broadly or loosely Socratic. It is not exactly what Socrates did, but you can see the likeness. In the original as well as its modified forms there is a teacher; there is a student or a number of students; the primary means of exchange is questions and answers, or dialogue; and so on. With the more modern versions the basic procedure is that the assignment is given and students are asked to go read, ponder, or figure, and return to talk about it, or demonstrate it on the blackboard. The simplicity of it is expressive of its essential rightness. It raises the only important issue: "Do you get what is going on here?" "Can you say what it is?" When that has been sufficiently addressed, class is over, or we move on to the next topic. This is what I have in mind when I talk about the Socratic method.

As soon as it is given a name, though—"Socratic" or "discussion-based" (as with "outcome-based" or ...)—any style of teaching takes on a certain aura or mystery, requiring special training at expensive workshops. Not here. Nor must you think this is about "the student-centered classroom" of *au courant* education theory, wherein students "construct their own knowledge" in small-group parleys about what they themselves want to learn.

In some ways (historically to be sure) it jumps over all that. Its name, recall, derives from the practice of a teacher who lived almost 2,500 years ago, and it was used for millennia before there was anything like what we now call educational research. To call it a method, therefore, or a technique, suggesting that it is the latest thing, supported by "the data," is to misrepresent it.

Suffice it to say that I value the Socratic method/approach/ style as an attempt to do what education, most fundamentally, is supposed to do. We sit down with a book and we read it. Why? So we can find out what the author is saying. Easy enough—or so it should be. I dare say, however, that that is exactly what a great many students cannot do: cannot read. I do not mean that they are incapable of sounding out words, or do not know what the words mean, or do not pause at commas or stop at periods (although those things are sometimes a problem as well). What I mean is that if I assign them a chapter in the history text and tomorrow ask them to tell me what it is about, they cannot tell me, let alone talk knowledgeably about the subject of the chapter—the theme or thesis or problem under consideration. But what else is there? If students can't do that, in science or math as well as Bible and English literature, it doesn't matter what else they can do. On the other hand, if they *can* do that, they can go to Harvard. I exaggerate, of course, for emphasis, because the ability to read and understand clearly what you have read so that you can talk about it (by which I mean write as well as speak)—that is the foundational ability of the academically competent.

THIS IS NOTHING NEW

How do we get students to read and know what they have read? is not a question that has never been asked before. Every thoughtful teacher, genuinely interested in the intellectual development of his students, has asked it in some form or other—because every thoughtful teacher cares that his students do more than memorize the list, fill in the blank, point to the right word, or otherwise "get the right answer." That is not to say that memorizing lists, filling in blanks, pointing to the right word, or getting the right answer are always useless exercises. It is only to say that unless they produce understanding or the skill that leads to understanding, they are unhelpful at best and pernicious at worst, because they teach students that by being able to do those things they are learning, when in fact they aren't—unless the teacher's goal is simply that students memorize a list, fill in a blank, and the like.

Agreed, there are times, at certain levels of student development or as a step in the process of understanding, when memorizing the parts of this or the sequence of that, lines of poetry or passages from the Bible, is not only useful or rewarding but necessary. You cannot discuss how a cell works unless you know the cell's parts. You cannot talk about how World War I may have led to World War II unless you have names, dates, and places at your fingertips. Not only is memorizing important, so are maps and charts and graphs and timelines and the rest. I am not advocating the abandonment of these things. To stop with them, however, is to stop short of the goal. We might say that the process of learning is more important than the product (if it comes to that), in the sense that getting to the answer (if there is one) is more important than the answer itself. The student might, after all, have just happened on the answer and have no idea why it is the right answer. But if she has learned how to do the problem, learned how it works, she will get the right answer, not only to that problem but to all others that work the same way. She might be on her way to figuring out those that don't work the same way. This is understood by all good teachers and is nothing new.

How Does the Socratic Method Help Us?

How then does the Socratic method as I have defined it help us? There are two ways primarily.

First, it puts the larger responsibility for learning on the student. The point of a class in chemistry is not to demonstrate that the teacher knows chemistry, but to ensure that the student does. To require students to struggle with the chemistry or literature text (or the calculus or biology problem), so that they are capable of talking intelligently about it, is therefore superior to telling them how they should think about it. If I know that tomorrow I will be asked to speak about a subject—decipher it or elaborate on it—my approach to studying will change dramatically. No more simply looking up the bold or italicized words in the book or waiting until the teacher or someone else explains it all in class. I may actually have to think about this. Learning should not be the teacher's travail, but the student's, and will not be effective until it is.

For the majority of my teaching career I labored under the conviction that being a good teacher meant that I was required to do most of the work: staying up late to write thorough and well-organized lectures and exams, meticulously grading papers, and so on. Teaching has moral and spiritual as well as technical obligations, including the obligation to model good work habits and a love of learning, plus a grasp of one's subject and the skill to articulate it. How else respond to the admonition to do everything well, as unto the Lord?

Scrupulousness, though, can sometimes be misguided. If it could be shown that by the teacher's doing nothing more than opening the classroom door at the beginning of class and closing it at the end students learned faster, understood to a greater extent, I submit that the teacher's responsibility should be nothing other than the opening and closing of doors—for which he should get very well compensated besides. I have been in classes where the teacher did little beyond just that, and they were some of the best I have ever seen, because it was the students who carried the load, who prosecuted the discussion, whose learning was on display—as it should be.

As in most things human, a great and lethal temptation in teaching is self-consciousness, taking oneself too seriously, so that the emphasis is on what I do rather than on what the student does, when it may be that the less I do the more the student learns. All parents know this in practice. In teaching my son how to fix the flat tire on his bicycle I am aware that the flat will get fixed quicker and better if I fix it myself. I also realize that to the degree that I fix the flat, to that degree my son does not discover how to fix it. At some point (after I have demonstrated the technique, guided him through it, and so on) I get out of the way. The same is true in the classroom. There is no need for the teacher always to teach, if we mean by "teach" disseminate information, or talk, or otherwise pull the weight.

A useful way to approach this may be to ask what, theoretically, is the most effective way for people to learn anything. One of the answers might be that they learn it best by learning it entirely by themselves. Take the flat fixing, for instance: we hand the child the disabled tire and the proper tools and leave him to figure it out. After who knows how many mangled tires and tubes, possibly bent spokes and rims, he will have solved the problem, not without considerable frustration, anger, self-doubt, damage to knuckles and fingernails, and time lost for other things—but he will know very well indeed how to fix a bicycle's flat, and a lot else besides.

In what I have just described I have also indicated why it is that we *don't* normally leave the young to figure things out for themselves, effective a means of learning as it might be. There is no need, apart from anything else, to reinvent the wheel (or in this case the means of repairing the tire and tube affixed to it). Why not simply tell or show someone how to do it? Why waste time and resources? Civilization is built on our capacity to learn from one another. We acknowledge, and thousands of years of experience have taught us, that teachers are absolutely necessary. Even the sparest application of the Socratic method, after all, required a Socrates to effect it. But somewhere between the teacher doing everything on the one hand and the student doing everything on the other is a place of maximum student learning, best weighted on the student's side, in my view, and ruthlessly focused on the essential point of whatever the topic is—and the Socratic method fits that description nicely.

Not that the Socratic method eliminates or dilutes the requirement for professional diligence, or in any sense makes teaching easier (more on that in a minute). Rather, responsibility takes a different shape as the teacher reevaluates what his job is, seeing it less as worrying about how to "get the subject across" or "make it interesting" and more as coming to grips with the substance of the matter at hand and directing his students to it, by means of questions or comments that will keep the discussion moving and on track.

That brings us to the second way the Socratic method helps students to understand, by discussing—because when students are able to talk about something, explain it, expand on it in response to well-formed questions from their teacher or comments by their classmates, the chances are increased greatly that they do really get it. All of us have heard the student excuse, "I understand it, but I can't explain it"—and the perceptive teacher's immediate reply, "If you can't explain it, you don't understand it." I agree. "When you know something," says Barzun, "you can tell it to somebody else" (1991, 34).

There are no doubt limits to what I am saying here. At the outer reaches of physics there are concepts, I take it, that refuse to be translated down. The same could be said for most disciplines, scientific and otherwise. Generally speaking, though, the ability to talk intelligently in everyday language about a complicated subject is pretty good evidence that you have it. That is the great use of essay exams as opposed to multiple-choice or fill-in-the-blank: they require students to explicate.

One of the places the Socratic method works best, by the way, contrary perhaps to what most of us might think, is in math. The most impressive demonstration of the Socratic method I have witnessed was in fact in a geometry class, where students were required to work out on the blackboard the proofs for the propositions in Euclid's *Elements*, step by step, sometimes twenty or more of them—and they could do it on the board because they had done it first in their rooms the night before. There was no teaching of the usual sort, except that what the student was doing was teaching of the best sort: not only was he working through the proof out loud, but the rest of the class was working through it with him. When he was stumped, his classmates (after a pause long enough to make it plain that he was stumped) might suggest that where he got off the track was "back at about step seven or so." A visitor would find it nearly impossible to know who the teacher was, so competent were the students at explaining themselves.

Geometry, because of its orderliness and the logicalness of its proofs, lends itself almost perfectly to a Socratic style of proceeding: such and such is given; we know from what is given that certain axioms apply; it follows therefore that ...; and because that is true, this is also true; and so on—all neatly set up to allow students to say how it works, and in so doing demonstrate their understanding. The same approach could be used with equal effectiveness in algebra or any math course: "*Why* does step four follow from step three?"—and the "why," after all, is what we're after.

Science too: "Now that you've memorized the names of the organelles, explain all the processes by which ATP is generated in an animal cell; also explain the relationship between the organelles." I am not attempting to dictate how biology should be taught (I hope it's not too obvious that I don't know much about it!), nor am I unaware that the teaching of science requires more than asking students to memorize and explain. I am saying only that a Socratic approach in science is not as difficult as it may seem, compared with, say, literature or history.

THREE MORE VIRTUES

Before I pass on to what the Socratic method is not, let me add three other virtues of this style of teaching that may be regarded as tangential, but are not insignificant nonetheless.

The first is that while the Socratic method does not create or demand leisure, it encourages the kind of thinking, or thoughtfulness, for which leisure is the most congenial circumstance. I think you would agree that they are natural partners.

The second is that it inculcates the skills and tempers required for civil discourse; and in a society in which civil discourse is conspicuously rare, giving young people an opportunity to participate in it can only be worthwhile.

By "civil discourse" I mean simply dialogue that is both informed and courteous, befitting educated people. Not that civil discourse can never entertain disagreement. Disagreement is often what discourse, civil and otherwise, is about, and that is not always a bad thing. Granted, the disagreement must be reasonable, but we expect that of academically supple men and women. That combination of informed equanimity and Christian forbearance fairly defines the style of converse for which the Socratic classroom so admirably provides the opportunity.

The third auxiliary or tangential virtue of the Socratic method is related to the second, for in giving students practice in civil discourse, it offers opportunities for the exercise of Christian charity. Love has good manners (as J. B. Phillips translates 1 Corinthians 13:5). At our school, students were required to refer to one another as "Mr." and "Miss" in the classroom (although not outside it): "Miss Sanchez's point is a good one, but I wonder if the author's comment on page 103 doesn't suggest to the contrary that ..." Courtesy is formalized, order reinforced, and everyone reminded that this is an exercise in polite as well as rational conversation. All are required to listen to another's point of view before responding; no talking while another is talking. This is not only good manners, but good sense, and avoids the embarrassment of having spoken about something I did not fully understand because I did not wait until it was fully expounded. Thereby will students learn to take other points of view, and other people, seriously, and to value the way in which dialogue, the mix and clash of opinions, works to sort things out, will learn how "iron sharpens iron, and one person sharpens the wits of another," as Proverbs tells us (27:17).

WHAT THE SOCRATIC METHOD IS NOT

It is true that such a classroom, poorly managed, could turn into a free-for-all, could become a forum for nothing more than pooled ignorance—and that takes us directly into what the Socratic method is not.

It is not, first of all, a means of allowing students to say whatever they want, a pedagogical device for making sure that students have the opportunity to "express themselves." (Remember that I said a moment ago that this is not about "the student-centered classroom" of progressive education theory.) A properly run Socratic discussion is governed from beginning to end by the text. The first requirement for any contribution is, Can it be supported by the reading? Precisely what you are not permitted is to offer an unsupported opinion, unless that is what is being asked for, as it sometimes is. The rules of good scholarship govern: what you say has to be defensible. Give us chapter and verse, page numbers, please. This is not a college dorm bull session, and not letting it become one is the responsibility of the teacher, whose thorough understanding of the material, careful evaluating of student comments, and well-thought-out questions and remarks ensure that the discussion does not lose its way.

Second, similar to the first, a Socratic classroom is not "students teaching one another" (as one of my parents claimed). Since it is the text that governs, even the teacher is more guide than dispenser of information. What is the meaning of *this* passage, the solution to *this* problem, the nature of *this* process? That's our focus.

Making the distinction between analysis based on careful reading and unsupported notion is part of the job of the teacher, although soon enough a savvy class will become attuned to making the distinction themselves and take a certain pride in ensuring that *their* discourse, at least, is not compromised by baseless opinion mongering. Again, "Page number, please, Miss So-and-So."

Nor is the Socratic method, third, a self-serving scheme devised by teachers to do away with their need to prepare or lead. The fact that the Socratic method puts the primary responsibility for learning on the student does not mean that the method eliminates the work of the teacher. Quite the opposite. Executed properly, this method requires more work than "ordinary" methods, although not work of the same kind. Just as it obligates students to begin to look at texts and problems in a different way, with more attention paid to *how* and *why*, so does it obligate teachers to prepare in a similarly different way. Before, I may have spent my evenings creating worksheets or pop quizzes or lectures (or charts or timelines or PowerPoint presentations); now I spend them rereading the text, thinking about it, trying to get inside it, seeing the parts in relation to the whole, the specific in relation to the general. By this means I formulate questions that lead students into the heart of what the issues truly are, or that provoke thinking that draws out of them insights that perhaps they did not know they had.

Is there in fact a *single* question that drives directly to the center of the subject and which, in attempting to answer, students will begin to see how all holds together—what the writer was on about, or (as in science or history) what links this phenomenon to that? In the attempt to form such questions the teacher is forced himself to come to terms with the essential nature of the material, to see it in ways he may not have done before, and so not only deepen his own appreciation of it and stimulate that of his students, but provide an example of the way the subject ought to be approached—the example, that is, of the careful thinker. Doing this may not appear to have been worked at, because the greater effort is intellectual, but its results are manifest—in the seemingly offhand remark or simple query that opens up the entire subject, informed as it is by ripened thought.

One of the reasons, I suspect, that the Socratic method may be difficult to get used to is that teachers are those who like to talk, and most of the time it is a good thing that they are. It is hard to teach if you are an introvert. But here teachers have to reinvent themselves, as it were, have to learn to see themselves as flies on the wall (or better, perhaps, as judges in a courtroom), to listen and observe, stepping in when needed, but no longer "the main speaker."

Fourth, this method does not make grading impossible or discriminate against the shy in favor of the gregarious. The difficulty in grading in a Socratic classroom is usually that assessing a student's participation in class discussion seems too subjective and arbitrary. But is not grading any work that is more or less open-ended—essays, for instance—subjective and arbitrary? In all such work we assume that the good teacher knows what she is looking for and can assess it fairly.

As for the naturally talkative versus the naturally taciturn: what we want is not volume of talk, but comment born of deliberation, and the teacher is, again, the judge of what is acceptable and what is not. Admittedly it will be easier for the temperamentally fluent or extrovert to discuss, but then it is always easier for the gifted to do what they are gifted for. For that reason they must be listened to with greater care, lest mere fluency be mistaken for familiarity with the subject. The reverse is also true: we listen to the shy with special attention, so as to hear what might be interesting or profound, aware that because they don't often talk we could be tempted to think they have little to say.

In a discussion-based classroom, while the diffident or less-outgoing may be at a disadvantage, so are they also in a place where they have the opportunity to make the style and skill of discourse their own. This is a learned ability, gained by competent instruction and disciplined practice, like dribbling a basketball or playing the violin. As I said to a father who complained that his son was doing poorly in such a classroom because he was shy: yes, some of us are shy, just as some of us are unathletic or unmusical or "mathematically challenged," but wouldn't it be wonderful if, under the guidance of a caring teacher and among classmates who had been taught that their discussion was required (in *this* Christian classroom anyway!) to be tempered by gentleness, the shy student learned how to offer an opinion and defend a proposition, confident in his claims because he had done the reading and thought it through? (That father's son, by the way, is currently at university studying English, preparing to be an English teacher.)

As intimated above, the Socratic method, even though it goes beyond the recitation of data—names, dates, places, particularity—does not, fifth, do away with the need for data. That is true of all good scholarship.

It does not, sixth, eliminate other styles of teaching, not necessarily. What is allowed is a matter of individual school policy. In some places nothing but the Socratic is allowed; in others there is something of a mix. If a school decides on this method, however, it must make sure that it does not deviate from it too much, otherwise students will never learn its virtues—because like any good discipline this requires working at; it will not in every case come naturally. Since what is being required is cogent thought and clear speech—no sloppy, half-baked explanations—some students, teachers too, will complain that it is too hard or too "intellectual." It disallows shallowness on the part of both teacher and student, and so must be encouraged and enforced until the aversion to it is overcome.

There is nothing sacred about a method, and to require rigid adherence to discussion-based pedagogy (or any other)—never an exception, no deviation—is a violation, it seems to me, of common sense. On the other hand, in order for it to work it must be the rule; everyone must be of one mind regarding its benefits, and committed to employing it as the standard. You cannot have one teacher given to worksheets, DVDs, and learning games while the rest of the faculty is working to train students to read carefully enough to be able to talk in an informed way about what they have read. Students should know that whatever the class, nothing less than understanding is the goal, and that that understanding will be both nurtured and demonstrated primarily by the Socratic method.

WRITING FOR STUDENTS AND LECTURING FOR TEACHERS

What then of writing assignments for students or lectures by teachers? The ability to write is so important—it is one of the ways by which students demonstrate understanding, in fact is a means of discussion—that I cannot see how any good instruction, in any subject, could neglect it. Writing is an exercise in thinking clearly. It is not an "English thing"—any more than logic is a philosophy thing or historical perspective a history thing—but a skill required of all educated people. You cannot do theology or literature or psychology, or math or science in some cases, if you cannot express yourself in writing. Einstein, we are told, wrote out his theories, in words, in longhand, because explaining them on paper helped him to think them through; and I once had a math teacher in my school who required her students to keep a math journal wherein they had to say in prose how they had done certain problems. The Socratic method, while not essentially "about writing," does not eliminate writing, rather should encourage it—largely because the skills developed in a Socratic classroom belong to a whole. "It cannot be too often repeated" wrote Barzun, "that reading, writing, speaking, and thinking are not four distinct powers but four modes of one power" (1991, 29).

Nor do I share the current disdain for lecturing. Even though teacher talk must not take up very much of a class where discussion is the norm, conceived rightly the lecture has its important uses. There are times when students need to be informed—about Emerson's theology or the background to Washington's "Farewell Address," or whatever. There is need to impart information, information not available in the reading under consideration but important to it. So the teacher says, "Today we'll suspend our discussion. I'm going to talk for an hour or so. You'll need to take notes."

There is another use of the lecture that I think we have forgotten, to our loss, in the contemporary opposition to it, namely, as an opportunity for the teacher once in a while to take on in a personal way some topic of his choosing, to "give a lecture" in something like the British manner. This would not be a mere ramble, off the top of the head, but a carefully thought-out and scripted comment on "The Virtues of the Socratic Method," for instance, or "The Importance of History for Christian Belief" or "The Christian and the Environment" or ..., demonstrating the kind of careful analysis and independent thought the teacher is wanting to encourage in his students.

Maybe it ought to be a requirement for all teachers to deliver such a lecture once a year. This would encourage them to think in a fresh way about their subject, and to model for their students what Christian scholarship should aspire to be. It might generate a new enthusiasm for their discipline among teachers for whom English or biology had begun to cloy. An athletic director of mine had a passage from *The Republic* posted on his office door that had to do with the importance of physical training for citizenship. What if every year the P. E. teacher demonstrated, by lecturing on "The Practical and Philosophical Basis of Physical Education," that he was no unthinking jock, but someone whose understanding of his craft was informed by his reading of Plato? Would that not radically alter students' appreciation of the nature of their school's vision, not to mention their view of physical education, not to mention that of their teacher?

What about quizzes, tests, and other traditional means of examination? There is no reason to abandon those either. It goes without saying, though, that all such would follow the line taken by your teaching. You wouldn't give a multiple-choice exam to students who have just been hashing out the extent to which early Christianity was or was not "communistic," or the United States' role in maintaining world peace.

Not that checking students on their grasp of the details is a bad idea—in fact it's a good idea—but, as Barzun has said, "nobody ever learned to write better by filling in blanks with proffered verbs and adjectives. To write is to fill in a totally blank sheet with words of your own" (1991, 34). "Passing a fill-in test in English composition [or any other subject] means nothing if the passer is power-*less*—not able—to write ten clear lines of prose" (29; italics in original).

SEVERAL FOOTNOTES

First, it is sometimes claimed that a Socratic style of teaching requires "smart" students and can work with no other. I would agree that it requires attentive, serious, caring students, but would deny that it requires those who are intellectually superior. Within reason (I am not talking about special-needs students, those with emotional or learning disabilities) what matters is discipline, work habits, paying attention, and so on. What matters especially for the Socratic method is their getting used to it, being taught how it works. Its success depends not on the intelligence of students or teachers, but on their having been schooled in a particular way of looking at things. (Perhaps you have seen the film distributed by the Junior Great Books people showing inner-city third graders holding forth Socratically.) No doubt smart students should be able to do this more easily than the rest of us, but that is true of almost everything. Smart students, after all, do better on worksheets and multiple-choice exams, but not, to be sure, always. Average students, working hard, in my experience, hold no less promise. In any case, both can learn how to think in the way required by the Socratic method.

Second, not only does the Socratic method not require smart students or reward only right answers, it positively encourages the admission of ignorance or confusion. "I don't get this at all" or "I don't understand how Mr. Lee gets from point A to point B" is a perfectly appropriate contribution to the discussion. For one thing, it signals the need for someone else to elaborate or clarify, and if that elaboration or clarification doesn't help, or is wrong, yet another someone can take a shot at it—all of which should encourage the timid or diffident or confused, because we're all in this together.

The confusion, it goes without saying, must not be the result of the student's having simply neglected to do the work, but rather of his having struggled with the text or problem to the place of knowing exactly what it is that confuses him. If a student can say what it is that he doesn't understand—he could follow one part of the argument but not another—he has already demonstrated a certain level of understanding; and everyone would agree that an honest failure to get it, arrived at after obvious intellectual effort, is a hundred times more valuable, and infinitely closer to what we mean by learning, than the ability to fill in a blank or make a list.

Third, not all subjects are equally amenable to the Socratic method, although, as I hope I have shown, some thought not to be are surprisingly well served by it, math being perhaps the best example. We can concede that literature or Christian doctrine classes more easily adapt to it than, say, physics; nor can you do physics without experiments and plenty of just plain working through the problems. There is a place, nonetheless, for Socratic dialogue, meant to encourage and test students' comprehension, even in a subject like physics, especially if that kind of comprehension is not being required under another name.

It should be just as obvious that Socratic, discussion-based teaching works best with smaller classes, but so does, by all measurements, any other kind.

The same common sense should apply to things like grade appropriateness. College-bound seniors will find a Socratic approach more comfortable than will frisky seventh graders, in part because seniors have more, five years more, to talk about. They will also have, if they have been trained in it, more experience, and thus greater comfort, in doing it—because another reason seventh graders will struggle with a teaching style that requires that they think with care and speak with precision is that they may never have been asked to do either.

Its successful implementation might also require instruction in its basic idea, and beyond that perhaps in the more specific matter of how good discussion questions are arrived at and followed up on. Old as the Socratic method is, it is not well-known today, except in a handful of schools and colleges where its virtues are extolled. It will require, therefore, to be gotten familiar with. After years of doing education in a lot of other ways, many of them acknowledged unfruitful, it may be time to allow the Socratic way an opportunity to demonstrate why, after almost 2,500 years, it is still doing, in some places, its good work.

CONCLUSION

Mark Hopkins was president of Williams College, 1836–72, the college's most famous and longest-tenured president, immortalized by the aphorism attributed to one of his students, James A. Garfield, twentieth president of the United States: "The ideal college is Mark Hopkins on one end of a log and a student on the other" (Rudolph 1990, 243). High praise indeed. Implied in the remark is the notion that the ideal college is *nothing more than* a great teacher and a willing student, with something for the two of them to sit on. (Another version of the comment has Garfield saying, "A pine bench with Mark Hopkins on one end and me at the other is good enough College for me.") But then Hopkins taught philosophy, not chemistry or music or theater, and so did not need Bunsen burners or centrifuges, or pianos or risers, or sets or soundboards—or any of a thousand things the modern school considers indispensable. Moreover, we have been told, he taught by means of the method we have been describing, the Socratic, and so might not have required even a blackboard, or whatever its nineteenth-century equivalent.

I am in no way suggesting that we can adopt wholesale an ancient style of teaching and the limited arrangements it required in a single discipline particularly suited to it, as if 150, or 2,000, years of technological progress and cultural evolution had never occurred.

But for all the exceptions that must be made to an attempt to apply the Socratic method across the curriculum, its basic idea is still a sound one: students are required to come to grips with the material, science or math or literature or history, and then asked to demonstrate their understanding by being able to talk about it. It has the added advantage of being simple and inexpensive, although by no means effortless. But then good things seldom are.

S e v e n

The Teaching Style of Jesus

And blessed is anyone who takes no offense at me.

—Jesus, Luke 7:23

At the beginning of the last chapter I remarked that I had once responded at length to the claim that the Socratic method was "the pedagogy of the Son of God." What I said in my response was that while I would agree that the Socratic method is a good method, in certain circumstances arguably the best method (as I have tried to show), it was not the teaching method of Jesus. Having said that, I am perhaps obligated to go on to say (a) in what ways Jesus' teaching differed from that of Socrates and (b) what Jesus' teaching method was.

The issue is not merely academic. Often in Christian education circles one hears the admonition that we should "teach as Jesus taught," or words to that effect. Recently in fact I heard it said that those of us in Christian schools need to model our teaching more on Jesus' teaching, particularly His use of stories and, most especially, questions. It is a natural Christian way of looking at things. Who, after all, *should* be the model for Christian teachers, if not Jesus? He is our model in everything else, is He not? We are told specifically that in our running of the race that is the Christian life we are to be "looking to Jesus the pioneer and perfecter of our faith" (Hebrews 12:2).

Moreover, Jesus was Rabbi or Rabboni, Great or Master Teacher. "Then he began to speak, and taught them, saying" (Matthew 5:2), the Evangelists inform us, or "when the Sabbath came, he entered the synagogue and taught" (Mark 1:21). Mark says that it was "his custom" to do so (10:1). A check of almost any concordance indicates, interestingly, that Jesus taught more than he preached, at least if we go by word count. In a discussion of teaching in Christian schools it would seem a singular omission, therefore, not to inquire into the teaching of Jesus.

DID JESUS TEACH SOCRATICALLY?

We might begin by addressing the question whether Jesus taught Socratically. Is it accurate to say that "the pedagogy of the Son of God" was the Socratic method, as has been claimed, and are we thus required to employ it ourselves? If not, as I have suggested—does that mean that we should therefore *not* use it?— what was it?

With the definition of the Socratic method employed in the previous chapter still before us, let me suggest that the issues for the purpose of comparing Jesus' teaching with Socrates' are three: (1) Does the master profess to impart no information, so that the dialogue is a mutual exploration wherein neither master nor pupil knows the outcome? (2) Is the exchange between master and pupil "a *sequence* of questions," again, truly an exercise in seeking or probing or, as we said, exploring? and (3) Is the master attempting to develop an idea latent in the mind of the pupil, as opposed, say, to telling him what it should be?

It is a fact that Jesus asked questions, lots and lots of them (someone has estimated that there are about 100 in the combined accounts). But are they Socratic questions?

I submit that in the four Gospels, with the exception possibly of one or two instances in which the adverb might be applied (albeit rather loosely), there is not a single instance of Jesus asking a question Socratically, that is, for the purpose of drawing out answers latent in the one questioned, while neither asker nor answerer is sure of the result. In the Sermon on the Mount, for instance, Jesus asks something like fifteen questions (not counting those that are included in a comment, such as, "On that day many will say to me, 'Lord, Lord, did we not prophesy in your name, and cast out demons in your name, and do many deeds of power in your name?"' [Matthew 7:22]). Every question is rhetorical, asked, as the dictionary says, "merely for effect with no answer expected" (Merriam-Webster, Incorporated 2003, 1069).

Is that because the Sermon on the Mount is a sermon? What is true of Matthew 5–7 is true of the entire Gospel, and what is true of Matthew is true of Mark, Luke, and John: there is no dialogue of a genuinely Socratic nature in any of them—perhaps least of all in the conversation on the road to Emmaus (Luke 24:13–32), where, in that eminently peripatetic teaching situation, we might most expect it. After two simple queries, "What are you discussing with each other while you walk along?" and (when one of the men asks, "Are you the only stranger in Jerusalem who does not know the things that have taken place there in these days?") "What things?" we are told that Jesus says, "Oh, how foolish you are, and how slow of heart to believe"—and immediately begins what must have been a very long (seven miles long?) explanation, starting with Moses and the prophets, of what was said in the Scriptures concerning Himself.

And as if to confirm that Jesus' companions did not come into the truth by means of His having drawn it out of them, Luke tells us that their eyes were opened in His act of breaking the bread, and what they remembered, what caused their hearts to burn within them, was Jesus' talking to them, His opening of the Scriptures for them, not their gradual enlightenment as they answered His round of questions.

The Socratic dialogues are by definition an exchange of ideas or opinions, in a sense open-ended. Furthermore, the exchange itself is what the exercise is mostly about. That is not at all the case with Jesus. When He asks a question He knows what the answer is, and the answer—that particular answer, and that answer alone—is what He is interested in, not the discussion as such. Even when He does seem to want a response, the response is often yes or no, or something similarly straightforward.

In the Gospel of Matthew, the longest answer to any of His questions is to His query, "Who do people say that the Son of Man is?" The disciples reply, "Some say John the Baptist, but others Elijah, and still others Jeremiah or one of the prophets" (16:13–15). It is a considerable stretch, in my view, to call this a Socratic question, as some have called it. (More on that in a minute.) It is meant to get at the truth, certainly, but not by means of extended dialogue. Rather, as in almost every case of Jesus asking a question, it is an opportunity for Jesus to speak. He doesn't elicit truth; He enunciates it.

COMPARING THE GOSPELS AND THE DIALOGUES

Probably the easiest way to demonstrate this is to compare any encounter of Jesus, with individuals or groups or crowds, to almost any of Plato's Dialogues, and the difference is dramatic. Open to the *Gorgias*, say, as I did at random: column after column of question and answer followed by question and answer. Then open a red-letter Bible to one of the Gospels and see page after page, in John chapter after chapter, of uninterrupted dominical monologue. Not only is there no Socratic dialogue, there is no dialogue at all.

What then can we say to Robert Stein's assertion that Socrates "by his use of questions ... forced his audience to become involved in the learning process," and that Jesus likewise used questions for the purpose of "drawing from his audience the correct answer he sought"? (1978, 23). Stein cites Mark 8:27–32 in evidence, the second Gospel's parallel account of the incident just referred to, wherein Jesus asks His disciples, "Who do people say that I am?" and they answer, "John the Baptist; and others, Elijah; and still others, one of the prophets," following which Jesus inquires, "But who do you say that I am?" and Peter responds, "You are the Messiah."

JESUS AND "ELICITING THE TRUTH"

We could start by wondering whether Jesus' seeking "a correct answer" doesn't of itself distinguish Him from Socrates, whatever the style of inquiry—given what we know of Socrates' probing, exploring, open-ended approach to issues, wherein "correct answers," if indeed there were any, were rarely if ever the point. Then we would want to ask further, While Mark 8:27–32 is plainly an instance of Jesus' use of questions, is even this really an attempt on Jesus' part to draw from His audience "the correct answer he sought"?

Jesus asks two questions. The first seems a pretty direct examination as to fact: What are people saying about Me? The disciples either know the answer or they don't. Whether they give a right answer or a wrong answer, there is no need to draw it out of them. The second concerns their personal conviction: What do you think or believe about Me? No doubt it is a different sort of question than the first—it is searching, deeply personal, and about a lot more than mere fact—but is it Socratic in the sense that (1) Jesus does not know the answer, (2) it involves a sequence of follow-up exploratory inquiries that lead the disciples to discover the truth, or (3) what they discover is that the truth was there the whole time, latent in them? To be honest, both questions are pretty straightforward and factual, although the second, as I've said, requires another order of self-evaluation and commitment. Nor does the conversation go any further than that. The dialogue, such as it is, is over with in two questions and two answers—one question and one answer really.

Admittedly the query, for Peter, had the effect of bringing to the surface or to consciousness something deep (latent?) within him, making articulate and concrete what was there but perhaps not well formed—provoking Peter, if you will, so that Peter in a sense would hear himself make his admission, also know that others had heard him make it. That may have been Jesus' intent. But even this looks like a much different thing from what is going on in the Dialogues. Peter's admission is a confession of faith, not the expression of an opinion in more or less tentative progress toward a conclusion.

A somewhat better example of Jesus' use of "Socratic questioning" cited by Stein (1978, 25) is Mark 8:15–21. Jesus, having fed the five thousand, and denying the Pharisees' request for a sign from heaven, says to His disciples, "Beware of the yeast of the Pharisees and the yeast of Herod," whereupon, not understanding, the disciples say to one another, "It is because we have no bread."

To this, Mark tells us, Jesus says, "Why are you talking about having no bread? Do you still not perceive or understand?" He then reminds them of His feeding the five thousand and asks how many baskets of bread and fish were left over, and, hearing their answer, asks, "Do you not yet understand?"

This is clearly a question calculated to make the disciples think, or so it appears; but, again, it's thinking of a personal, self-examining, or introspective sort rather than thinking that ends in a judgment or an idea needing further to be explored or discussed. In any event, no record of any answer by the disciples, not even yes or no, let alone an extended comment, is given.

All of Stein's other examples (Mark 10:38, Matthew 17:25, Matthew 21:31, Luke 10:36, Luke 22:35) are questions of this self-examining kind (1978, 23), where the answer is personal, short, and while not predictable in every case, requires no further probing that "draws forth more and more definite answers by means of pointed questions" (Runes 1972, 295)."

Even in those more memorable instances in which the question seems as if it might have a Socratic intent, might be designed to generate a response, it doesn't—or if it does the response is not recorded. A perfect example is Matthew 9:2–8 (Luke 5:17–26). It's the touching story of the paralyzed man lying on a bed, brought to Jesus by his friends for healing. When Jesus says to the afflicted one, "Take heart, son; your sins are forgiven," some of the scribes who are looking on say, "This man is blaspheming"—meaning, as Luke tells us, that no one can forgive sins but God. To this Jesus replies, "Why do you think evil in your hearts? For which is easier, to say, 'Your sins are forgiven,' or to say, 'Stand up and walk'?"

If ever there was a Socratic moment this is it. What a wonderful question to work on dialectically, worthy of Socrates himself: ease of saying versus ease of doing, ability to forgive sins versus ability to heal bodies, the relationship between the two, etc. So what does Jesus do with it? Absolutely nothing. He discusses it not at all. As soon as He asks it He says, "But so that you may know that the Son of Man has authority on earth to forgive sins ..." and tells the paralytic to get up, take up his mat, and go home.

Case closed—and the perfect opportunity for Socratic dialogue dismissed. (Whether Jesus' way with the scribes had something to do with their being scribes is perhaps important, but Jesus' use of the Socratic method is no less difficult to find in any case.)

There are other occasions of what seem to be, or might have been, Socratic questions and Socratic responses in the Gospels. In Matthew 12:27 Jesus asks the Pharisees, "If I cast out demons by Beelzebul, by whom do your own exorcists cast them out?" and in 19:16–22, the story of the so-called rich young ruler, Jesus, in answer to the inquiry, "Teacher, what good deed must I do to have eternal life?" replies, "Why do you ask me about what is good?" One can imagine the beginnings in the second case of a long back-and-forth on the meaning of "good," whether good for God means the same as it does for men, and the like, Socratic mode; or in that of the Pharisees' accusation, debate about the uses and abuses, or limitations, of demonic power. Not in either case does Jesus even pause for a rejoinder. In the first He goes right on, declaiming on how it is that He casts out demons by the Spirit of God, and the sin of blasphemy against the Holy Spirit; in the second He answers Himself ("There is only one who is good"), then proceeds to expose the young man's apparent preference for earthly treasure over heavenly. Again, no dialogue.

What we have in Stein's analysis, I think, is a logical fallacy, a fairly common one it may be, that goes something like this: the Socratic method is a style of teaching that is based on questions; in His teaching Jesus asked questions; therefore Jesus used the Socratic method. The error in reasoning thus is that it fails to consider the *kinds* of questions Jesus asked. Not all questions are Socratic questions; just because a teacher asks questions doesn't mean he is using the Socratic method.

JESUS AND THE RHETORICAL QUESTION

It is admittedly not easy to categorize Jesus' questions, and I claim no expertise or precision in attempting to do so. But if you count those in Matthew's Gospel (to take but one of the Synoptics), and if you eliminate the ones that demand a simple factual answer, such as "How many loaves have you?" (15:34); and if you further take out those meant, seemingly, to stimulate self-examination, such as "You of little faith, why did you doubt?" (14:31) or "Are you also still without understanding?" (15:16) or "Have you not read ...?" (19:4)—which might be interpreted "Don't you know ...?"—you end up with something like forty questions asked by Jesus, the vast majority of which, as I have said, are rhetorical, meant not to be answered, but to make a point, or, again, as one dictionary says, "solely to produce an effect or to make an asseveration and not to elicit a reply." (The number can vary, depending on how refined your categories, but the distinction holds.)

An asseveration is "an emphatic assertion" (Random House, Inc. 1997, 125), a positive statement or declaration. Isn't that exactly what Jesus is doing with His questions most of the time, making an asseveration? The Sermon on the Mount is full of such: "If you love those who love you, what reward do you have?" (Matthew 5:46); "Is not life more than food, and the body more than clothing?" (6:25); "Are you not of more value than [the birds of the air]?" (6:26); "How can you say to your neighbor, 'Let me take the speck out of your eye,' while the log is in your own eye?" (7:4); and so on. No answer is expected and none is given. Again, Jesus is simply making a point.

Stein is much more on target, in my view, when he says that "the most frequent use Jesus made of the question was as a rhetorical device. By using a rhetorical question Jesus sought not so much to draw a verbal response from his audience as to produce an effect. At times the effect sought was the assent of his listeners to what he was saying, for Jesus assumed that only one answer was possible" (1978, 24). I would go further and say that it is easier to argue that all of Jesus' questions are in some sense rhetorical than it is to argue that any is in any sense Socratic. But, on the whole, from this point on in his argument, I tend to agree with Stein.

THE VARIETY OF JESUS' QUESTIONS

Specimens of Jesus asking questions of various sorts abound (I'm not attempting to cover them all!), but in none of them does He appear to be trying to elicit truth, or even engage the questioner in conversation. The rhetorical formulas of Jesus—"It is said" and "It is written," but, most especially, "You have heard that it was said ... but I say unto you" and "Verily, verily, I say unto you," provide the clearest antithesis to Socratic elenchus.* It is "Then Jesus told them," "Then Jesus cried out," "Jesus answered," "He began to teach them, saying ..."—but never, "And Jesus, in an attempt to get them to see the truth of the matter, asked yet another question, this time from a different angle."

Think, for illustration, of Jesus' remarkable encounter with the woman at the well (John 4:7–30), one of the more extended conversations of His recorded in the Gospels. Here we have questions, all right, but every one is asked by the woman. And while there is a wonderful and definite, but definitely not obvious, logic in the way Jesus guides the exchange from opening request to concluding declaration by means of an extraordinary series of profound replies to a series of seemingly mundane queries, this is, again, not what we would commonly describe as debate or dialectic. The woman's final remark suggests as much: when she leaves her water jar and goes back into the city she says to the people, not "I have met a man whose logic is irrefutable," but "Come and see a man who told me everything I have ever done!" It is not Jesus' persuasive but His prophetic powers that convince her.

Or consider the equally remarkable interchange between Jesus and Nicodemus (John 3:1–21). What is astonishing about it, among other things, is that for all of its pregnant possibilities for long and deep rumination on matters of the profoundest religious significance—doing signs and the presence of God, being born again, flesh and Spirit—there is no real give-and-take to speak of. Nicodemus comments or asks questions; Jesus, however, does not follow up with counterquestions—except in verse 10 ("Are you a teacher of Israel, and yet you do not understand these things?")—but rather, as so often, with emphatic declarations, in every instance attended by "Very truly, I tell you." It is startling how un-Socratic it all is, especially if we are accustomed to thinking

---

Elenchus is a Greek word meaning "refutation" or "cross-examination; thus the Socratic method is sometimes called the elenctic method.

of Jesus as reasoner or disputant. Tête-à-tête, perhaps, but hardly argumentation of a Platonic sort.

At this stage someone might object that in many of the instances I have cited Jesus was not really *teaching;* He was simply interacting (we might say) with people. We can't properly characterize His pedagogy on the basis of such incidents, therefore, in comparison with Socrates or anyone else. Here, though, I have only followed others who have commented on Jesus' teaching, wherein "teaching" is used in the broadest sense and includes most of Jesus' encounters, whether conversation or controversy or repartee. If we are allowed to allude only to those instances in which the word *teaching* (or *taught*) is used, we'll find barely a handful in which Jesus asks questions (Luke 5:17–26, already noted above, and Matthew 21:23–27, for instance). In a sense, then, we must expand our definition if we are to have much to talk about.

JESUS IN CONTRAST TO SOCRATES

The differences between Socrates and Jesus must surely be attributable to this, that Jesus, unlike Socrates, whose noble life was spent inquiring after wisdom, Jesus was Himself the one "in whom are hidden all the treasures of wisdom and knowledge" (Colossians 2:3). He came not to educate (in the sense of drawing or leading out), but to reveal. Jesus' pedagogy derives from who Jesus was and is. Jesus' pedagogy is a Christological issue.

Something like this distinction is being made in Soren Kierkegaard's *Philosophical Fragments,* chapters one and two, which Peter Kreeft calls "the most illuminating comparison I know between the two greatest men in history" (2002, 4).

Socrates, says Kierkegaard, understands all learning and inquiry to be interpreted "as a kind of remembering; one who is ignorant needs only a reminder to help him come to himself in the consciousness of what he knows. Thus the Truth is not introduced into the individual from without, but was within him" (1946, 5). Socrates therefore "entered into the role of midwife and sustained it throughout" (6). In *Theaetetus,* for example, Socrates says, "Well, my art of midwivery is in most respects like [the real midwives']; but differs, in that I attend men and not women, and I look after their souls when they are in labour, and not after their bodies: and the triumph of my art is in thoroughly examining whether the thought which the mind of the young man brings forth is a false idol or a noble and true birth" (*Theaetetus* 150; Jowett 1952, 516). So it is that in his imaginary dialogue between Socrates and the students and faculty at a twentieth-century American divinity school, Kreeft at one point has Socrates say to a class in Comparative Religions, "I do not tell you what you do not know, just what you know but don't know you know" (2002, 94). Socrates did not see himself as begetting Truth, but, much more modestly, merely delivering or (as we might say these days) facilitating it. Begetting for Socrates, according to Kierkegaard, "belongs to God alone" (1946, 6).

That, in Kierkegaard's reckoning, is the difference between Socrates and Jesus: Socrates draws out truth from inside one who "must have the Truth in himself, and be able to acquire it by himself" (1946, 8); Jesus, on the other hand, reveals the truth that man cannot know by himself, but only by new birth mediated by the Teacher who is also his Servant and Savior (9–14). Socrates and Jesus had different roles, and so, we may take it, different teaching styles. The subtitle of Kreeft's book fairly sums it up: *History's Greatest Questioner Confronts the Claims of Christ*. Socrates questions; Jesus makes claims that must be confronted.

OTHER DIFFERENCES BETWEEN SOCRATES AND JESUS

There are other important differences between Socrates and Jesus—on the matter of authority, for one. "Socrates, despite the contrary claims of his contemporaries, insisted many times that he was not an authority regarding anything," says Norris Archer Harrington. "Almost without exception, he held that he was simply trying to understand the essence of whatever issue or question was at that time being discussed" (2000). In Kreeft's imagined dialogue, Socrates says to Flanagan the janitor, "I learn again that my surest surety lies in learning that I am *not* sure" (2002, 10; italics in original).

Harrington and Kreeft are echoing Socrates' famous description of himself as wise only to the extent that "I do not think that I know what I do not know" (*Apology* 21d; Hamilton and Cairns 1961, 8). "Real wisdom [Socrates says] is the property of God." Because it has been Socrates' business to disprove others' wisdom, people assume that he knows everything and is a "professor of wisdom," an appellation he regards as one of "various malicious suggestions." So when the divine oracle says that Socrates is the wisest man in the world,

> he is not referring literally to Socrates, but has merely taken my name as an example, as if he would say to us, The wisest of you men is he who has realized, like Socrates, that in respect of wisdom he is really worthless.
>
> That is why I still go about seeking and searching in obedience to the divine command, if I think that anyone is wise ... I try to help the cause of God by proving that he is not. (*Apology* 23b; Hamilton and Cairns 1961, 9)

This reluctance or refusal of Socrates to be dogmatic about what he knew is nicely rendered by Walter Pater in his classic treatment, *Plato and Platonism*. Pater contrasts Socrates' courage and independence of mind in declining to take advantage of the legal appeal that might have saved his life with what he calls "a genuine diffidence about his own convictions which explains some peculiarities in his manner of teaching." Pater goes on to say: "The irony, the humour, for which he was famous—the unfailing humour which some have found in his very last words—were not merely spontaneous personal traits, or tricks of manner; but an essential part of the dialectical apparatus, as affording a means of escape from responsibility, convenient for one who has scruples about the fitness of his own thoughts for the reception of another, doubts as to the power of words to convey thoughts, such as he thinks cannot after all be properly conveyed to another, but only awakened, or brought to birth in him, out of himself" (1905, 88).

Whether or not we agree with Pater on this aspect of Socrates' character and teaching, I don't think it could ever be said of Jesus that He was unsure of His own convictions, or that His use of irony was a means of escape from responsibility, "convenient for one who has scruples about the fitness of his own thoughts for the reception of another." In starkest contrast to Socrates' insistence that he was not an authority, it is Jesus' authority that for many of His hearers *defined* His teaching: "He taught them as one having authority, and not as their scribes," Matthew reports (7:29). Not as Socrates, either, we might add. To say that Jesus was dogmatic and uncompromising is not to put it too bluntly, telling people exactly what they should and must think or believe and what the consequences are if they don't. Is it not precisely Jesus' authority that is the crux of His saying, "You have heard that it was said ... but I say to you"—which is to say, "You may have heard such and such from other authorities, but my authority trumps them all"?

There is the related question whether Socrates was even a teacher, in the usual sense of dispensing knowledge or wisdom. He says himself, "I have never set up as any man's teacher" (*Apology* 33a; Hamilton and Cairns 1961, 18) and "I have never promised or imparted any teaching to anybody, and if anyone asserts that he has ever learned or heard from me privately anything which was not open to everyone else, you may be quite sure that he is not telling the truth" (33b; 19). Socrates' duty, rather, in obedience to the oracle (as he tells us), is to "examine those who think that they are wise when they are not" (33c; 19). Humor or irony on Socrates' part? Perhaps. But still a long way from Jesus, whose entire ministry, seen from one side, might be summed up by the simple observation, "Then he began to speak, and taught them, saying ..."

Was Jesus a Philosopher?

"The Socratic Method is a conversation, a discussion [says Harrington], wherein two or more people assist one another in finding the answers to difficult questions" (2000). Did Jesus ever ask for or require assistance in finding the answers to difficult questions, those, I mean, of a more or less philosophical sort? In reply to what is arguably the most genuinely philosophical question in the Gospels, noteworthy in my view for its peculiarity if not uniqueness, Pilate's "What is truth?" (John 18:38), Jesus says exactly nothing. It may be that Jesus' silence was conditioned on what He knew to be Pilate's cynicism or hardness of heart, but we are not told that. Or we may say that Jesus declined to be drawn into a discussion of "Truth" in the abstract because, as He said, He *was* the Truth (John 14:6). But that only underscores the point: Jesus was not Socrates.

True enough, C. S. Lewis once remarked, "Our Lord, if we may so express it, is much more like Socrates than Shakespeare" (1967, 4), referring to Jesus and the particular parable of the Unjust Judge (Luke 18:1–8). "Some of the parables do work like poetic similes," said Lewis; "but then others work like philosophic illustrations." His purpose was to counter the view that Jesus was a poet and His parables the evidence. "And I dread an over-emphasis on the poetical element in His words," Lewis continued, "because I think it tends to obscure that quality in His human character which is, in fact, so visible in His irony, His *argumenta ad homines*, and His use of the *a fortiori*, and which I would call the homely, peasant shrewdness" (1967, 4; italics in original). In my opinion, Lewis was arguing only that on occasion Jesus' style is more like that of the philosopher Socrates than that of the playwright Shakespeare, but not that He was therefore a logician or dialectician.

I am not a philosopher, though, and so not an authority here. If anyone who is a philosopher wants to insist that Jesus was also a philosopher, in some sense, I will not resist too much. In his little book *The Philosophy of Jesus*, for example, Kreeft claims that in fact Jesus was a philosopher, but of a very specific kind. "Would He give a lecture at Harvard, or engage in a long Socratic dialog in Plato's Academy, or write a critique of Kant's *Critique of Pure Reason?*" Kreeft asks. "Obviously not," he answers. "And everyone knows that." Was Jesus a philosopher then in the sense that everyone is a philosopher, since everyone has a "philosophy of life"? Yes. "Even Homer Simpson is a philosopher," says Kreeft (2007, 3).

"But Jesus was a philosopher in a meaningful middle sense," Kreeft maintains, "the sense in which Confucius, Buddha, Muhammad, Solomon, Marcus Aurelius, and Pascal were philosophers" (2007, 3). He then quotes C. S. Lewis (in a letter to Dom Bede Griffeths, repeating the sentiments of "Christianity and

Literature," just cited), saying that Jesus' "'type of mind' ... stands at just about the same distance from the poetic as from the philosopher," and that in Jesus' irony, repartee, argument, repeated use of the *a fortiori*, and appeals to our reason "we recognize as the human and natural vehicle of the Word's incarnation a mental complexion in which a keen-eyed peasant *shrewdness* is just as noticeable as an imaginative quality—something in other words quite as close (on the natural level) to Socrates as to Aeschylus" (4; italics in original). I would have no reason to disagree. But, again, unless I am mistaken, what Lewis is claiming is simply that Jesus was no less "philosophic" than he was "poetic"; he stands at "just about the same distance" from one as the other.

Nor am I saying that there is nothing in common between the life of Jesus and that of Socrates. Anyone reading the *Apology* will be struck immediately by both obvious similarities and dissimilarities, as has been remarked often enough. My point is a much more limited one, regarding their teaching styles: they are not the same, so far as I can see, and the reason is that Jesus wasn't teaching "the same sort of thing" Socrates was teaching, if indeed Socrates was teaching at all.

So What Was Jesus' Teaching Method? The Rabbinical Context

In attempting to get a handle on Jesus' pedagogy it is crucial to remember that it was cast in a rabbinical mold. Jesus, as we mentioned, was "Rabboni." What that meant was two things at a minimum.

It meant, first, that His teaching, like all early Jewish teaching, was not academic or intellectual in either the ancient Greek or modern Western sense. "The primary purpose of education in Bible times was to train the whole person for lifelong, obedient service in the knowledge of God (Prov. 1:7; Eccl. 12:13)," writes Marvin Wilson (1989, 279). "To the Greek," he says, "knowledge was the main way to virtue; the path to the good life was through the intellect. But to the Hebrew, wisdom went beyond intellectual pursuit; it was practical" (282).

This difference between the ethical/devotional purposes of Jewish teaching and the more strictly academic way of the Greeks I develop in *Piety and Philosophy: A Primer for Christian Schools* (chapter 1). The idea here, related, is that it was this rabbinical context out of which Jesus came and in which He needs to be understood. "During New Testament times the landscape was dotted with itinerant teachers and their disciples," Wilson tells us. "Jesus was one such teacher in the scribal tradition (cf. Matt. 13:52)" (1989, 299). At the heart of the Christian revelation is of course the truth that that is not all that Jesus was, but it is not inaccurate to say that He was that at least, and the fact informs our understanding of how He taught.

The second thing that Jesus' being a rabbi meant for His teaching was that His *method* was of a certain sort. "Rabbis interpreted the Torah, explained the Scriptures, and told parables," Ann Spangler and Lois Tverberg remind us (2009, 27). Jesus was not, in other words, the *only* rabbi who told parables (30). Similarly, in His employment of paradox He may well have been following Old Testament writers (Dickson 2003, 69). He belonged, as Wilson has said, to a tradition.

Most notable perhaps: "Along with instructing the crowds, a rabbi's greatest goal was to raise up disciples who would carry on his teaching.... As important as knowledge of Scripture was, there was one thing more important—a rabbi's moral character." And for the disciple: "Even more than acquiring his master's knowledge, he wanted to acquire his master's character, his internal grasp of God's law" (Spangler and Tverberg 2009, 33–34). Again, this is instruction of a peculiarly (uniquely?) Jewish and biblical kind.

THE FORMS OF JESUS' TEACHING

When you get to more technical descriptions of Jesus' teaching, how He spoke, what I have called His rhetorical formulas, you find words and phrases like *logia*, discourse, parable, parabolic proverb, allegory, aphorism, pronouncement story, antithetical parallelism, irony, paradox, hyperbole, illustrated story, even pun and poetry—but not, significantly, dialogue or dialectic. In his famous

The Formation of the Gospel Tradition Vincent Taylor argues that "the arrangement [of Jesus' sayings] is that which we find repeatedly in Proverbs, Ecclesiastes, and the Wisdom of Sirach" (1949, 92). Taylor was speaking about the *arrangement* of Jesus' sayings rather than the sayings themselves, but you can see that the character of the sayings themselves is necessarily involved. That Jesus' teaching is described as "sayings" is itself significant—and takes us back to Jesus' purpose: to declare or reveal the Truth, about the kingdom of God, about God and man and the relationship between the two, the relationship of men and women to one another, and so on.

In summarizing the forms of Jesus' teaching, Stein reminds us that "Jesus was born, raised, and lived in a culture quite different from the scientific culture of our day." Jesus' words "were not meant to be photographic portraits or laboratory descriptions for a scientific culture but rather impressionistic stories and sayings that sought in a storytelling culture to describe the arrival of the kingdom of God." What we learn from this is that "scientific description is merely one method of describing reality. At times and in certain contexts it is no doubt the best method, but in other contexts it is inappropriate, or, at least, less suitable than others." In a society that places a premium on text-message brevity and fast-food efficiency and what Stein calls "computer accuracy," it is helpful to remember that "the form or vehicle that Jesus used to convey his message is clearly not the language of twentieth- [or twenty-first-] century science but rather the metaphorical, exaggerating, impressionistic language of a culture that loved to tell stories" (1978, 32). We can't fully appreciate the force of what Jesus is saying unless we understand something of its form.

There is also the other side to it. Can we teach twenty-first-century physics—or chemistry, or biology, or geometry or calculus—using "the metaphorical, exaggerating, impressionistic language of a culture that loved to tell stories"? We don't even teach stories, history, or literature that way, not usually. Or the Bible. Telling the story is one thing, studying it another. The parable, "the most famous form used by Jesus in his teaching" (Stein 1978, 34), would not for that reason be the obvious choice of instruction in math or science or foreign language, just as the equation or formula would not best carry the truth expressed in Jesus' illustrations.

One could certainly make a case for questions, as we have done. They seem hardly ever out of place. But in doing so we must keep in mind what we have said about Jesus' questions vis-à-vis Socrates'. It is the Socratic style of question we want, is it not—seeing that it is the Socratic style of teaching we are most engaged in? Yes, the rhetorical question, especially perhaps in Jesus' employment of it, is also effective. If it's a response we're after, however, getting students to talk, "eliciting the truth," the bulk of our questions can't be rhetorical, even if Jesus' were.

Jesus, we might say, was involved in a first-order activity, we in a second-order—to the extent that we are teachers and learners. If we become writers or artists or research scientists or philosophers, as opposed to students of philosophy, we become practitioners of first-order work as well. But even then ours is a very different role from the Word-revealing role of Jesus. Given that for which He Himself said He had been anointed—"to bring good news to the poor … to proclaim release to the captives and recovery of sight to the blind, to let the oppressed go free, to proclaim the year of the Lord's favor" (Luke 4:18–19)—Jesus' "method" seems eminently appropriate, although who am I, or is anyone, to say? Surely it was appropriate because that is what it was. He alone knows what means best suited His ends.

Do His means, though, suit *our* ends? I think the answer must be, sometimes they do, sometimes they don't. It would seem unlikely that stories and questions (if that is how we decide to characterize Jesus' teaching) would always and everywhere be appropriate to what we are attempting to do. Which is to say that for a variety of reasons we may not in all cases be able to "teach like Jesus."

Jesus' pedagogy was determined by His person and purpose, who He is and what He came to do. He was a teacher, to be sure, but not after the manner of Socrates or Plato or Aristotle or Quintilian or Cicero. He was the Word made flesh, the revelation of God, Himself the Good News, the New News, which, as Kierkegaard reminds us, we could not have come to on our own, not even with the best of Socratic midwives to assist us. Thus did Jesus declare and proclaim and utter and preach and pronounce and say. What He announced was not to be found in men themselves, latent or dormant, waiting to be birthed or cultivated by the insightful or especially skilled teacher. It was revealed, and made operative through the power of the Spirit, by whom men are born anew, "the eyes of [their] understanding being enlightened," as the apostle Paul puts it (Ephesians 1:18, KJV).

JESUS' INTERPERSONAL STYLE

We move on to what we might call the personal or psychological, as opposed to the methodological, aspect of Jesus' teaching, the way in which He dealt with those He taught, interpersonally we could say. Was He, for instance, personable, open, and (as we like to have it these days) vulnerable; also patient, gentle, and welcoming? Frequently we are told that He was approachable or accessible. He was someone we would feel comfortable with, and in that way a model teacher in the modern sense. We might even be tempted to say that He was "there for" His pupils.

In "The Practical Teaching Methods of Jesus Christ," a paper by Edward P. Shuppe, we are encouraged to think that "Jesus had a unique intimacy with His students.... He established confidence and esteem between Himself and His students," says Shuppe. "He never ridiculed His pupils. He did not appear to them as overbearing or haughty. He was never impatient or tactless, and never showed discourtesy towards those who approached Him, not even to His enemies.... He was approachable and friendly. Even His voice was well modulated. We read that the people wondered at the gracious words that proceeded from His mouth." Later we are told that "He was always patient," that "He commended His students," and that He "let no effort go unnoticed" (1–3). It is not an uncommon portrait of Jesus as popularly drawn.

WAS JESUS THE MODEL MODERN TEACHER?

But all this seems too obviously an effort to picture Jesus as State Teacher of the Year rather than to come to terms with what the Gospel accounts actually say about Him. I wish Shuppe had provided Scripture references, but, alas, he did not—largely, I suspect, because there are none. How would we know, among other things, whether Jesus' voice was well modulated, as that would not necessarily follow from the graciousness of His words?

How about Jesus "was never impatient"? In Mark 9:14–29 (Matthew 17:14–21, Luke 9:37–43) we are told that after being on the Mount of Transfiguration, Jesus, Peter, James, and John come down from the mountain and are met by a man whose son is an epileptic, whom Jesus' disciples could not cure. In response to the man's plea Jesus declares, "You faithless generation, how much longer must I be among you? How much longer must I put up with you? Bring [the boy] to me" (Mark 9:19).

At least one commentator sees in Jesus' response on this occasion "infinite forbearance" and "infinite compassion" (Davidson 1954, 824). For whom? The father? The son? The disciples? Jesus healed the boy, all right, but if there was forbearance and compassion in His ministrations, there was something else. J. B. Phillips translates Jesus' retort as, "Oh, what a faithless people you are! How long must I be with you, how long must I put up with you? Bring him here to me," and Eugene Peterson (The Message), "What a generation! No sense of God! How many times do I have to go over these things? How much longer do I have to put up with this? Bring the boy here." Stein finds in the incident evidence of Jesus' "exasperation and frustration" (1978, 24). There was that at least. I would call it rebuke.

What of Jesus' ridding the temple of the money changers (Matthew 21:12–13), or His comment to Peter, "Get behind me, Satan! You are a stumbling block to me" (Matthew 16:23)? Not impatience? Was it then disappointment or dissatisfaction or discontent?

We must believe that Jesus never ceased loving anyone, even those He chastised—as parents never cease loving their children even when they are angry with them. All the same, I am not sure it helps our understanding, in particular cases, to try to paint Jesus' actions as kinder or gentler than they plainly were.

Likewise the view that Jesus "never showed discourtesy towards those who approached Him, not even to His enemies." On one occasion He calls the Pharisees "You brood of vipers!" and follows up with, "How can you speak good things, when you are evil?" (Matthew 12:34). On another He refers to them as "blind guides" (Matthew 15:14); on yet another as "blind fools" (Matthew 23:17). Numerous times He addresses them as hypocrites (Matthew 6:2, 22:18, 23:23–29). Jesus may not have been discourteous, "even to His enemies," but He was hardly endearing. One of them, it is reported, felt insulted by Jesus' remarks (Luke 11:45).

In what sense then was Jesus "approachable and friendly"? When the Canaanite woman cries, "Have mercy on me, Lord, Son of David," He doesn't bother to answer at first, then tells her, "I was sent only to the lost sheep of the house of Israel." Even after she kneels before Him, imploring, "Lord, help me," He says, "It is not fair to take the children's food and throw it to the dogs" (Matthew 15:22–28). In the end He grants her request and praises her faith, but would any of us think His manner with her approachable and friendly? Does He encourage her, build her confidence or esteem? In some sense, perhaps, but it is not obvious how.

Similarly when He is told that His mother and brothers are waiting to speak to Him, He says, "Who is my mother, and who are my brothers?" and, pointing to the disciples, "Here are my mother and my brothers! For whoever does the will of my Father in heaven is my brother and sister and mother" (Matthew 12:46–50)—as if not to acknowledge His own family.

And the further claim that Jesus "commended His students" and that He "let no effort go unnoticed"? Again, I submit that this is an attempt (for no references are given here either) to depict Jesus as the teacher we might wish Him to be, rather than a description of the teacher He was according to the biblical accounts.

Consider the woman who says to Him, "Blessed is the womb that bore you and the breasts that nursed you!" (Luke 11:27), intending no doubt the highest praise. Jesus' reply? "Blessed rather are those who hear the word of God and obey it!" (11:28)—end of comment. No "Thank you for your kind remark" or "You are generous to say so" or "You are certainly on the right track." No encouragement at all of the sort we would expect from a teacher who commended His students and let no effort go unnoticed. It is true that in reply to one of the responses of the rich young ruler He said, "You have given the right answer" (Luke 10:28); similarily, to the woman at the well, "You are right in saying ..." (John 4:17). But the overwhelming impression, for me, is that Jesus is not an "encourager" of the modern sort. As for His enemies: once anyway, so far from being drawn into further dialogue they were enough startled or offended or devastated by His comments that they didn't dare ask Him any more questions (Matthew 22:46).

In *Teaching Like Jesus*, La Verne Tolbert, in a kindred attempt to fit Jesus into a modern mold, says that He "established relationship" with those He taught. She cites in support the story of Zacchaeus, whom Jesus famously visited in the tax collector's home (Luke 19:1–10). "By identifying with the learner he was able to effect change in his behavior" (2000, 28). This must surely be true, as it is hard to imagine that Zacchaeus was anything other than deeply and lastingly, not to say eternally, affected by a personal visit from the Savior of mankind, as the text tells us he was.

But in citing the story of Zacchaeus do we not demonstrate how rare such occurrences are in the Gospels? Except for Peter and (one assumes) the other disciples, except for Mary and Martha and Lazarus, how many examples are there of Jesus "identifying with" the learners by visiting them in their homes, or in other ways? In the vast majority of the cases recorded, Jesus heals or rebukes or prescribes and moves on. Nor would it have been possible for Jesus to establish a relationship with each person among the multitudes we are told He taught on occasion.

Tolbert further contends that "Jesus taught each age group in keeping with its developmental level." She references the feeding of the five thousand, wherein "by using a little boy's lunch, Jesus fed five thousand men, plus women and children (John 6:9–13)" (2000, 29). But Jesus wasn't teaching the little boy—no more than He was the crowd. Wasn't it principally the disciples? The only "age group" Jesus ever taught, so far as I can see, was adults. That

Jesus taught "developmentally" is no doubt a fair assumption, but it is nowhere supported by the biblical record.

There are other attempts on Tolbert's part to demonstrate that Jesus was the Master Teacher and that He modeled methods that will "help us become more effective teachers" (2000, 27), but all require the same critical scrutiny. That Tolbert's is a book for church workers, as opposed to teachers of algebra or English, does not eliminate that requirement.

In the interests of charity and truth it must be said that the intentions of those who idealize Jesus' teaching in the language of twentieth- or twenty-first-century educational psychology or methodology are clearly above reproach. They mean nothing less than honor, adulation, reverence. If Jesus was who He claimed to be, Son of God and Son of Man; if He is our only Savior, our friend, and the lover of our souls; if He was in addition the greatest teacher who ever lived—wouldn't He be the supreme, it may be the only, model for our own teaching? That's the tacit and no doubt natural assumption, devotionally speaking.

Who Jesus Was—the Crux of the Issue

Tolbert rightly says of Jesus (2000, 27) that "who he was—God Incarnate—was the basis from which he taught." I wonder though if it isn't precisely that fact that forbids us from teaching like Jesus most of the time. If any of us, for any reason, ever said to a single soul who approached us, "My mandate is not to teach you, but others" ("I was sent only to the lost sheep of the house of Israel") or, upon her persistence, "It is not fair to take the children's food and throw it to the dogs," we might well worry whether we would have our contract renewed. We might be dismissed forthwith on the grounds that we had failed to treat people "as Jesus would"!

Please do not mistake what I am saying. I do not question whether Jesus was the greatest teacher who ever lived or whether He loved as only their Redeemer could those He taught or healed or otherwise ministered to. God's surpassing love in Jesus is the essence of the Good News. Moreover, we are told a number of times that Jesus had compassion on the crowds or on one He healed. I am asking only whether our characterization of His teaching in terms of contemporary pedagogical categories is not too easy or self-serving, whether it doesn't fail to see Him as He is portrayed by the Gospels themselves.

Jesus cannot be made to conform to our standards, no matter how lofty the standards or laudable our motives in attempting to analyze Him in this way. To try to assess Him by means of contemporary categories, pedagogical or otherwise, is in my view to try to fit Him for our own purposes, to domesticate Him perhaps, to make Him less formidable, or less offensive, or less terrifying, than His contemporaries found Him. "It has been left for later generations to muffle up that shattering personality and surround Him with an atmosphere of tedium," wrote Dorothy Sayers. "We have very efficiently pared the claws of the Lion of Judah, certified Him 'meek and mild,' and recommended Him as a fitting household pet for pale curates and pious old ladies" (1949, 6). How much claw paring is involved in endeavoring to portray Jesus as the model modern teacher, commending and encouraging, approachable and friendly, ever establishing "confidence and esteem between Himself and His students"? "Aslan," as Peter Kreeft reminds us, referring to "the great lion-lord" of C. S. Lewis' Narnia, "is not a tame lion" (2002, 5–6).

Assuredly it is the Christian's obligation to "look unto Jesus," to be like Him to the degree that that is possible. Whether that includes teaching as He taught, however, seems to me doubtful, especially if what we mean by "teaching" is what most of us in schools do most of the time: reading, writing, and arithmetic, inculcating general knowledge and general intellectual capacities. If it is Sunday school we are talking about (an equally noble calling!), we have a different situation, I would agree. But even there I take it that we will not be so much teaching *as* Jesus taught as teaching *what* He taught.

There is comment elsewhere in the New Testament about teaching: teachers are mentioned among those to whom Christ gave gifts for the work of ministry (Ephesians 4:11–12); teachers are appointed by God in the church (1 Corinthians 12:28); the

Lord's servant must be "an apt teacher, patient, correcting opponents with gentleness" (2 Timothy 2:24–25); and so on. But that is teaching of a special variety. The extent to which its techniques apply to Christian schools I would think is limited; at best they would have to be applied with careful attention paid to the peculiar requirements of discrete disciplines.

CONCLUSION

If what we intend by "teaching as Jesus taught" is caring about people, having compassion for them, understanding "where they're coming from," and the like, then we must teach as Jesus taught, no less than we must act in love toward everyone, as we are commanded to do throughout Scripture. If we have in mind, however, that our style of teaching should emulate Jesus', I am not at all sure what that might mean in practice. It seems to me more sensible, because more suited to our curriculums, to advocate that we teach like Socrates, or according to the method named after him—for the reason that it is "Socratic material" that we are dealing with most of the time, not "Jesus material." That in no way abrogates our responsibility for "Jesus material," certainly not in Christian schools. But it does require, I think, that we distinguish between that which befits us as followers of Christ in general and that which is our obligation as teachers of a traditional and academic sort.

The Christian who is an aeronautical engineer at the Jet Propulsion Laboratory has no less a duty to be generous, kind, and respectful, as well as principled, loyal, and diligent, at work than he does when he is serving as elder at First Presbyterian Church. At the same time, it is clearly his obligation *not* to be conducting Bible studies when he is being paid to design space modules. The fact that his Christian profession obliges him to be like Jesus does not mean that he must always be doing exactly or only what Jesus did, in just the way Jesus did it. His Christian commitment to honesty and integrity as an employee may in fact be what prohibits him, as a Christian disciple, from witnessing to colleagues during the workday—not to mention that his honesty and integrity may be the best witness of all.

By the same token, our commitment as Christian teachers to the best academic education for our students as is possible may be what prohibits us from preaching or evangelizing or counseling when we are being paid to teach Pythagoras or Chaucer. The ministry of Jesus was unique in all the world, because of course Jesus was unique in all the world. There may be times when His teaching style suits us; there may be times—most times, I reckon—when it doesn't. Ours is a derivative and lesser calling, but not unimportant for that reason by any means.

What that calling is, with special reference to what I have called the liberal arts, I want to take up in the next two chapters.

Eight

"For Their Own Sakes"

Nay, Sir, it is wonderful what a difference learning makes upon people even in the common intercourse of life, which does not appear to be much connected with it.

—James Boswell, *Life of Johnson*

In chapter 1 I tried to argue that the point and purpose of education, academically speaking, was the liberal arts, those studies that foster general knowledge and general intellectual capacities. In chapter 4 I argued further that it was this sort of education that America's Founders had in mind when they insisted on the importance of education for the maintenance of liberty. In several places throughout I have said that for the liberal arts to do their good work they must be pursued "for their own sakes."

I'd like now to try to say what that phrase means. I'd like also to address the related problem of how such studies can serve the purposes of self-government or virtue, or whatever, at the same time that they are pursued for their own sakes. If a thing is done truly for its own sake, how can it be done *for* anything else?

What the Phrase Means

The meaning then of the phrase. As applied to the disciplines of the liberal arts, "for their own sakes" means, first of all, not for the purpose of earning a living. I mention this at the beginning because it is so contrary to the current view of education in the

United States. In this country you could hardly have a conversation about almost any academic subject—or about "why children should stay in school," or in response to the familiar student complaint, "Why do we have to study this?"—without preparation for vocation being brought up. The college educated, we are often told, earn more money than those not so educated. That is apparently true, and would not be unexpected. On the other hand, I seem to recall surveys from fifty years ago indicating that over the course of a lifetime blue-collar workers earned more than those with college degrees. And what if a liberal education did *not* guarantee a better income? Should we consider it not worth our while? For many the answer is clearly that we should not. The importance of literature, history, abstract math and science, and the rest therefore requires defense, sometimes long and labored; it is by no means understood by most people. I alluded earlier to the statistics: 60 percent of all college students, according to a 2001 report from the Carnegie Institute, are pursuing a technical or preprofessional degree, and business majors are leading the way. Most are *not* studying subjects "for their own sakes." They're studying them to prepare to earn a living. The 2005 American Freshman Survey reports that 71 percent of students attend college "to be able to make more money" (Bauerlein 2008, 67).

It is true that the number of business majors seems to be declining. It is also true, according to yet another recent survey, that English is seventh among the ten most popular majors, with psychology second, elementary education third, biology fourth, education sixth, and political science tenth. The rest are nursing (fifth), communications (eighth), and computer science (ninth). The question would be to what extent psychology, elementary education, education, and political science are liberal arts strictly speaking, since the Princeton Review, which conducted this research, describes each in terms of its usefulness for vocation— although I would agree that that does not, by itself, make them "nonliberal" (Princeton Review 2007).

It is likewise becoming more accepted to come at the subject from the other end, to herald the fact that those with liberal arts degrees sometimes make a great deal of money—in large part because of their liberal education. I am looking now at an article that says just that. An English and psychology graduate who has held senior executive positions at various Fortune 500 companies and currently owns her own marketing and development firm tells an interviewer: "My majors taught me some invaluable skills. I learned how to write in different voices and at different lengths. Whether I'm posting on a blog or writing a white paper, I never freak out about how to write." She and two others, one with a degree in philosophy and another who graduated in history, says the writer, are laughing all the way to the bank (Snyder).

I would concur that, as one of those interviewed said of her liberal arts degree, "It enabled me to acquire a real education versus just preparation for a specific career path or vocation. As a result, I tend to have a more holistic view of business and of life" (Snyder). That is what I have been saying all along.

But to contend that, having acquired "a more holistic view of business and of life," you are, or may be, enabled to make more money misses the point entirely. Further, it reinforces the kind of popular notions it is the purpose of this chapter to counter. The liberal arts may or may not earn you more money, but whether they do or don't is wholly irrelevant, because that is not at all why they should be studied, in fact is exactly the wrong reason to study them.

That there may be advantage in taking courses that are neither "practical" nor "necessary," nor (perhaps especially) "useful" in the sense that they help anyone get a job, is in our day an almost completely foreign, if not heretical, concept. In modern America it is practically assumed, an article of faith, that the reason children go to school is that they will one day be able to be "successful."

Education and Usefulness

This was decidedly not the view of the ancients. Indeed such a notion was explicitly repudiated. Aristotle included music in the curriculum, but not because it was useful. Rather, "it is of no practical use whatever, and yet in spite of that—or even because of that—it is an essential part of education" (Barclay 1959, 82; see *Politics* 8.3; McKeon 1941, 1306–08). "The test of utility is anathema to the cultured Greeks," says Barclay; "anything that is learned to be used for practical purposes is not education; anything which enables a man to make money is necessarily an ungentlemanly thing; and anyone engaged in making money is *ipso facto* unfit to be a citizen" (1959, 82). "Wherefore we call those arts vulgar which tend to deform the body," said Aristotle, "and likewise all paid employments, for they absorb and degrade the mind" (*Politics* 8.2; McKeon 1941, 1306). Even the utilitarian Romans shared this view. Quintilian (AD c. 35–c. 95), for instance, says, "I trust that there is not one even among my readers who would think of calculating the monetary value of such studies" (1.12.17; 1989, 199), and Cicero (106–43 BC) similar things (Barclay 1959, 83).

We can be thankful that times have changed, for the reason that most of us are not gentlemen in the ancient sense (and half of us not men in any sense), and under ancient conditions would have been condemned to earning a living by means of business or the trades, and excluded thereby from citizenship. It was among just such people, moreover, that the Christian gospel took root and flourished. It was also the Christian gospel that first asserted the worth of all men equally and led eventually, albeit slowly and often against entrenched institutions (sometimes in alliance with the Church), to the educational enfranchisement of women as well as men, poor as well as rich, slaves as well as free, as we saw in chapter 1. Neither could a Christian but acknowledge that legitimate labor is honorable as well as necessary, and "to work with your hands" biblically ordained (1 Thessalonians 4:11).

At the same time, I think we can rejoice that we are heirs of an educational tradition, however circumscribed by cultural mores, that has placed a premium on the life of the mind and imagination, on art and music and literature as well as philosophy, history, pure math, and pure science—on an education that is given, as Aristotle concludes, for no other reason than that it is liberal and noble (*Politics* 8.3; McKeon 1941, 1308). Nor is it any compromise of the Christian concern for just those classes that the cultured

Greeks deemed unfit for civic duty, to agree that it may likewise be a Christian concern to advocate the pursuit of the "highest things"—for their own sakes and without any reward beyond the things themselves, and regardless of whether they help anyone advance a career.

The irony is this: unless you study a subject for its own sake in the first instance you will not truly arrive at whatever your desired end—practical, transcendent, or otherwise—in the second. If you study calculus only for the purpose of getting it over with in pursuit of your ambition to be a successful engineer, the chances are that you will neither learn calculus nor be a successful engineer. If you study history only to get a good grade, you will likely neither learn history nor get a good grade. By the same token, if you genuinely care about history—if you can forget about the grade long enough to be concerned about the subject—you will learn history and get a good grade besides. A fundamental principle, a paradox, is at work here: he that loses finds.

There must be a place in society, especially but not only in a democratic society, for the asking of questions about meaning and truth, unhindered by any requirement that they serve some purpose beyond their own worth. "To translate the question into contemporary language," says Pieper, "it would sound something like this: Is there still an area of human action, or human existence as such, that does not have its justification by being part of the machinery of a 'five-year plan'?" (1998, 22).

Should there not also be a largeness of soul, especially among Christians, that can appreciate whatever it is simply for itself, with no qualification that it somehow pay us back? When the object is another human being we call such magnanimity love. It might well be the same here.

In a modern America obsessed with success (measured almost always in terms of income), the importance of the *artes liberales*, the "free arts"—we might say the "useless arts"—is liable to get lost, and often does. But in a democratic society, somebody—one hopes that it is everybody at one time or another in the exercise of their political obligations—must be asking and answering the questions,

"What do we mean by 'a democratic society'?" "What guarantees that it is free?" "What is the importance of 'the rule of law'?" "How is freedom consistent with responsibility?" And answering those questions requires that the citizenry have both the educational means and the time to do so, if only for a season. That is one of the primary reasons schools and colleges exist. This is the most idealistic of ideals, and at best only partially realized anywhere in this country, I grant, but that difficulty I try to speak to in chapter 10. That is not to mention the myriad other questions the human spirit demands be answered by philosophical and scientific inquiry of every conceivable sort.

Then there is the way in which careerism can either deaden an interest in liberal learning or simply leave no time for it. Asks Bauerlein, "Has the undergraduate plan become so pre-professionalized that the curriculum functions as a high-level vocational training that dulls the intellectual curiosity that encourages outside book reading?" (2008, 56).

The tendency in tough economic times is for students to neglect the liberal arts in favor of studies that will guarantee employment. It seems a perfectly obvious and sensible response. But that way of looking at the matter only strengthens the notion that education is really (however much we protest otherwise) about livelihood; it follows the market. I agree with Derek Bok, former president of Harvard: "There's a lot more to a liberal education than improving the economy" (Cohen 2009)—because of course it is one of the uses of the liberal arts to teach us exactly that. It is in tough economic times that they are needed most.

Although my point is the importance of a broad liberal education of the sort that produces a "cultivated intellect," I am in no way decrying the need for technical or vocational training. To do so would be absurd. No modern society can succeed without highly trained, highly skilled, very smart, very creative engineers, technicians, researchers, artisans, craftsmen, and the like, as well as their counterparts in management, finance, and entrepreneurship—not to mention perhaps the most important class in the everyday scheme of things, the laborers and bus drivers and busboys and sanitation workers and legions of unskilled workers without whom the entire machinery of daily life would come to a halt. We owe our quality of life, envied the world over, largely to just such people.

My own view is that the men and women who design and build bridges, airplanes, and skyscrapers, or space stations and artificial hearts, along with those who train them, are among the most fascinating people there are. What would many of us, me included, do without the various medications we ingest daily, in the absence of which we would have died long ago? I am not saying that occupational or professional training is bad and liberal education good. I am saying only that a strictly utilitarian approach to learning is shortsighted. The health of the cultivated intellect, especially in a society whose preoccupations are almost entirely on the side of what is practical and profitable, needs particular and constant attention paid to it.

Is it not also true that the practical and profitable, and most of the privileges we enjoy, would not be possible apart from the ideas, the philosophy or theology, that is their intellectual lifeblood—ideas about free enterprise, the right to own property, human dignity and equality, liberty, democracy, and so on? Neglect or deny the theory and the practice expires.

Two Great American Heresies

What we are advocating here are two great American heresies: (a) the necessity of thinking about "useless things" and (b) the importance of "doing nothing," which was the subject of chapter 5. Possibly a third: doing both at the same time, for they belong to one another. We have already seen that what we mean by "doing nothing" is not mere "idleness," and we shall see in a moment that what we mean by "useless" is not "without value." I think it helpful nonetheless to address these subjects as they are commonly understood.

To say that the liberal arts are useless is a hyperbole meant to underscore that they are not useful in the ordinary sense; they don't help make things or make money. They are useful in the most profound sense, however, in that they have to do with the most fundamental issues of human life. The true, the good, and the beautiful is the ancient way of categorizing them. As Henry Edmondson, in his commentary on the philosophy of John Dewey (generally regarded as the author of utility in American education) puts it: "Here we have a paradox: In making utility the chief goal of education, we sacrifice much of its usefulness. A merely utilitarian education is largely ineffectual precisely because it does not seek to make a student good, or at least to teach him what is good, or even to provide him with those principles that guide good behavior—all of which qualities are essential aspects of true utility" (2006, 80).

E. D. Hirsch, Jr., contends that a general education is in fact more useful and practical, even in the popular sense, than a technical or professional one. Contrary to 150 years of anti-intellectualism, developmentalism, progressivism, and what he calls "other naturalistic fallacies" in American education, he says, "Today, it is no longer possible to assert that learning algebra is inferior to learning how to select an occupation. With the nature of jobs shifting every few years, it has become obvious that algebra is in fact the more practical study.... With jobs having become highly changeable, no one knows how to teach for specific occupations. In the present, ever-shifting economic scene, the student needs the ability to learn *new* occupations. Hence, a general ability to learn, based on broad general knowledge and vocabulary, is a more practical tool than direct vocational training" (1996, 110; italics in original).

But even though success in one's occupation may be the result of a liberal education, I do not think that that in any way means that success in one's occupation is the *purpose* of such an education. Its purpose remains "cultivated intellect," and that happens to be the most useful sort of education for everything.

On Not "Using" the Curriculum

The second thing studying the liberal arts "for their own sakes" means is also negative. It means not "using" them, not enlisting them in support of what you may believe to be your "larger agenda"—tolerance or world peace or environmentalism or self-esteem—no matter how convinced you are of such an agenda's rightness. As I said in chapter 2, we in Christian schools are under the strictest obligation to intellectual integrity, dealing with the subject matter on its own terms, for what it is, no more and no less. When our scholarship does support our views—in our case, perhaps, of theism or morality or cosmology—it will be because we have dealt with the subject absolutely honestly. Likewise when it does not support our views. In this we pay tribute to the importance of the subjects themselves, and in doing so acknowledge the millennia-old and civilization-shaping contribution of the liberal arts, so determinative in the forming of Christian—no less than secular—thought.

We also give expression to our God-given humanity. We are created with the capacity and desire to know, but not primarily because we can get something out of the objects of our knowing; rather because we are the only one of God's creatures possessed of the capacity to wonder and be awed. Not only do we seek the truth of things with no expectation of reward beyond truth itself, but we come to the mysteries of the natural world and the human experience as seekers, in part because it is our Christian responsibility to exercise dominion, and care, over creation, but also because we recognize that we are ignorant; we are required to learn. The academic disciplines of the liberal arts are the formal educational means of doing so, and they lead us to knowledge or understanding best, perhaps only, if we are humble enough.

Learning and Worship

You can see that the language we use to describe the act of learning is not unlike the language we use to describe the act of worship. Of course I do not mean that intellectual curiosity can be confused with adoration of the eternal God. But I do think they are similar, or related, in that both have as their object nothing other than the object itself. We worship God, not because we must, not because in doing so we curry His favor, but for no other reason than that God draws forth and deserves our worship. So too the desire to learn: it becomes us, and the created order is worthy of our interest. (When I speak of "the created order" I mean the whole of reality, not only that which inspires the natural sciences, but also that which animates philosophy and history and literature and psychology, and the rest.)

Both worship and learning also do us the inestimable favor of taking us out of ourselves—blessed thing!—and afford us the privilege of being partakers in a common enterprise, a fellowship, if you will, of like-minded seekers after truth.

THE PROBLEM OF LIBERAL EDUCATION AND SELF-GOVERNMENT

We come at last to the vexing question of liberal education and self-government; also that of virtue, intimated at the beginning of the chapter. The first is two questions really: (a) How does the intent of an academic education to prepare citizens to participate in a democracy square with such an education's pretensions to be without particular intent, to be "free" or "useless," its own reward; and, related (b), How can a liberally educated citizenry be both loyal to its government and allowed or encouraged to reprove it? Or as Edmondson suggests, "Jefferson might argue that to achieve a proper civic education is the most challenging educational problem of all, for the citizen must be taught simultaneously to revere and to criticize his government, neither allowing his patriotism to soften his judgment nor permitting his criticism to weaken his civic pride" (2006, 70).

These are, admittedly, tough questions. I will do my best to answer both simultaneously. The issue of education and virtue will follow.

As regards (a), Jacob Klein, longtime tutor at St. John's College, Annapolis, puts it like this: "How often is the phrase 'education for citizenship' used in our schools today! I need not mention the present-day pressure for change in the educational system of the country to be undertaken for the sake of political ends. The demands of the political community to which we belong are indeed inexorable. It is important to understand, however, that the idea of liberal education cannot be easily reconciled with those demands. It is important to see that there is a definite tension between the exigencies of political life and the self-sustained goal of liberal education. This tension is very great" (1985, 169).

Klein framed the problem in possibly its most extreme form. But he was writing in 1940, following the societal upheavals of the '30s and on the eve of America's entry into World War II, when the calls in certain quarters for an education for faithful citizenship must have been especially urgent. His point remains a good one nonetheless: Is a liberal education true to itself if its ends are political? Isn't education's end "beyond politics," or, as we have said, for its own sake?

An answer, in small part, might be something like this: while the ends of liberal education must not be self-consciously political (or anything else), they nonetheless may serve political purposes, indeed cannot help doing so. While you cannot circumscribe education, cannot require it to drive in a certain direction or produce certain results—for then it would no longer be liberal in any meaningful sense—neither can you be unaware of the ways in which the results of your "searching and questioning" (as Klein calls it [1985, 170]) not only must impinge on or inform politics (and every other area of our life), but have always done so. "Ideas have consequences," as per the title of Richard Weaver's famous book. That, in a sense, is the lesson of Western civilization: the most practical and political of policies is rooted in the most philosophical or theological of doctrines. The right of men and women to vote is grounded in ancient and Christian views of human equality; the abolition of slavery in the dignity of all men; the "free arts" in the human desire simply to know; and so on.

Furthermore, in answer to (b), is it not the case that our belief in liberal education is basic to and protected by the very forms of democracy to which such an education gave rise? In other words, is there not some interest in preserving both democracy of a Western sort and education of a liberal sort at the same time and together, because they are bound up with one another? It may not be the stated purpose of the *artes liberales* to "educate for citizenship," but our American experience over the last 400 years has been, as Jefferson and Mann and others insisted, that responsible citizenship is both necessary to democracy and dependent on a proper education. The arrangement has served us nobly thus far.

Where else in the world, except in Western-style democracies, is there such liberty to criticize one's government—which criticism, we believe, when legitimately expressed, works to improve that government? The exception—every rogue dictatorship or Marxist state—proves the rule. Should there come a time when either the citizenry refuses to be educated or its education leads it (in the interests of some deformed manifestation of "intellectual freedom," say) to destroy the very political system that has sustained it, we shall have been the victims of our own folly and sin and will deserve our fate.

EDUCATION AND VIRTUE

The tougher question is, If the liberal arts are not meant to cultivate citizenship, not at least in the first instance, are they meant to cultivate virtue, as is often claimed? Rather, *do* they cultivate virtue? Here too I think we must answer in the negative. "I ask what evidence there is," says Barzun, "that a good book has ever prevented a bad action, or a fine sonata a foolish deed.... It is also true that in modern as in ancient times the persons reared in the humanities have been exemplars of individual and social unrest. It is men brought up on art, literature, languages, history and philosophy who have been the ambitious and the intriguers, the rebels and the tyrants, the libertines and the agitators, as well as the great tragic figures of discontent in the biographical history of art" (1958, 58). If a liberal education were conducive to moral betterment, wouldn't the most liberally educated be the most moral?—which is plainly not the case.

But neither is that reason not to learn great art, literature, history, and philosophy—or biology, chemistry, physics, and math. The reality that the contemplation of "the best which has been thought and said in the world," as Matthew Arnold famously put it (1994, 5), cannot guarantee rectitude is no good ground not to be exercised by it. The biblical equivalent of the ancient triad of the true, the good, and the beautiful, after all, is "whatever is true, whatever is honorable, whatever is just, whatever is pure, whatever is pleasing, whatever is commendable, if there is any excellence and if there is anything worthy of praise" (Philippians 4:8). Why would we not allow ourselves to be exposed to these things, especially in schools? We may have no surety as to their effects, but we can do no less. Good sense, as well as the Scriptures (we might say), requires it.

What we do know is that children who have the advantage of rigorous academic training are better able to think well, those informed by the reading of good literature may be more inclined to noble sentiments, those disciplined by regular exercise will be sensitive to the importance of a healthy body, and so forth.

As soon as that is said the mind is invaded by a host of examples that urge otherwise. But that was my point: while it seems obvious, as it always has, what should be the content of our teaching, as well as the necessity of it, and just as obvious that there can be no guarantee about its effects, there is wisdom still, born of the experience of centuries, in doing what sensible teachers and sensible schools have ever done.

We do not know, as we said in chapter 2, the exact relationship between good learning and good people, how much of the first is required to get the second, or if it works quite like that. What we are certain of is that there is a relationship, and that in the absence of good learning, in the vacuum provided for its opposite, the chances are greatly increased that we will not have good people.

CONCLUSION

It may be that this chapter would be unnecessary if it were not for the American obsession with "usefulness," most especially that usefulness that translates into earning a living. Even so, I would not for a minute, as I have said, dispute the enormous value of things, maybe most things, being useful, or the requirement that considerable attention be paid to vocation. No less an authority than the apostle Paul has admonished us about how serious it is for a person to "provide for relatives, and especially for family members" (1 Timothy 5:8). In a day and age when, probably as never before in history, young people have the opportunity to make career choices—both a heretofore unimaginable luxury and an invitation to indecision and what Dorothy Sayers called "that artificial prolongation of intellectual childhood and adolescence" (1947, 1)—there can hardly be too much wise counsel, preferably from parents, about what their children are "going to do" when they leave school or college.

But as I hope I have made plain, that is not what I am talking about here. I am not saying that the practical can be ignored. The exigencies of daily life will soon enough dispel any doubt about that! My concern has been, rather, to reassert the age-old conviction that some things—most of the really important things—are not at all practical in the usual sense, and if we fail to engage them on those grounds we will have denied our students and ourselves both the contemplation of what is highest and best and the primary purposes of a proper education. No matter how well we prepare young people to "succeed in today's economy," if we have failed to direct them to what is exalted and sublime, we will have been negligent in our duties. Worse, we will have reinforced in their minds what is arguably the reigning falsehood of our age: that the coveted life has mostly to do with income, job security, material well-being. Neither in the interests of time-honored wisdom nor Christian piety can we afford to do that.

One of the ways we might begin to provide an antidote to the poison of materialism and Mammon is by stressing over and over again that not everything has to do with "treasures on earth" or "what you will eat or what you will drink, or about your body, what you will wear" (Matthew 6:19, 25). As the life of every noble man or woman down the ages, preeminently Jesus Himself, has taught us, what are most to be prized, what make a difference, what dignify men and exalt nations, are the affairs of mind and spirit: ideas and ideals, sentiments (not to be confused with sentimentality) and affections, insight and understanding—what a man or woman thinks and is, not what he or she has. There is indoctrination aplenty for all of us in the wisdom of the world, day in and day out, by means of every possible medium. The young therefore need constant immersion in better things, and in those disciplines that train them in discerning what those better things are.

And although, as we have acknowledged, we have no assurance that such immersion will have the desired effect—sometimes it does, sometimes it doesn't—of this we can be reasonably confident, that if we do not do our duty, the world will readily enough seize the opportunity afforded by our negligence.

Nine

The Liberal Arts: What Are They, and What Do They Do?

A perfectly vigorous and intelligent young American, equipped with all the latest devices of mechanics and chemistry, bursting with all the latest business tips about salesmanship and mass psychology, is not an educated man. He is not educated because he has only been educated in all modern things, and not even in all mortal, let alone all immortal, things. In a word, he has not been made acquainted with human things, and that is what we mean when we say that he has neglected the humanities.

—G. K. Chesterton, "Bernard Shaw and America"

In a completely rational society, teachers would be at the tip of the pyramid, not near the bottom. In that society, the best of us would aspire to be teachers, and the rest of us would have to settle for something less. The job of passing civilization along from one generation to the next ought to be the highest honor anyone could have.

—Lee Iacocca, *Where Have All the Leaders Gone?*

We come now to what I suppose is the *pièce de résistance*: the question of what the liberal arts are and why we should study them. Throughout this discussion I have asserted that what I mean by "education" is an academic (as opposed to a technical or vocational) education, and that the substance of such an education is "the liberal arts." I have taken for granted that readers understand what I intend by the phrase—and generally speaking they probably do. I am pretty sure that in most places you can talk about the liberal arts without much protest from anyone requiring you to define your terms. People use the phrase all the time, and the majority will likely understand it to mean what I said it meant in chapter 1, "language, philosophy, history, literature, abstract science"—the humanities so-called with pure math and pure science added in.

MORE THAN ONE APPROACH

But now, with the much-lamented "failure of the public schools" in the last generation or two, and the concomitant increase in the number of private and charter schools—all attempting in their own ways to do something about the crisis in American education—we have seen a remarkable increase in the variety of elucidations of what it means to educate rightly, not a few harking back to traditional or other interpretations of the liberal arts, many identifying themselves by that very phrase. The definition often seems less than straightforward.

There is, for instance, the "classical and Christian" approach. Some apologists for this approach trace their lineage to Dorothy Sayers's famous lecture "The Lost Tools of Learning," which was an argument for a return to the ancient and medieval trivium and quadrivium, the trivium most importantly. (The trivium, remember, consisted of the three disciplines of grammar, dialectic, and rhetoric, taken in that order; the quadrivium of arithmetic, geometry, astronomy, and music.) Sayers' point in that lecture is that while the quadrivium consists of "subjects" ("and need not," she says, "for the moment concern us"), the trivium, two of its subjects at any rate, "are not what we should call 'subjects' at all: they are only methods of dealing with subjects" (1947)—thus they are the *tools* of learning, and the pedagogical focus or methodology, of a number of those schools calling themselves "classical."

That is one way of interpreting the liberal arts. Another, also calling itself classical, is found in schools that ground their set of courses in the study of Latin (sometimes Greek) and ancient history and literature, regarded as foundational to any appreciation of Western Civilization. They also make a good case.

Then there are the Great Books curriculums, based on the reading of the enduring texts of, again, the Western tradition, often as given in the Great Books of the Western World series, first published in 1952 by Encyclopedia Britannica in conjunction with the University of Chicago and edited by Chicago's former president Robert Maynard Hutchins, along with coeditor Mortimer J. Adler. The Great Books curriculum is now the staple, perhaps most famously, at St. John's College, but, as well, at several Christian schools and colleges, both Catholic and Protestant (Thomas Aquinas College and the Torrey Institute at Biola University, respectively, to name but two). There are also the Junior Great Books for younger readers, but devoted less exclusively these days to the Western tradition. (What would Hutchins and Adler make of that?)

Finally, there is plain old "liberal arts," as commonly understood.

So if we ask, What exactly is meant by *liberal arts?* several answers are admissible in the current environment. (There are of course others besides the ones I have named, including combinations of the ones I have named.) The same seems to be true historically; there has apparently been no consensus on the subject down the ages. Donald Levine tells us, for instance, that distinguished University of Chicago classical scholar Richard McKeon "showed that interpretations and uses of the liberal arts have changed continuously over the past 2,500 years" (2007, 186). But in light of the many and able attempts to argue for *The Great Tradition* (Gamble 2007), or what Hutchins (1952) called *The Great Conversation,* one wonders if the disarray is as pronounced as Levine's comment seems to suggest. We will have to come to terms with the fact that not everyone defines, or has defined, through the centuries, *liberal arts* exactly the same way. We will also have to see if there is something common to all the definitions and, if so, what that something is.

"A More Ominous Threat"

While there is apparently some confusion about the exact meaning of *liberal arts*, there are more serious problems in persuading parents and students of their importance. As intimated in chapter 8, if part of what we mean by the liberal arts is what is studied "for its own sake," as opposed to what is studied for the purpose of earning a living, we are up against, as Levine puts it, "a more ominous threat: a tendency to deal with questions of educational content in terms of the increasingly fashionable business notion of a bottom line" (2007, xiii). What Levine is referring to, I think, is the demand, often for purposes of survival, for colleges primarily, but schools no less, to tailor their course offerings to the needs or wants of those they serve. If those paying your tuition prefer computer programming or business math over British literature or calculus, how can you argue with that? It is a huge problem for many private, including Christian, schools; for as Jeffry Davis and Leland Ryken of Wheaton College put it, "The most palpable rhetoric which operates within the heads and hearts of most of our students is not the rhetoric of the church or the Bible, but the rhetoric of consumerism." These are they who are regularly tempted to believe that "ultimate security in life comes, not from God, but from Mammon" (21).

"The Things Most Students Don't Want to Know"

There is also this: "Among the things most students don't want to know [claimed David Bouchier in 1989] are history (the dead past), literature (dull), other languages (too difficult), philosophy (all questions and no answers), and art (incomprehensible and elitist)—in other words, the traditional product line of the liberal-arts college." This is an attitude supported by what Davis and Ryken call "the myth of the contemporary" and "the disparagement of the past" (18), both related to that denial of any culture outside the student's own that Bauerlein warned us about in chapter 3.

There are other obstacles as well. Not only are there the "technicians," according to Michael Bauman, "those who could or would train us only to program (or even to design) a VCR" (or whatever its up-to-the-second equivalent—or is it even possible in this constantly changing technological environment to get that reference current?), there are the "self-esteem peddlers of our day" who teach students that "to feel good is at least as important as to do good, and that to get a job and make money is the central purpose of an education and the chief means to happiness." Both "bow in abject servitude to the tyrannous and impotent dictates of the so-called affective domain when they ought to banish it forever from the classroom" (2004).

But vocationalism, consumerism, and pop psychology are only several of the more obvious of the barriers to mounting a compelling case for the liberal arts. For Christians there is what Davis and Ryken call "the long-standing tension which Christian teachers and students have felt as they have sought to use a curriculum derived from the pagan past, converted to serve Christian purposes" (1). That tension I hope I have dealt with in chapter 2. It has been resolved most satisfactorily in the concrete historical development that is Greco-Roman/Judeo-Christian civilization, which includes many of the greatest thinkers and most of the greatest colleges and universities in Europe and America, all bearing, at one time anyway, testimony to faith in Christ.

Having admitted the seeming confusion, or vagueness, that surrounds the phrase *liberal arts*, and having indicated some of the problems for their implementation, we must turn now to the primary concern of this chapter, and try to give answers to the questions, What are they? and What do they do?—and that requires, as with most things, a bit of history.

ANCIENT DISTINCTIONS

By almost every account the liberal arts were born in Athens in the fifth century BC, with roots running back perhaps into the sixth century. The principal education theorists of that day, as we saw in chapter 1, were Isocrates and Plato. Isocrates emphasized a curriculum primarily of literature and rhetoric, his goal being the training of virtuous citizens for Athenian democracy; Plato, on the other hand, emphasized math and philosophy, what Bruce

Kimball calls "the speculative and endless pursuit of truth" (1986, 33), the kind of thing we see going on, most famously, in the Socratic dialogues. The first we might call the pragmatic, the second the analytical, approach to learning. This difference Kimball develops into a paradigm for understanding the entire history of the liberal arts.

According to the paradigm, it was the Isocratic or rhetorical, or oratorical, view, rather than the Platonic or philosophical, that almost immediately came to dominate education, not only in Greece and Rome, but throughout most of our history. It was the Roman orator Cicero (106–43 BC) who first used the phrase *artes liberales*, although, Kimball argues, that is no proof that he invented it: "There is evidence that *liberalis* had direct antecedents in Greek" (1986, 13). So while it was the Greeks who effectively created the disciplines we know as the liberal arts, it was "the Roman penchant for cataloging and prescribing" that "must be recognized as a major factor in the evolution of the liberal arts into a coherent program of study" (Davis and Ryken, 3). The liberal arts thus became the seven liberal arts (*septum artes liberales*), organized further into the trivium, the three subjects concerning language, plus the quadrivium, the four mathematical or "scientific" subjects, mentioned above, a curriculum that remained more or less standard throughout the Middle Ages.

RENAISSANCE HUMANISM

When we come to the fifteenth and sixteenth centuries we discover that the Renaissance humanists, according to Kimball, introduced their own modifications of the *artes liberales*, which they referred to as the *studia humanitatis* (humane studies). These included "the disciplines of grammar, rhetoric, poetry, and history, often combined with moral philosophy" (1986, 78)—very like, though with a somewhat different contour than, the medieval trivium and quadrivium. But because of Renaissance humanism's devotion to the "continual refinement of the human personality" (that sounds familiar, does it not?), some Christian men of letters had difficulty reconciling their faith with the spirit of the prevailing scholarship.

Among them was the famous Desiderius Erasmus (1469–1536), one of the most influential education theorists of the period; also renowned editor of the Church Fathers and the Greek New Testament, as well as celebrated author of *The Praise of Folly*, his widely read satire on the corruption of the Church, and a variety of other learned works. Like many of the great Christian thinkers before him, Erasmus, says Kimball, "experienced great tension between his Christian commitment to humility and the humanist value assigned to pride and praise, between the Christian desire for pure, simple belief and the humanist respect for sophisticated refinement" (89).

It is a tension that runs all through the history of Christian accommodations to secular learning, starting with the Fathers—or should we say the apostle Paul? Interestingly, and instructively, the greatest Christian thinkers seem to have felt it most acutely. What they were seeking, nonetheless, might be summed up in the motto of the school founded in Strasbourg in 1538 by Johannes Sturm (1507–89): *sapiens et eloquens pietas*, "wise and eloquent piety." A lovely phrase, is it not, which Sturm drew, remarkably, from Cicero (Kimball 1986, 94)—evidence, again, of the union that was seen to be possible, even natural, between Christian faith and liberal learning.

REFORMATION GIANTS

As for the two Reformation giants, Martin Luther (1483–1546) and John Calvin (1509–64): both expressed admiration for classical authors, especially Cicero and Quintilian. In 1524, we are told, Luther appealed to German mayors to rejuvenate education, and "in sermons and letters he recommended the 'liberal arts,' asking; 'Where are the preachers, jurists and physicians to come from, if grammar and other rhetorical arts are not taught?'" (Kimball 1986, 92). Philipp Melanchthon (1497–1560), Luther's great ally and the foremost humanist among the Lutheran Reformers, for his part, "provided the model of school organization (*Schulordnung*), whereby the Latin grammar school became normative for Protestant municipal schools throughout central

Europe" (93). Says Kimball, "It is not surprising to learn that nearly all of the top two-dozen leaders of the Protestant revolt had counted themselves Renaissance humanists" (92). The alliance between Protestantism and liberal learning in Europe and, eventually, America is underscored by Davis and Ryken's remark that "the phrases that the Reformers and Puritans used in talking about schools and education reveal their profound rejection of any antagonism between knowledge and faith" (13).

THE ENLIGHTENMENT

As we turn to the period of the Enlightenment, especially the latter part of the eighteenth century, we do seem to recognize what appear the beginnings of a more drastic alteration in the notion of liberal education. Largely as a result of the advance of the New Science associated with the empiricism of Francis Bacon (1561–1626), there was pressure in some European universities, especially in Germany, to replace the classics with the natural sciences and the ancient languages with modern vernaculars. Proponents of the New Science and New Philosophy objected to the abstract and "useless" disputations of the universities, "their scholastic and gentlemanly preoccupations," as Kimball calls them. They were equally critical of "the adulation of Greek and Latin letters" (1986, 125–26). Included in their proposals were similarly radical notions of emphasizing research over time-honored wisdom and training the intellect over the cultivation of noble virtue—all of this signaling the stress on human liberty, intellectual and otherwise, that so characterized the Age of Reason.

Neither in England nor in America did such reforms take root without considerable resistance, however. In defense of maintaining the traditional curriculum against proposals to drop the classical languages, the Yale *Reports* of 1828, for instance, declared that "classical letters were the indispensable basis of 'liberal education'" (Kimball 1986, 150). Many at Harvard concurred, and as late as the 1850s similar views were expressed in the official reports at Oxford and Cambridge (150–51).

IN AMERICA

In America it was not until after the Civil War and sometime before World War II that the meaning of "the liberal arts" actually changed, in some quarters. Following the lead of the German universities, more and more American schools embraced the growing scientific disciplines and the concomitant emergence of specialization, a move that one commentator of the time described as from "humanistic and religious" to "scientific" (Kimball 1986, 175). Others refer to it as an "intellectualized" approach to liberal learning, the accent more on the enhancement of critical intellect than on character or virtue—on "making minds" more than on "making men," although the distinction was not always clearly articulated, and in some cases amounted rather to "an effort at rapprochement between two ideals" (177–78).

Some of these differences are expressed, nonetheless, in the modern distinction between a (liberal arts) college and a (research) university, between the educational purpose of cultivating understanding (and perhaps virtue) based on "the best which has been thought and said in the world" and that of advancing the frontiers of knowledge—differences that have led in some cases to questioning whether the traditional liberal arts are still relevant or in others to their abandonment. For if there is no consensus regarding even what the liberal arts are, especially in the urgency of more practical and pressing or popular concerns, why bother?

Or maybe the liberal arts *are* a continually evolving species. They never were fixed, it could be said, and never will be. Why then should we not be exploring new ways of doing them, all the while recasting the paradigm? Levine, for instance, wants us to think about going from seven arts toward eight "powers," from trivium and quadrivium (or *studia humanitatis* or ...) to "audiovisual powers" and "kinesthetic powers," to powers of "creating a self" and "sharing meanings with others," with several like "powers" in between (2007, 188–89).

That development is not what those in what Kimball calls the rhetorical or oratorical tradition had in mind, though, as that tradition, broadly speaking, can be identified, he says, by these seven characteristics: (1) "the goal of training the good citizen to lead society"; (2) "the prescription of values and standards for character and conduct"; (3) "respect for commitment to the prescribed values and standards"; (4) agreement on the values and standards provided by "a body of classical texts"; (5) "identifying an elite who achieve greater merit by adopting the personal and civic virtues expressed in the texts"; (6) a "dogmatist epistemology," a "belief that truth can be known and expressed"; and (7) a conviction that the oratorical ideal was an end in itself, that "the personal development which resulted from a study of the classics [was] sufficient justification for the labour involved" (1986, 37–38).

But Kimball's book, perhaps the most thorough treatment of the subject available, is throughout an attempt to demonstrate that this dominant oratorical tradition—descended from Isocrates and Cicero and Quintilian and manifested variously down the ages in the *septum artes liberales*, the *studia humanitatis*, and more contemporarily in curriculums such as the "classical"—has been fundamentally at odds with the other tradition in Kimball's paradigm, the philosophical tradition of Socrates and Plato, "the speculative and endless pursuit of truth" (Kimball 1986, 33), which might be described as not so much informing the student about the virtues as teaching him how to search for them (38), and which has become the basis of much modern practice.

MODERN APPROACHES: THE NEW LIBERAL ARTS IDEAL

This post-Enlightenment approach to liberal education replaces the seven characteristics of the old rhetorical/oratorical tradition with seven characteristics of its own: (1) "an emphasis on freedom, especially freedom from a priori strictures and standards"; (2) "an emphasis on intellect and rationality," including Descartes' "basically Socratic view that evil arises from ignorance"; (3) "a critical skepticism," not least about final answers to almost anything; (4) tolerance; (5) "a tendency toward egalitarianism"; (6) an "emphasis on volition of the individual rather than upon the obligations of citizenship found in the *artes liberales* ideal"; and (7) the new ideal's "standing as an ideal, an end in itself," for, "since conclusions are always subject to criticism, it is not the truth that is finally desirable, but the search" (Kimball 1986, 119–22).

These characteristics of the new liberal arts give an entirely unprecedented meaning to the word *liberal*, which Kimball defines, in an interesting use of language, as "liberal-free" (1986, 119), in contradistinction to the older *artes liberales*. Is it true, then, as Kimball says, that "American higher education in the second half of the twentieth century [and beyond?] holds Socrates, rather than Cicero, as its paragon" (11), and that inherent in the idea of liberal arts is the notion that they can and perhaps should be continually re-thought? Levine's "new goals for the liberal curriculum," his "eight powers" (2007, 188–89), would seem to be an outworking of such a notion.

REACTIONS TO MODERNISM

Whatever we make of that way of formulating the issue, it is pretty clear that most of those attempting to establish the case for a renewed interest in the liberal arts take a different view altogether. What they mean by liberal arts is precisely that such studies are *not* forever evolving. On the contrary, references to The Great Tradition are meant to indicate that something—in fact a great deal, in a sense everything important—has been handed down. References to The Great Conversation are likewise meant to indicate that there is real dialogue taking place across the millennia, wherein the parties are speaking, essentially, about the same things. It all holds together, is of a piece. That is why it is appropriate to use the definite article in speaking of "Great Tradition" or "Great Conversation." It is "the rootedness of traditional liberal arts education in the past," as Davis and Ryken call it (18), that they are contending for—contra what Richard Gamble describes as "the modern tendency to value the past merely as a precursor to the present" (2007, xvii). Gamble goes on to quote Herbert Butterfield, great Christian historian at Cambridge half a century ago: "Whether our establishment is a new one or an old one, we ought to have the sense of belonging to a single great tradition"

(Butterfield 1962, 26–27). Newman likewise spoke of "a specific idea" of liberal education, "which ever has been, and ever will be.... It is illustrated by a continuous historical tradition, and never was out of the world, from the time it came into it. There have indeed been differences of opinion from time to time, as to what pursuits and what arts came under that idea, but such differences are but an additional evidence of its reality" (5.5; 1982, 83).

There is then *a* tradition, truly *the* tradition, of which we are heirs. It is one thing and can be identified; it has certain characteristics. While it may not have been interpreted in exactly the same way at all times and in all places, neither is it a constantly emerging work in progress.

Before I try to say what in my estimation those characteristics are, we must attend to the wisdom of one final commentator on the subject. As you will see, I saved the best for last.

THE BEST FOR LAST: JOHN HENRY NEWMAN

For my money the preeminent explication of liberal learning belongs to John Henry Newman. His *The Idea of a University*, which I have quoted generously already, was first published under that title in 1873 and is the expanded version of his *Discourses on the Scope and Nature of University Education: Addressed to the Catholics of Dublin*, the first edition of which appeared in 1853 on the occasion of his appointment as founding rector of the new Catholic University of Ireland. Although the university did not succeed, *The Idea* has not only survived but soared in critical estimation. The historian G. M. Young, we are told, "has ranked it with Aristotle's *Ethics* among the most valuable of all works on the aim of Education," and Sir Arthur Quiller-Crouch "told his students at Cambridge [in the first half of the last century] that 'of all the books written in these hundred years there is perhaps none you can more profitably thumb and ponder'" (Svaglic 1982, vii).

What makes *The Idea* so valuable in my view are two things: first, Newman's brilliance at getting at the essence of a thing, paring a subject down to its core, and, second, related to the first, his profoundly Christian, even Pauline, insights. Like no one else he seems able to articulate the virtues of a liberal education at the same time as he is able to appreciate, from a Christian perspective, its limitations. And while there are in Newman echoes of what has been said by others—this is, after all, as Newman himself reminded us, "a continuous historical tradition"—I don't think *The Idea* can be matched, either for its perspicacity or psychological and spiritual sensitivity. For Christian educators this is the book to read.

So what is Newman's view of the liberal arts and what they do?

Like many other commentators Newman prefers to define liberal learning not so much by specific subjects as by its overall purpose. In one place, however, he does talk at some length about the sort of academic discipline he thinks is required as preparation for university. "I hold very strongly [he says] that the first step in intellectual training is to impress upon a boy's mind the idea of science, method, order, principle, and system; of rule and exception, of richness and harmony. This is commonly and excellently done by making him begin with Grammar." He also recommends mathematics, "still with the same object, viz., to give him a conception of development and arrangement from and around a common centre. Hence it is that Chronology and Geography are so necessary for him, when he reads History, which is otherwise little better than a storybook." Similarly metrical composition, "in order [when he reads poetry] to stimulate his powers into action in every practicable way"—all in the interests of gaining "this habit of method, of starting from fixed points, of making his ground good as he goes, of distinguishing what he knows from what he does not know" (1982, xliv–xlv).

"THE CULTIVATION OF INTELLECT, AS SUCH"

By and large, though, as I have said, Newman's interest is less in prescribing courses than in ascertaining what liberal education is, and it is here that his genius is especially manifest. "Liberal Education, viewed in itself," he says, "is simply the cultivation of intellect, as such, and its object is nothing more or less than intellectual excellence" (5.9; 1982, 92).

What is singular about Newman's take on this is its economy, for want of a better word. He says what is fitting and no more. As physical exercise promotes physical strength or coordination, but does not make us more reasonable or thoughtful, so intellectual exercise promotes intellectual competence, but does not make us more decent or honorable. Just where we might expect a Christian advocate for liberal learning to go on to extol its efficaciousness in nourishing moral virtue, he stops. Intellect has its own beauty, he says, and that is in and of itself a goal worthy of education. We don't need to require of it anything more. "To open the mind, to correct it, to refine it, to enable it to know, and to digest, master, rule, and to use its knowledge, to give it power over its own faculties, application, flexibility, method, critical exactness, sagacity, resource, address, eloquent expression, is an object as intelligible (for here we are inquiring, not what the object of a Liberal Education is worth, nor what use the Church makes of it, but what it is in itself), I say, an object as intelligible as the cultivation of virtue, while, at the same time, it is absolutely distinct from it" (5.9; 1982, 92–93).

All through there is the highest praise, in the most eloquent terms, of the benefits of education. There is also the most zealous care in making sure that those benefits are not misunderstood or education given credit for what it cannot do. Liberal knowledge is a wonderful and necessary thing, he argues, but

> For all its friends, or its enemies, may say, I insist upon it, that it is as real a mistake to burden it with virtue or religion as with the mechanical arts. Its direct business is not to steel the soul against temptation or to console it in affliction, any more than to set the loom in motion, or to direct the steam carriage; be it ever so much the means or the condition of both material and moral advancement, still, taken by and in itself, it as little mends our hearts as it improves our temporal circumstances.... Knowledge is one thing, virtue is another; good sense is not conscience, refinement is not humility, nor is largeness and justness of view faith. Philosophy, however enlightened, however profound, gives no command over the passions, no influential motives, no vivifying principles. Liberal Education makes not the Christian, not the Catholic, but the gentleman. (5.9; 1982, 90–91)

Not that such an education is therefore less important for Newman. On the contrary, its value is everywhere apparent in his remarks. Here is his description of the young who have yet to be educated: "This is an emblem of their minds; at first they have no principles laid down within them as a foundation for the intellect to build upon; they have no discriminating convictions, and no grasp of consequences. And therefore they talk at random, if they talk much, and cannot help being flippant, or what is emphatically called 'young.' They are merely dazzled by phenomena, instead of perceiving things as they are" (1982, xlii–xliii; italics in original).

Nor is it only the young who cannot help revealing their lack of "real cultivation of mind": "What is more common than the sight of grown men, talking on political or moral or religious subjects, in that offhand, idle way, which we signify by the word *unreal*? 'That they simply do not know what they are talking about' is the spontaneous silent remark of any man of sense who hears them" (Newman 1982, xliii; italics in original).

The distinguishing trait of the liberally educated by contrast is "intellectual culture," "health ... of the intellect," "intellectual illumination" (Newman 6.2; 1982, 95–96). The uneducated "generalize nothing" (6.5; 102); for them "nothing has a drift or relation." Such a man "has no standard of judgment at all, and no landmarks to guide him to a conclusion." "True enlargement of mind," on the other hand, "is the power of viewing many things at once as one whole" (6.6; 103); and "the intellect, which has been disciplined to the perfection of its powers ... knows, and thinks while it knows ... has learned to leaven the dense mass of facts and events with the elastic force of reason" (6.7; 104).

LIBERAL KNOWLEDGE IS "ITS OWN END"

Knowledge, moreover, "is capable of being its own end" (Newman 5.2; 1982, 77); truly, "that alone is liberal knowledge, which stands on its own pretensions, which is independent of sequel, expects no complement, refuses to be *informed* (as it is called) by any end, or absorbed into any art, in order duly to present itself to our contemplation" (81; italics in original).

As for useful versus liberal knowledge, Newman pretty much follows the tradition, but is perhaps more elegant, and more expansive, in his handling of it: "This process of training, by which the intellect, instead of being formed or sacrificed to some particular or accidental purpose, some specific trade or profession, or study or science, is disciplined for its own sake, for the perception of its own proper object, and for its own highest culture, is called Liberal Education" (7.1; 1982, 115).

Sacrificed to some specific trade or profession. That's the problem. In attempting to train for professional skill, education gives up its higher purpose, "Thought or Reason exercised upon Knowledge, or what may be called Philosophy" (Newman 6.7; 1982, 105), "that perfection of the Intellect, which is the result of Education" (6.6; 105).

Nowhere does Newman denigrate either professional skill or specialization. He is saying only that that is not education's aim. So far from disparaging "usefulness," he claims, "I will show you how a liberal education is truly and fully a useful, though it be not a professional, education" (7.5; 1982, 124). How? Such an education "gives a man a clear conscious view of his own opinions and judgments, a truth in developing them, an eloquence in expressing them, and a force in urging them.... It prepares him to fill any post with credit, and to master any subject with facility" (7.10; 134–35). That idea was the subject of the previous chapter.

The virtues of liberal learning from Newman's pen show exceedingly attractive indeed. Among them are consequences "to a man's immediate society, how he talks, as how he acts" and "simply that of speaking good sense in English, without fee or reward, in common conversation" (7.8; 1982, 130). Every page is crowded with wisdom and Christian sanity.

But I must end, and do so by returning to what is necessarily one of the main themes of this book, the relationship of the kind of education Newman has explicated so winsomely to the Christian faith for which he was such an engaging apologist. It is a theme we touched on at the beginning of the chapter. It is a fitting theme on which to conclude, as it was upon this theme that Newman himself chose to conclude.

"KNOWLEDGE VIEWED IN RELATION TO RELIGION"

What Newman has to say here can be summed up in his delineation of "the radical difference indeed of this mental refinement from genuine religion." This, he says, "in spite of its seeming relationship, is the very cardinal point on which my present discussion turns" (8.4; 1982, 144–45). The problem as Newman sees it is that so impressive are the powers of intellect and in some cases so like moral virtue that we are tempted to forget how fundamental and absolute is the contrast between the merely educated man (the gentleman, as Newman calls him) and the Christian. Even "the scorn and hatred which a cultivated mind feels for some kinds of vice, and the utter disgust and profound humiliation which may come over it, if it should happen in any degree to be betrayed into them"—even of this it may be said, "there is nothing really religious in it, considered by itself" (8.5; 145). This phenomenon, familiar to all of us, Newman refers to as "the substitution of a moral sense or taste for conscience in the true meaning of the word," wherein "virtue is nothing more than the graceful in conduct" (146–47).

There is a basic, crucial difference between the gentleman and the Christian, says Newman, even though both appear to be possessed of an admirable moral propensity, or, to be candid, the gentleman sometimes more. The one may have "intellectual religion" or "philosophical virtue" (8.6; 1982, 147), even "of a liberal and generous character"; the other in contrast is moved by a faith often given to less than congenial convictions. "This was the quarrel of the ancient heathen with Christianity, that, instead of simply fixing the mind on the fair and the pleasant, it intermingled other ideas with them of a sad and painful nature; that it spoke of tears before joy, a cross before a crown; that it laid the foundation of heroism in penance; that it made the soul tremble with the news of Purgatory and Hell; that it insisted on views and a worship of the Deity, which to their minds was nothing else than mean, servile, and cowardly" (8.5; 147).

Newman calls to remembrance Julian the Apostate, mentioned in chapter 1, distinguished by his "simplicity of manners, his frugality, his austerity of life,... his modesty, his clemency, his accomplishments," which, in Newman's view, "go to make him one of the most eminent specimens of pagan virtue which the world has ever seen." But for all that, says Newman, "how shallow, how meagre, nay, how unamiable is that virtue after all, when brought upon its critical trial by his sudden summons into the presence of his Judge!" Julian's last hours, as reported by a sympathetic eyewitness, comments Newman, illustrate "the helplessness of philosophy under the stern realities of our being" (8.6; 1982, 147–48).

ENDING ON A POSITIVE NOTE

Liberal knowledge may have "a special tendency," as Newman calls it, "to impress us with a mere philosophical theory of life and conduct, in the place of Revelation," that is, to become a substitute for faith (9.2; 1982, 165). At the same time, he says, speaking of what he calls Secular Literature, if we fail to refine a student's taste under conditions we have ourselves set, we plunge him into the world without the advantages that such literature—we would add all liberal studies—afford, and "without the honest indulgence of wit and humour and imagination having ever been permitted to him, without any fastidiousness of taste wrought into him, without any rule given him for discriminating 'the precious from the vile,' beauty from sin, the truth from the sophistry of nature, what is innocent from what is poison" (9.8; 177). Illuminating these distinctions is therefore our job—which would no doubt be included in presenting a Christian worldview.

Knowledge in the form of the liberal arts is a marvelous, indisputably beneficial, even necessary, thing, the good gift of a loving God. Apart from grace it may have "a special tendency," it is true, to divert or distract us from faith, but that is not the whole of it. The Church, says Newman, "fears no knowledge, but she purifies all; she represses no element of our nature, but cultivates the whole.... Her principle is one and the same throughout: not to prohibit truth of any kind, but to see that no doctrines pass under the name of Truth but those which claim it rightfully" (9.8; 1982, 178). That is her educative role at its best.

When Newman spoke of the Church, he meant of course the

Roman Catholic Church. No Protestant need dismiss his insights on those grounds, however. His understanding of both the importance of liberal education and its limitations from a Christian perspective are an invaluable contribution to the literature of Christian schooling—for all of us. In this chapter I may have quoted him too much. No, he can hardly be quoted too much. Rather, he should be read entire.

THE CHARACTERISTICS OF A LIBERAL ARTS EDUCATION

I said a moment ago that even though the facts forbid us to force the liberal arts into a single mold; even though they have been interpreted variously as *septum artes liberales*, *studia humanitatis*, humanities, "classics," in some places Great Books, and so on— these diverse interpretations share certain general characteristics. I must now try to say what I think those characteristics are.

The **first**, as we've already seen, is their "rootedness ... in the past," as Davis and Ryken put it. Peter Leithart of the Classical Christian Education movement describes it like this: "True education is an initiation into our full humanity. It is not so much a leading-out as a passing-on of the skills necessary to participate in culture. True education is really *traducation*" (2008, 3; italics in original). Leithart also speaks of the importance of "the role of tradition" (4) and "the ongoing conversation of Western civilization" (5). "Questions of education are questions about the relation of a culture to its past and to its future," he says, and Classical Christian Education "represents, more or less overtly, a protest against contemporary society, as well as contemporary education." Classical educators, he claims, "take aim at a range of contemporary values: professionalization, bureaucratization, standardization, deference to 'expert' authority, the whole Weberian apparatus of rationalization." Such an education "is not about maintaining the cultural status quo." It is rather "a reaction to the educational failures of the last century" (9).

That reaction takes the form of what Davis and Ryken describe as "a shared conviction that the fund of knowledge most worth having reaches back from the contemporary into the past history of Western civilization. Historical depth of field is a hallmark of the liberal arts tradition, and the reading lists ... begin with Plato and Aristotle as well as the Bible" (14). His selection of readings from the Great Tradition, says Richard Gamble, "is intended to supply an arsenal of the liberal arts for those who would wage war—covertly or openly—on the side of an education rooted in the classical and Christian heritage.... Readers looking for up-to-the-minute advice about innovative teaching methods and classroom technology, or about how to prepare students for the 'real world' and tomorrow's top-ten careers, will be gravely disappointed" (2007, xvi). Of "that unbroken chain of literary and intellectual tradition which extends from the ancient to the modern world," Irving Babbitt wrote:

> It is by bringing home to the mind of the American student the continuity of this tradition that one is likely to implant in him, more effectually, perhaps, than in any other way, that right feeling and respect for the past which he so signally lacks....

> The American, it is true, is often haunted, in the midst of all his surface activity, with a vague sense that, after all, his life may be deficient in depth and dignity; it is not so often, however, that he succeeds in tracing this defect in his life to its lack of background and perspective, to the absence in himself of a right feeling for the past,—that feeling which, as has been truly said, distinguishes more than any other the civilized man from the barbarian. (1908, 159–60)

"Classical and Christian," "Plato and Aristotle as well as the Bible": this view of the liberal arts is rooted not only in the past, but in the Western past. That is their **second** general characteristic as I see it. When we speak of The Great Tradition and The Great Conversation, it is the Greco-Roman and Judeo-Christian tradition and conversation we are talking about, what James Schall describes as "the two origins of our culture, the Greek heritage and the revelational response to its brooding questions to itself." Schall goes on to say,

And these origins belong together, however different each is. What is known as patristic and medieval thought is designed to explain how this relationship is possible, how the best in Athens can be seen as related to revelation and its unique terms.... What is known as "modern" thought is largely the attempt to solve the classical human questions without recourse to either tradition. Any adequate concept of "liberal arts" and "liberal education" would, to be intellectually complete and honest, have to attend to the Greek and Roman classical traditions, to the Hebrew and Christian revelation, to the patristic and medieval experience, and finally to modern claims, especially those arising from science and politics, even when they claim to be "autonomous." (2006, 26–27)

That does not mean that the liberal arts are exclusively Greco-Roman and Judeo-Christian, as if nothing worthwhile was ever thought or said in the Islamic or African or Asian traditions, or that we have nothing to learn from them, or that we may not be improved and edified by becoming more "international" in our outlook—or that we might not be *required* to do so, practically speaking. It could mean, however, given the speed of the so-called knowledge explosion and the enormous pressures applied by the proponents of multiculturalism (and the very real fact of the multiplicity of competing cultures itself!), that we will have to recognize, as Davis and Ryken suggest, that "the ideal of a comprehensive education that covers all known knowledge cannot sustain itself" (17). We cannot do everything. Besides, we are already making choices about these kinds of things: between vocational and academic courses, between teaching "life-skills" and cultivating intellect, between (in certain Christian circles) what is "spiritual" and what is "merely scholastic." Why not a choice between the liberal arts and their competitors, especially when (a) it is the liberal arts that along with Christianity have been the intellectual and spiritual staple of what is best in the Western tradition, (b) that tradition is our tradition, and (c) that tradition has been the source of so much that is undeniably good in the world? Or as Hutchins well put it over fifty years ago, "At a time when the West is most often represented by its friends as the source of that technology for which the whole world yearns and by its enemies as the fountainhead of selfishness and greed, it is worth remarking that, though both elements can be found in the Great Conversation, the Western ideal is not one or the other strand in the Conversation, but the Conversation itself" (1952, 1–2).

As for the angry charge of Western narrowness and self-absorbed ignorance of the wider world (remember "Hey, hey, ho, ho, Western Civ. has got to go"?) leveled by "those leaders of opinion who out of unspent hatred are bent on war against the West," as Barzun put it:

> The provincialism of the West is a myth. It is the West, and not the East, that has penetrated into all parts of the globe. It is only the West that has studied, translated, and dis-seminated the thoughts, the histories, and the works of art of other civilizations, living and dead. By now, the formerly shut-in peoples do take an interest in others, but this recent development is in imitation of Western models. By good and bad means, Western ideas have imprinted themselves on the rest of the world, and one result is that cultural exchange and mutual instruction are at last consciously international; this, just at the time when we are told to repudiate our achieve-ments and consign our best thoughts to oblivion.

This, Barzun concludes, is a "form of moral suicide" (1991, 131–32).

The **third** general characteristic of liberal learning is that it is broad and not narrow, universal and not specific. In a sense it is about everything, for the purpose of equipping us for everything. "Liberal education is not a 'specialty,'" says Schall. "It is not what is called a 'major.'" Rather, it is fixed in what he calls "intellectual *eros*" (2006, 39; italics in original). That is why almost everyone who has ever written about this has argued, as I tried to show in chap-ter 8, that it is not about training in a particular skill, professional or otherwise, but about requiring us to think deeply and broadly about the nature of men and things, about life, from a wide range of perspectives, ancient and modern, philosophical and historical, literary and scientific. It is "a reflection into the heart of things," as Schall has it (2006, 30).

That leads to what I think is another, the **fourth**, general characteristic of a liberal education: it is about "the big issues." This is not often discussed, so far as I can see, but it seems obvious and implicit in much of what is said on the subject. The most important questions, after all, are "philosophical," are they not? While they may not be the most urgent questions, in the sense of the most immediate, they are the most important nonetheless: "Does God exist?" "Are there moral absolutes?" "What does it mean to be human?" Our answers here shape our worldview, indeed *are* our worldview. They govern our everyday lives whether we are aware of the fact or not. If you talk about almost any issue long enough you end up at these or questions very like them.

The Great Conversation, by and large, is about what Schall refers to as "the highest things" (2006, 33). Or as Michael Bauman puts it, "If you desire to become educated rather than to remain merely trained, then you must remember that an educated person can give careful and insightful answers to the fundamental, or diagnostic, questions of life, questions like: 'What is a good life, and what good is life?' 'What is a good death, and what good is death?' 'What is a good love, and what good is love?' 'What is a human being?'" Bauman goes on to say, by way of contrast, that "such preliminary questions do not include the questions professors most often hear from students, questions that seem naturally to arise from the indoctrination those students receive from the technicians and job trainers of our day—questions like: 'Will this be on the test?' 'Will this help me get a job?' 'Will this make me feel good?'" (2004, 2–3).

We come then to what I consider the **fifth** general characteristic of liberal education, which is that it is not so much about learning "subjects" as it is about cultivating intellectual virtues. Important as the liberal disciplines are, they are not themselves the point. The point is the cognitive skills they nurture, "the intellectual tools to understand the world," as Schall puts it (2006, 32)—"what survives when what's been learned has been forgotten," as someone has said (I have seen the remark attributed to Albert Einstein, B. F. Skinner, the Marquis of Halifax [1630–95], and the English poet

John Dryden [1631–1700]), the intellectual range and suppleness that is the consequence of having done the academic exercise, even though the facts, the data, are no longer remembered.

Woodrow Wilson, when president of Princeton, "claimed that the drift toward specialization was producing 'a new ignorance' produced by 'separate baronies of knowledge, where a few strong men rule and many ignorant men are held vassals'; he defended the 'generalizing habit' based on a broad survey of the field of knowledge, without which 'it is hard to see how a man is to discern *the relations of things*, upon the perception of which all just thought must rest'" (Levine 2007, 30–31; italics in original).

Writers on the effects of liberal learning frequently talk about this ability to see "the relations of things," often in conjunction with the "generalizing habit." Hutchins said that "the substance of liberal education appears to consist in the recognition of basic problems, in knowledge of distinctions and interrelations in subject matter, and in the comprehension of ideas. Liberal education seeks to clarify the basic problems and to understand the way in which one problem bears upon another" (1952, 3). Others speak of the importance of the liberal arts in cultivating "broad modes of thought" or "mental methods" or "intellectual virtues" (Levine 2007, 182–83). Newman specified the abilities to analyze and discriminate. A droll twist on this is given by Irving Babbitt in his recollection of Voltaire's sketch of the noble Venetian lord Pococurante—"the type of scholar who would be esteemed, not like the man of today by the inclusiveness of his sympathies, but by the number of things he had rejected. Pococurante had ... rejected almost everything except a few verses of Virgil and Horace. 'What a great man is this Pococurante!' says the awe-stricken Candide; 'nothing can please him'" (1908, 80). This is intellectual discrimination with a vengeance!

The benefits of liberal learning have traditionally been accounted in moral as well as intellectual terms. We have already seen, in chapter 1, that, from the beginning, education has meant "essentially, moral training, character-training, a whole way of life," as Marrou reminded us (1956, 147). Other ways of putting it include "to realize ever more perfectly the human ideal," "a particular style of living," "culture," "character and taste," and so on. With the triumph of Christianity we have the marriage of pagan notions of educational purpose and biblical standards of virtue; thus the goal of teaching often becomes something like "wise and eloquent piety" or, as David Newsome has characterized the aims of early Victorian English public schools, "godliness and good learning" (1961, 2).

We could describe the liberal arts from the other end, as well; that is, not by the intellectual or moral virtues that are their result but by the way in which, psychologically or spiritually, they are approached. According to Jacob Klein, this is exactly the way they ought to be defined. Says Klein, "The idea of liberal education ... whether you accept or reject it, is not definable in terms of some peculiar subject matter. Some applied sciences may well fall outside its scope. But, by and large, any formal discipline may form its vehicle and basis. It is not subject matter that determines the character of studies as liberal studies. It is rather the way in which a formal discipline, a subject matter, is taken up that is decisive: whenever it is being studied for its own sake, whenever the metastrophic way of questioning is upheld, whenever genuine wonderment is present, liberal education is taking place" (1985, 166).*

To illustrate, Klein goes on to say, "Foremost among the formal liberal disciplines are, of course, the mathematical disciplines, the physical sciences, the science of life, the sciences of language—grammar, rhetoric, and logic—and also the great works of literature, those incomparable mirrors of man. But it is a rather fantastic idea to equate liberal studies with the so-called humanities; as if mathematical and scientific disciplines were less human than historical or poetic or philosophical studies. And do we not

---

Metastrophe is the Greek word for "to turn around." What Klein means by "the metastrophic way of questioning" may then be the sort of questioning that turns one around to see the essence of a thing; as Plato says, "the conversion [turning around] from the shadows to the images that cast them and to the light and the ascent from the subterranean cavern to the world above" (*Republic* 532a–b; Jowett 1952, 764). Or as Klein himself says, "The formal disciplines come into being as a result of our human ability to detach ourselves from our familiar and conflicting experiences, to turn about, to ask the radical question 'Why' and to persist in it" (1985, 164).

know that philosophy itself can be studied in the most illiberal way?" (1985, 166).

I think we could say that a liberal education is, **sixth**, largely a literary education. What I mean is that it has to do at base, but not exclusively, with reading, writing and, in the ancient world, speaking. It has to do with words, "the close-fitting dress of ideas." "The question of a proper education follows the question of what to read," says Schall. "The two, reading and education, are clearly related, though which comes first can well be disputed" (2006, 24). Hutchins reminds us that it is not only reading but the reading of certain books, the Great Books of the Western World. "Until very recently these books have been central in education in the West," he tells us (1952, 3). "It would be an exaggeration to say that Western civilization means these books. The exaggeration would lie in the omission of the plastic arts and music, which have quite as important a part in Western civilization as the great productions included in this set. But to the extent to which books can present the idea of a civilization, the idea of Western civilization is here presented…. These books are the means of understanding our society and ourselves. They contain the great ideas that dominate us without our knowing it. There is no comparable repository of our tradition" (2). Jacob Klein has forcefully, and rightly, reminded us that liberal education is not purely literary, but I wonder if even he would dispute that it is largely so.

Finally, **seventh**, the liberal arts are those studied "for their own sakes," or as Newman put it, knowledge "which stands on its own pretensions, which is independent of sequel, expects no complement, refuses to be *informed* (as it is called) by any end, or absorbed into any art, in order duly to present itself to our contemplation" (5.4; 1982, 81; italics in original). But that characteristic of the liberal arts was the subject of chapter 8 and has been implicit throughout this discussion.

CONCLUSION

What are we to make then of Bruce Kimball's paradigm, his exposition of the liberal arts in terms of the two broad categories of Ciceronian orators and Platonic-Socratic philosophers and their mutual exclusivity? Are the liberal arts to be seen as one or the other, the oratorical having been dominant for most of our history but the philosophical in the ascendancy now?

My own limited understanding would suggest that while Kimball's paradigm is an excellent means of getting a handle on an obviously not-uncomplicated topic, and his book a wonderfully thorough piece of scholarship, his juxtaposition may be too neat. Or as Richard Gamble said to me (in an e-mail in December 2007), "The best of the Western tradition, like Cicero, combined the oratorical and philosophical traditions and did not allow them to be sealed off into warring camps." That certainly seems to be the case with the various assertions of the liberal arts in our own time. Whether "humanities" or "classical" or "Great Books"—or simply "liberal arts"—all would claim to be neither merely "oratorical" nor "philosophical" but both. Plato is as much a part of it as Cicero, just as are their differing ways of seeing things. (Professor Kimball's further take on this, as he said to me on March 2, 2008, also in an e-mail, is that the oratorical tradition "has predominated in terms of duration over time, but both have been equally influential in how educators have thought about the liberal arts.... I would say that the 'Great Conversation' does and has always continued in the tension between the two traditions, neither of which can remain predominant.")

In a sense then it doesn't matter too much by what name you designate your preferred interpretation of the liberal arts. If the point and purpose of your curriculum is "cultivation of intellect" or "general knowledge and general intellectual capacities," taken up in the right spirit ("whenever genuine wonderment is present"); and if in addition it does not deny or disavow The Great Tradition, but embraces it, and honors for its own sake the wisdom it affords—it seems to me you are on the right track. Your curriculum, while it may not be identical to another calling itself "liberal arts," will nonetheless be informed by a kindred spirit and so have like results. To put it in pragmatic terms: I do not see how it would be possible at this stage to require that every school advocating liberal learning adopt exactly the same program of study. That would involve way more reshuffling administratively (retraining or rehiring, for instance), not to mention the evangelization and conversion of ways of thinking, than is practical or possible. (Imagine switching from "classical" to "Great Books," for instance, or the other way around.) I think it more sensible, and not at all a compromise of convictions, to plead that all who share the views of learning enumerated above should be blessed. Those who are not against us are for us. One of the salient lessons of this investigation, after all, has been that not everyone who has prosecuted the liberal arts tradition down the ages has prosecuted it in the same way—although the differences "are but an additional evidence of its reality," as Newman said (5.5; 1982, 83).

I finish with a paradox. No one would want to deny that our educating should be in some important sense "relevant"—"about life," "applicable to everyday affairs." We do not teach to produce recluses or misanthropes, rather men and women who can "speak to our condition." But how does an education "rooted in the past" and not at all "practical" propose to do that? By immersing us in what is universal and timeless and therefore always contemporary. "Students who read Plato, Aristotle, St. Paul, and St. Augustine," says Schall, "often are struck to find themselves brought more up-to-date, in a way, than when they read the New York Times or the latest textbook. The former sources possess a freedom and an intelligence that the latter somehow lack" (2006, 27). Most of those so educated could bear similar witness.

At the same time, one of the purposes of a liberal education is to disabuse us of contemporary illusions, to immunize us against "the great cataract of nonsense that pours from the press and the microphone of [our] own age," as C. S. Lewis said of the use of studying history (1949, 51); to take us out of ourselves and our culture long enough to allow us to see both for what they are, through other and better eyes; to get us out of the trees long enough to see the forest. The idea is incisively summed up in an amusing but no less telling, and entirely relevant, anecdote. In the introduction to his excellent *The Great Tradition: Classic Readings on What It Means to Be an Educated Human Being*, Gamble quotes this conversation from Evelyn Waugh's story *Scott-King's Modern Europe*. The headmaster of Granchester, a fictional English public school, is talking to Scott-King, a classics teacher there.

> "You know," [the headmaster] said, "we are starting this year with fifteen fewer classical specialists than we had last term?"
>
> "I thought that would be about the number."
>
> "As you know I'm an old Greats man myself. I deplore it as much as you do. But what are we to do? Parents are not interested in producing the 'complete man' any more. They want to qualify their boys for jobs in the modern world. You can hardly blame them, can you?"
>
> "Oh yes," said Scott-King. "I can and do."
>
> "I always say you are a much more important man here than I am. One couldn't conceive of Granchester without Scott-King. But has it ever occurred to you that a time may come when there will be no more classical boys at all?"
>
> "Oh yes. Often."
>
> "What I was going to suggest was—I wonder if you will consider taking some other subject as well as the classics? History, for example, preferably economic history?"
>
> "No, headmaster."
>
> "But, you know, there may be something of a crisis ahead."
>
> "Yes, headmaster."
>
> "Then what do you intend to do?"
>
> "If you approve, headmaster, I will stay as I am here as long as any boy wants to read the classics. I think it would be very wicked indeed to do anything to fit a boy for the modern world."
>
> "It's a short-sighted view, Scott-King."

"There, headmaster, with all respect, I differ from you profoundly. I think it the most long-sighted view it is possible to take." (2007, xv–xvi; Waugh 1998, 375–76)

That should give us plenty to think about.

Ten

But Is Academic Education for Everyone?

He is to be educated, because he is a man, not because he is to make shoes, nails, or pins.
                    —William Ellery Channing, "Self-Culture"

The self-educated are marked by stubborn peculiarities.
                    —Isaac Disraeli, *The Literary Character*

Wile trying to say what the liberal arts are may be the *pièce de résistance*, the most deeply practical and soul-searching problem for education at large is perhaps whether such studies are for everyone. By that I mean two things primarily: (a) Is everyone *capable* of appropriating a liberal and academic education? and (b) Will everyone *want* to appropriate it?

As for (a), do not vast differences in upbringing, learning styles, and just plain IQ suggest that probably everyone is *not* capable of such an education? As for (b), are we not seeing, at almost every level, a slackening of interest in traditional liberal arts studies among the young? That was a good part of Mark Bauerlein's complaint about "The Dumbest Generation" in chapter 3.

That leads to the question whether an academic education is elitist; or to put it the other way around, even though a democratic society requires an educated citizenry, is the kind of education required for a democracy itself democratic? (For the moment I am using "elite" and "elitist" to mean the same thing; we will get to the distinction shortly.) And if an academic education is the education we require for everyone, what does that imply for the training of skilled workers, whether in business or medicine or the trades, which is just as required?

Is Academic Education Possible for Everyone?

First, is everyone both capable and desirous of an academic education? The powers that be, to a certain extent anyway, still seem to think so. Every scheme of secondary schooling in the United States that I know of, public or private, insists that those benefiting from it meet certain basic requirements in the liberal arts. In my own city, Los Angeles, the school board in 2005 mandated that every student graduating from high school have met University of California entrance requirements: so many years (not the same number for each) of English, history, math, laboratory science, foreign language, and art, plus a "college prep elective." The reason for their action, it is true, was to ensure that all students, especially minority students, have equal access (at least as regards academic preparation) to a college education, and thus, perhaps more important from their point of view, to an increasingly competitive job market. The decision could also be seen as an attempt to guarantee that all citizens are equally prepared to participate in a democratic republic. However interpreted, the results, one hopes, will serve both ends.

There is powerful evidence to suggest that the ideal is very far from the real, however. The high school dropout rate in Los Angeles is now, I understand, about (if not over) 50 percent; in most major cities it is not much better, or worse. Is that reason for national soul-searching about whether we can continue to pursue the Jeffersonian vision, or is it cause for an intensified recommitment to it?

For Christian schools the course, in my view, is clear. We must continue to press the case for the importance of academic education, to the continuance of a free society certainly, but for learning's own sake as well. We have the best of reasons, in Christianity's foundational role in both the development of democracy and the Western intellectual tradition, to do so.

Is It Elite/Elitist?

Is it then time, second, for us to ask ourselves whether academic education is in fact elite, in the sense that while its importance must regularly and relentlessly be laid before the entire community, not everyone will appreciate or take advantage of, and so will be denied, its benefits? That may be one of the risks of a free society. At the same time, and for that reason, the responsibility of those of us committed to such an education to do our work well is increased. Because such an education is freely offered, even required, is no guarantee that it will be appropriated. It may be derided or deprecated or ignored, but that is no reason to forget its importance or falter in its prosecution for the broadest possible spectrum of the populace.

And is it not true that Christian education *is* elite? It costs money, for one thing. That means that unless we can begin to create ways to make it available to those who cannot afford it, it will remain elite in the sense that it is accessible to a restricted segment of the population, those who can afford it. Ninety percent of America's students attend public schools, 10 percent private, and of that 10 percent one-tenth independent Christian schools. We are not competing with public schools, not even with nonsectarian private schools. Should we not then settle into our role of educating a special 1 percent in a special way, and do it excellently?

What about the epithet "elite" anyway? If it means belonging to a particular or restricted group, well, then, as we have already admitted, we *are* elite, and can hardly help being so. Nor would it be a bad thing if we were seen as elite in the sense of "choicest" or "best," because of the acknowledged quality of our work. "Elitist," or "elitism," on the other hand, usually has the connotation of consciousness of or pride in belonging to a select or favored class, and frequently includes discrimination against those who do not belong in favor of those who do—and that of course we are forbidden. We do well to remember our roots: "Not many of you were wise by human standards, not many were powerful, not many were of noble birth" (1 Corinthians 1:26). Still, there could be only relief and freedom in being honest about who and what we are. As others have urged, we should perhaps be elite, but not elitist.

WHAT ABOUT THE NEED TO TRAIN SKILLED WORKERS?

What then of the third question, the training of skilled workers, without whom we cannot survive, any more than we can without an educated citizenry?

In this country, the answer is that even those trained in business or the trades will have some academic education, good or not so good, because they (unlike in the Greece of old) belong to the polis, and it is well they should. That in part is what we mean by modern Western democracy. Nor would anyone want to alter that arrangement, not least because you and I are members of that very class that in ancient Greece would have had to earn a living and therefore been denied participation in the affairs of state. We are beneficiaries of democracy's impulse to educate everyone. For that we can be deeply thankful.

THE PROBLEMS OF "EQUALITY"

But there are problems, summed up by C. S. Lewis in this way: "When societies become, in effort if not in achievement, egalitarian, we are presented with a difficulty. To give every one education and to give no one vocational training is impossible, for electricians and surgeons we must have and they must be trained. Our ideal must be to find time for both education and training: our danger is that equality may mean training for all and education for none—that every one will learn commercial French instead of Latin, book-keeping instead of geometry, and 'knowledge of the world we live in' instead of great literature. It is against this danger that schoolmasters have to fight, for if education is bested by training, civilizations dies" (1939, 82).*

The greater problem, practically speaking, Lewis maintains in another place, is this: "Democratic education, says Aristotle, ought to mean, not the education which democrats like, but the education which will preserve democracy. Until we have realized that the two things do not necessarily go together we cannot think clearly about education" (1986, 32).

What Lewis was referring to are the proposals, recurrent in every generation for the last sixty or seventy years, to, as he puts it, "make the curriculum so wide that 'every boy will get a chance at something.' Even the boy who can't or won't learn his alphabet can be praised and petted for *something*—handicrafts or gymnastics, moral leadership or deportment, citizenship or the care of guinea-pigs, 'hobbies' or musical appreciation—anything he likes. Then no boy, and no boy's parents, need feel inferior" (1986, 33; italics in original).

This is a refrain we all know by heart, although not always put as bluntly as Lewis has put it. Likely it constitutes an aspect of our own thinking, so often have we heard it said. With all due respect for what are genuine learning disabilities in a certain percentage of the population (what those are and how widespread I'll have to leave to the experts), we may still have to come to terms with the issue as Lewis has formulated it: "An education on those lines will be pleasing to democratic feelings. It will have repaired the inequalities of nature. But it is quite another question whether it will breed a democratic nation which can survive, or even one whose survival is desirable" (1986, 33). That is putting it pretty bluntly indeed, is it not?

The way in which Lewis develops this idea, especially on its psychological or spiritual side, is so interesting and so unmodern that I must let him speak, at some length, for himself. On the attempts to level or equalize education he says,

---

*It is remarkable how closely Lewis' description of this danger parallels the recommendations of American educationist Charles Prosser, whom E. D. Hirsch Jr. describes as "an influential opponent of bookishness." Writing in 1939, the same year as Lewis, Prosser said, "business arithmetic is superior to plane or solid geometry; learning ways of keeping physically fit, to the study of French; learning the technique of selecting an occupation, to the study of algebra; simple science of everyday life, to geology; simple business English, to Elizabethan classics" (Hirsch 1996, 109).

The demand for equality has two sources; one of them is among the noblest, the other is the basest, of human emotions. The noble source is the desire for fair play. But the other source is the hatred of superiority. At the present moment it would be very unrealistic to overlook the importance of the latter. There is in all men a tendency (only corrigible by good training from without and persistent moral effort from within) to resent the existence of what is stronger, subtler or better than themselves. In uncorrected and brutal men this hardens into an implacable and disinterested hatred for every kind of excellence. The vocabulary of a period tells tales. There is reason to be alarmed at the immense vogue today of such words as "high-brow", "up-stage", "old school tie", "academic", "smug", and "complacent". These words, as used today, are sores: one feels the poison throbbing in them. (1986, 33)

The schemes to achieve equality in education, when their intent is simply (as it often is) to "appease envy," are bad, says Lewis, for two reasons. The first is that "no attitude of humility which you can possibly adopt will propitiate a man with an inferiority complex," and the second that "you are trying to introduce equality where equality is fatal" (1986, 34).

What Lewis means by "fatal" is this: "Equality (outside mathematics) is a purely social conception. It applies to man as a political and economic animal. It has no place in the world of the mind. Beauty is not democratic; she reveals herself more to the few than to the many, more to the persistent and disciplined seekers than to the careless. Virtue is not democratic; she is achieved by those who pursue her more hotly than most men. Truth is not democratic; she demands special talents and special industry in those to whom she gives her favours. Political democracy is doomed if it tries to extend its demand for equality into these higher spheres. Ethical, intellectual, or aesthetic democracy is death" (1986, 34).

In language everywhere forbidden in contemporary discussions of the subject, Lewis goes on: "A truly democratic education—one which will preserve democracy—must be, in its own field, ruthlessly aristocratic, shamelessly 'high-brow'. In drawing up its curriculum it should always have chiefly in view the interests of the boy who wants to know and who can know. (With very few exceptions they are the same boy. The stupid boy, nearly always, is the boy who does not *want* to know.) It must, in a certain sense, subordinate the interests of the many to those of the few, and it must subordinate the school to the university. Only thus can it be a nursery of those first-class intellects without which neither a democracy nor any other State can thrive" (1986, 34; italics in original).

That was written in 1944. It may well be argued, and certainly will be, that advances in education psychology and philosophy, not to mention social consciousness, render much of what Lewis says obsolete or (more damming should we adopt it) uncaring and hopelessly out-of-date. But apart from our instinctive modern reaction to what he says, there is a certain logic in it that merits our consideration, and that logic has nearly everything to do with what we think about academic education and the way we manage it.

We could add that while what Lewis wrote over half a century ago might be viewed as insensitive or old-fashioned, we should remember that he was writing against a background of German Nazism and Italian Fascism, possibly Russian Communism, at the time very real and immediate dangers to Western democracy and civilization, especially in Europe. Our unwillingness to be so pointed in our views may have a good deal to do with our distance from those dangers. That fact alone should be a caution.

What Then of the "Dull Boy"?

Having almost certainly aroused our indignation by his references to "the dull boy" or "the stupid boy," the one who doesn't attain to a "high-brow" education, Lewis hastens to emphasize that same boy's nonetheless indispensable place in a democratic society. If the educated ultimately become the "big men" in such a society, as almost surely they will, then it is also true that "democracy demands that little men should not take big ones too seriously; it dies when it is full of little men who think they are big themselves" (1986, 36). The "little men" keep the "big men" in check, as it is well that they should. True enough in experience, to be sure, but is this not mere patronizing on Lewis' part? I find it hard to believe that he intended it to be. There is plenty of evidence to show that Lewis had no small regard for "little men."

In *Screwtape Proposes a Toast*, in a long and perceptive, and prophetic, comment on the same theme, Lewis dilates on both the perverse intent and the deleterious effects of attempting, in schools as elsewhere, to make everyone equal, all in the name of "democracy." "The scene [Lewis tells us] is in Hell at the annual dinner of the Tempters' Training College for young devils. The principal, Dr. Slubgob, has just proposed the health of the guests. Screwtape, a very experienced devil, who is the guest of honour, rises to reply" (1961, 163). In the course of his extended toast, Screwtape gets onto the topic of the effects of perpetuating, in the name of equality, "the most degrading (and also the least enjoyable) of all human feelings," namely, "the feeling ... which prompts a man to say *I'm as good as you*" (174; italics in original). Screwtape continues:

> What I want to fix your attention on is the vast, overall movement towards the discrediting, and finally the elimination, of every kind of human excellence—moral, cultural, social, or intellectual. And is it not pretty to notice how "democracy" (in the incantatory sense) is now doing for us the work that was once done by the most ancient Dictatorships, and by the same methods? You remember how one of the Greek Dictators (they called them "tyrants" then) sent an envoy to another Dictator to ask his advice about the principles of government. The second Dictator led the envoy into a field of grain, and there he snicked off with his cane the top of every stalk that rose an inch or so above the general level. The moral was plain. Allow no preeminence among your subjects. Let no man live who is wiser or better or more famous or even handsomer than the mass. Cut them all down to a level: all slaves, all ciphers, all nobodies. All equals. Thus Tyrants could practise, in a sense, "democracy." But now "democracy" can do the same work without any tyranny other than her own. No one need now go through the field with a cane. The little stalks will now

of themselves bite the tops off the big ones. The big ones are beginning to bite off their own in their desire to Be Like Stalks. (1961, 177–78)

Barzun recognized the same phenomenon: "Everybody keeps calling for Excellence—excellence not just in schooling, throughout society," he wrote. "But as soon as somebody or something stands out as Excellent, the other shout goes up: 'Elitism!' And whatever produced that thing, whoever praises that result, is promptly put down. 'Standing out' is undemocratic" (1991, 3).

As for the kind of education such a disposition produces, says Lewis,

> The basic principle of the new education is to be that dunces and idlers must not be made to feel inferior to intelligent and industrious pupils.... These differences between the pupils— for they are obviously and nakedly *individual* differences— must be disguised. This can be done on various levels.... At schools, the children who are too stupid or lazy to learn languages and mathematics and elementary science can be set to doing the things that children used to do in their spare time. Let them, for example, make mud pies and call it modelling. But all the time there must be no faintest hint that they are inferior to the children who are at work.... The bright pupil thus remains democratically fettered to his own age group throughout his school career, and a boy who would be capable of tackling Aeschylus or Dante sits listening to his coeval's attempts to spell out A CAT SAT ON A MAT. (1961, 179–80; italics and capitals in original)

It is difficult to imagine, as I have suggested, any twenty-first-century American thinking Lewis' remarks anything other than condescending or inappropriate at best, downright malign at worst. We just don't refer to students these days as dull or stupid, or as dunces and idlers. And I, like everyone, have known too many who were neither dull nor stupid in the usual sense of "unintelligent"— they were more often than not quite intelligent and not at all dull— who were totally uninterested in schoolwork of any kind, academic work least of all. There were reasons why they were uninterested, having to do, usually, with the way they were brought up—but it was not, so far as I could tell, for lack of brains. Nor could we forget that Christians, no less in our educating, have a profound obligation, at some point, to all our children, dull as well as bright, or however we decide to talk about the subject.

Inevitably, though, to be candid, there may be a real question "whether every citizen is capable of such an intellectual education," as Kimball puts it. Is what we're up against here "the conflict between intellectualism and egalitarianism," or "the tension between the desire for intellectual leadership and for equality" (1986, 178–79)? Are we talking about something like what Kimball calls "the intrinsic elitism of the intellectual" (189)? We may well be. It might simply be a fact of life we have to deal with as assiduously as we can—which could mean, as in so many things, doing our best and settling for less than the ideal.

There is too the disconcerting likelihood that the very attempt to grant universal education may be the reason for a lack of interest in it. T. S. Eliot (admittedly no egalitarian!) framed the issue like this:

> People can be persuaded to desire almost anything, for a time, if they are constantly told that it is something to which they are entitled and which is unjustly withheld from them.... It is possible that the desire for education is greater where there are difficulties in the way of obtaining it—difficulties not insuperable but only to be surmounted at the cost of some sacrifice and privation. If this is so, we may conjecture that facility of education will lead to indifference to it; and that the universal imposition of education up to the years of maturity will lead to hostility towards it. A high average of general education is perhaps less necessary for a civil society than is a respect for learning. (1949, 176–77)

More disconcerting is Eliot's cheerless prophecy: "And we know, that whether education can foster and improve culture or not, it can surely adulterate and degrade it. For there is no doubt that in our headlong rush to educate everybody, we are lowering our standards, and more and more abandoning the study of those subjects by which the essentials of our culture—of that part of it which is transmissible by education—are transmitted; destroying our ancient edifices to make ready the ground upon which the barbarian nomads of the future will encamp in their mechanized caravans" (1949, 185).

There is a good deal in what Eliot says to give us pause, and plenty to ponder. But, again, I do not think we are in a position, practically speaking, seriously to entertain the prospect that universal education is somehow inherently impossible, or that universal education necessarily means poor education, or one to which the many will inevitably be hostile—although, I confess, the prospect looks all too real, frighteningly so.

Just here it seems to me Christian schools have something to offer. Is our obligation to academic/intellectual excellence or to academic/intellectual equality? Or is it somehow to both? We are committed to doing all things well, and that must surely include teaching and scholarship, as has been the case down the centuries. Are we not likewise committed to seeing that "the least of these," not part of the "intellectual elite," also partake of the blessings of an academic education, especially when such an education is requisite for the fullest participation in a democracy? Of course we are free to remain unconcerned about these things, but even for our own sakes it behooves us, and becomes us, to try to see that as many of our brethren as possible are so educated. That too has been a Christian priority down the centuries, as we saw in chapter 1. Everywhere the gospel has gone there have followed two eminently Christian institutions: the hospital and the school, healing for the body and enlightenment for the mind.

Neither has my experience yet convinced me—again, genuine learning disabilities aside—that academic education is the province solely of the intelligent or bright or otherwise intellectually superior. I have seen too many students, very average students, handle it perfectly well, and too many obviously capable students handle it poorly by comparison. What made the difference was nearly everything other than natural competence: interest; willingness to be taught and to work hard; especially an upbringing that values education, whether the parents are educated or not. "Poorly" and "well" do not break down along IQ lines—or whatever language we prefer to use.

The difference has a good deal more to do with educating parents than it does with educating students, more with convictions about the importance of academic work than the ability to do it. It is therefore with the Christian community's understanding of the seriousness and benefits of liberal studies, in my view, where we must begin. I am no expert, certainly not in the complex and highly sensitive field of learning disabilities, nor do I know personally the frustration and pain parents go though whose children struggle with education of any bookish kind. I speak now only from admittedly limited personal experience as a father, a teacher, and an administrator, and only in a general way.

Whatever one makes of Lewis', or Eliot's, analysis, one must agree, surely, on one thing at least: that even in an American democracy, where everyone is expected to be educated, many will need to be vocationally trained and not all will *want* to be educated. We may have to confront the reality that wherever the line is drawn—natural ability versus upbringing, training versus a lack thereof—a line will be drawn. But that in no way should be allowed to dampen our enthusiasm in pressing for academic education for as many as possible.

CONCLUSION

Contrary as it may be to appearances, none of the foregoing is meant to suggest that every Christian school should have as its exclusive purpose an academic education of the sort we have been discussing here. The variety of Christian styles of piety, their differences in theological or devotional emphasis and sense of vocation, is so vast that no one could presume to prescribe what any group or school should do. No one size can or should fit all. Nor would a Christian deny that a gospel whose results include that "there is no longer Jew or Greek, there is no longer slave or free, there is no longer male and female; for all of you are one in

Christ Jesus" (Galatians 3:28) could neglect, in the interests of an "aristocratic education," no matter how valuable that is, those for whom such an education, for whatever reason, does not work. But to be fair to Lewis, he was not talking about Christian education, only education proper to democracy. As I have said, this is not an uncomplicated issue.

I have meant only to alert us to the trend toward valuing technical or professional training over academic education, to reiterate the fundamental importance of the latter to democratic society, indeed to "high civilization" of any kind, and thereby to suggest that those schools, Christian and otherwise, whose charter is liberal arts have the noblest of reasons to carry out their task diligently and without compromise.

Conclusion

The test and the use of a man's education is that he finds pleasure in the exercise of his mind.
—Jacques Barzun, "Science vs. the Humanities"

One of the main purposes of this book is to point us in Christian schools back to first things, and in so doing to simplify our task. In refocusing our attention we may also find that we are able, as a kind of added extra or by-product, to do our work less expensively. Given that Christian schooling in some places has priced itself (or been priced?) out of the range of the average American family's ability to pay for it, that should be a preeminent concern of us all.

Just as important: we do not have time or energy, in my estimation, for too much more than doing what we are meant, most fundamentally, to do. The world too badly requires the virtues of trained Christian intellect for us to dissipate our energies in the plethora of activities that fairly defines much of modern education. The irony is that the more desperately Christian intellect is needed the more tempted we are to give ourselves to other things. The successful Christian school, it must be said, is not now everywhere known for its singular devotion to the life of the mind. More often than not it is known for its ability to offer a multitude of activities given to almost everything else.

That there is a crisis in American education is beyond doubt. From the government's *A Nation at Risk* report of the elder Bush's administration to the No Child Left Behind program of the younger's, there has been an almost continuous reiteration of the urgency of the situation. Only the tragedy of 9/11 has caused us to divert our attention from what for all intents and purposes was and is our foremost national concern. The success of private schools, both Christian and nonsectarian, has been one of the most significant aspects of that crisis. That they are now becoming too expensive for many families is, in my view, a shame.

The root of the crisis is a failure to understand the point and purpose of education, especially as it relates to the training of intellect by means of the academic disciplines, more especially perhaps as such an education is related to the maintenance of culture.

At some length I have tried to spell out what we mean by "academic education," what are its antecedents in ancient Greece, and how it was first accepted, then baptized, by the Christian church, and became, as Marrou puts it, the means by which classical education "fertilized our whole European tradition" (1956, 97).

It is especially important that Christians, principally Christian educators, understand this, for the reason that we are the heirs of that very tradition of which Marrou speaks. That is why I included a chapter on "the Christian response" to the scheme of *paideia* bequeathed to us by the Greeks—because there are some in Christian schools who are fearful of or otherwise opposed to it still, or who think that Christian education began sometime in the middle of last century.

What I am particularly concerned to say in this book, though, is that the learning I am advocating requires a kind of focus and a kind of leisure not often found even in those schools dedicated to it. Thus the chapters "We've Got Too Much Going On" and "Leisure, the Basis of Culture"; also "The Socratic Method," because that too is an attempt to simplify and thereby improve what we are doing.

On a larger scale there is more to it than that. If a democracy requires for its maintenance a liberally educated citizenry, then we have precious persuasion to do our job exceedingly well, in Christian schools more than elsewhere. We have obligations to our history, the relationship of Christianity to democracy, to fulfill.

Can we, though, to be nothing more than honest, afford (perhaps literally) to cut back, slow down, concentrate in the ways I have been suggesting? If our graduates cannot include on their transcripts, not only a 4.3 grade point average, but as well those umpteen activities and honors I mentioned in chapter 3, will they in fact be getting into Harvard, or indeed a lot of other colleges and universities in this insanely competitive academic marketplace? Is it prudent and practical, to put it no worse, to make changes in the direction of less is more?

Of course I have no idea what the answer is, but I can speculate, along two lines. First of all, as most of us know, increasing numbers of homeschooled children, Christians and non-Christians alike, are finding acceptance at the more prestigious institutions of higher learning. This suggests to me that solid academic training, even in the absence of the extracurricular bells and whistles, is often recognized for what it is, and that the failure to present a résumé loaded with a dozen or twenty interests or aptitudes beyond evidence of the abilities to read, write, and think well is no necessary barrier to educational progress.

But, second, should it come to that—should acting on our convictions about what constitutes good education in the best Christian sense, with our graduates for that reason perhaps being denied access to Harvard or wherever—I am afraid we will have to do what Christians have ever done, namely, set out boldly, confidently, on the road less traveled. Nothing really worthwhile was ever accomplished in this world, after all, by those bound to the status quo, to what "works," to what is expedient or sure.

Then, almost always, those looking on begin to wonder, "Why didn't we think of that?" and, perhaps tentatively at first, they emulate. And is there not now, for strictly academic as well as Christian reasons, plenty of room for serious reevaluation of the way we do education?

As I say, I have no idea what the practical consequences of fundamental change might be in the way of matriculation rates at prestigious colleges and universities, for example, or other such gauges of success, but whenever those become the sole or primary means by which we assess ourselves we have clearly lost our effectiveness to be salt and light. That way of thinking too may need reevaluation.

As I read what I have written, three things stand out. The first I intimated in the introduction: the distance, intellectual and maybe moral, between what I have been talking about in these pages and the problems, deep-down, huge, and in some cases systemic, mostly in government schools and mostly among the educationally disadvantaged. I do not mean that there is not good and heroic work being done in those places by men and women of enormous intelligence, ability, and courage, or that there are not excellent schools there too. Nor do I mean that talk of liberty, leisure, and good learning is not relevant even in those circumstances. It would be less than honest, however, to pretend that such talk is not a long way from the needs of high school seniors unable to do basic math or understand the difference between an adjective and an adverb—in "a wasteland where violence and vice share the time with ignorance and idleness," as Barzun put it a quarter century ago (from a reprinted essay titled "Teacher in 1980 America: What He Found"; in Barzun 1991, 7). It could be no better now. What vast tracts of terrain must be gotten over, or so it would appear, before most of what this book is about could seriously be entertained in some areas. That, as I've said, is in no sense an effort to appear superior. On the contrary, it is an admission of a kind of helplessness before difficulties of such magnitude and complexity. One would desire to be of help, ideally where help is needed most. But for that task wiser heads and larger souls than mine are required.

The second thing is that it all could seem to be pushing the envelope a bit. Not only the chapter on the liberal arts, but the one on leisure, perhaps that on the Socratic method, even on liberty—those chapters for some may be asking of junior high and high school teachers and students more than it is fair to ask.

I am pretty sure that that is not the case, for two reasons: (a) there are plenty of teachers at the secondary level who have thought about these things as much as I have, probably more, and (b) what is certain is that they are far better teachers than I am. For those reasons I do not think I have misunderstood who my audience is. The students? They can usually be counted on to rise to expectations.

The third thing may be another way of seeing the second; that is, a number of the writers I have quoted are writing about college rather than junior high or high school. The reason I have used them is that so widespread is the emphasis on preprofessional training in colleges and universities, as I said in the introduction, that the responsibility for liberal education has devolved on us. What used to be higher education's stock-in-trade is becoming ours. The obligation, and privilege, is thereby increased.

Those who read these pages will include many for whom this is, if not urgent or new, then maybe an encouragement, as they are doing outstanding work already—rigorous, Christian, focused. For others, there will be ideas that are strange or novel, seemingly incompatible with their understanding of what Christian education means, but interesting (I hope) nonetheless. I can only trust that in the inevitable mix there will be some who find here and there a helpful word.

Regarding "Christian Civilization"

Throughout this discussion I have referred to the Western tradition or to Western civilization, which I described as Greco-Roman and Judeo-Christian. I haven't much used the phrase *Christian civilization*, but that is no less what I have in mind—for in its most practical political, legal, and social manifestations, Western civilization has been Christian civilization. That that may no longer be the case—that we may, in Europe and North America perhaps in particular, be becoming predominantly secular or predominantly pluralistic (if I may be permitted what looks like an oxymoron), or predominantly nothing very much at all—is indeed behind a good deal of the agitation in some quarters for a return to Judeo-Christian values, or a biblical worldview: a return or reinvigoration that in fact has been among my primary purposes to advocate in this volume.

It may be in order, therefore, to spend a moment thinking about "Christian civilization," to sharpen the focus a bit on this broadly interpreted and easily misunderstood phrase.

Fortunately that sharpening has already been done in a brilliant little book by John Baillie titled *What Is Christian Civilization?* which is a compilation of the Riddell Lectures for 1945.* It is to Baillie and his little book then that I want to turn.

The questions, it seems to me, are two: What do we mean by "Christian civilization"? and Is it what we as Christians really want? Perhaps for present purposes a third: Is it therefore what Christian education should in some sense be about?

Baillie traces the relationship of Christianity and civilization through what he considers its three stages. The first was the period of the early Church, during which Christians were an uninfluential and often persecuted minority, required by Scripture to submit to their rulers (Romans 13:1–7 and 1 Peter 2:13–17), but also to obey God rather than man (Acts 5:29). Thus the Church's attitude toward civilization was that "it combined a necessary and not disloyal participation with a very large measure of spiritual detachment" (1945, 8).

This stage was followed by what Baillie calls the Constantinian chapter, the conversion of the emperor (most significantly Constantine [288?–337], Theodosius [346?–395], and Justinian [483–565]) and the triumph of Christianity, generally speaking, throughout the Roman world. And although there was not yet any attempt to reorder society along Christian lines, there is no doubt, Baillie says, that in this period "a new conscience about many things began to develop in the West" (1945, 21).

"The beginning of a new synthesis between Christianity and civilization" came, as Baillie sees it (1945, 21), with Charlemagne (742–814) in this same period. This was the Middle Ages, which "represent the brave attempt to bring the whole of life under the control of Christian standards," wherein "what was attempted ... was not to exchange the existing social institutions for others but rather to permeate them more and more with a Christian spirit" (22). Christian faith was compulsory (often accomplished

---

*The Riddell Memorial Lectures were founded in 1928 in memory of Sir John Buchanan Riddell with the intention that they should explore the relation between religion and contemporary thought. The best known of the Riddell Lectures, for many of us, are perhaps those given by C. S. Lewis in 1942, which were published as *The Abolition of Man*, probably Lewis' best book on education— more specifically, the deleterious impact on education of moral subjectivism.

by mass conversion), and civil rights were made dependent on baptism. This medievalism was thus the fuller flowering in the Middle Ages of what began under Constantine and Theodosius. The same relationship obtained, in large part, through the period of the Reformers, as "the whole range of life was brought under the sway of radical Christian ideas to a greater extent than previously" (23). This was most especially and obviously the case, perhaps, in Calvin's Geneva.

The third and final stage is that from the latter part of the eighteenth century to the present, which Baillie calls an "open type" of Christian civilization (1945, 41), wherein no one is compelled to believe, the Constantinian chapter is closed, and while Christian ideas may still hold sway in a broad and vague sense, men and women feel no obligation to profess Christian faith, and many are quite openly anti-Christian, or make no profession of anything. Unlike in an earlier era, "the alternative they envisage is therefore not between being Christian and being pagan, but between being Christian and nothing in particular.... Such is the tragedy that has overtaken so much of our common life—that it belongs nowhere, has no spiritual home, no ultimate standards of reference, and little definite conception of the direction in which it desires to move" (39). That, as I said, was written in 1945. It could have been written yesterday.

Our present dilemma is perhaps that we do not want a system in which men and women are forced in any way to be Christians (were that even possible!), but we nonetheless want a "Christian" society of some kind. Many of us, perhaps especially in Christian education, are further constrained by the prospect of children, born into Christian homes, who are "to be educated in spiritually neutral schools and then launched into a spiritually neutral society fed by neutral newspapers and a neutral [media]" (Baillie 1945, 40). "I cling [says Baillie] to what is left of this civilization, believing the hope of the future to lie in such a reinvigoration of it as can result only from its regained hold upon the fundamental Christian ideas" (40). In other words, even though men and women may or may not be believing Christians in anything like a personal and saving sense, still we desire a society, as not very long ago, in which, for most people, "the Christian view of man, the world and God, formed the unquestioned background of their minds and provided the framework within which their lives were lived" (44). They shared, in short, a Christian worldview. Such, as I say, was European and American civilization until fairly recently.

For all of its seeming virtues, however, it may well be asked, first, Is such a civilization what we truly want? Is that not a civilization of superficial and sham Christianity, which tends "so to inoculate men with a mild form of Christian religiosity as to render them immune from the grand infection" (Baillie 1945, 31)? Would it not be infinitely better, from the point of view of the gospel, to have a completely secular society in which righteousness was clearly distinguishable from wickedness, sinner from saint, where the Church made its pilgrim journey through this world as an alien people whose real home was elsewhere; where, that is, real repentance and conversion were more likely, and understood to be more needed? Second, Is it even possible to have Christian moral standards without genuine Christian belief, even Christian worship?

As for the first: no matter how "Christian" a society may be, whether seemingly obviously so or hardly recognizable as such, the community of the saints, those whose trust is in Christ and whose lives are animated by His grace and peace, have always been a relatively small percentage of the whole; that is, it is never the case that "Christian society" is coterminous with "the saved of God." As for the second: although genuine Christian conviction requires involvement in earthly life in its social and political dimensions (for Christian conviction affects the way we think and act with regard to everything), mere Christian ideals cannot endure cut off from Christian faith. Or as Baillie puts it, "It is unlikely ... that the Christian conscience of the West can long survive its present disseverance from its original setting of belief and its original nourishment of worship. There must either be some return to the integrity of the Christian outlook or a still further disintegration"—because what is ever upholding the Christian ideal is nothing less than "Christian belief about reality" (1945, 49).

More important is the truth that Christian faith has an impact upon civilization only when the hope of Christian men and women is primarily in something else. "The Christian's attitude to civilization must be a double one," Baillie writes. "He must strive to bring it as near to the Christian ideal of life in community as is possible in a world of sinful men, but he must never give it his absolute approval or unconditional loyalty; he must place in it only such a strictly qualified hope as would, even if it were to suffer complete shipwreck, leave his ultimate hope as securely anchored as before" (1945, 56).

Are we then in some sense still a Christian civilization? Will we remain one? Only to the extent that Christian ideas continue to be our compass; but those ideas will continue to prevail only to the extent that they are fastened in genuine Christian belief and a concomitant "nourishment of worship"—as well as a thoroughly Christian view of time and eternity. "The historical permeation of our society by Christian ideas and ideals is a development for which we must be profoundly thankful to the Lord of all history," says Baillie, "and for the furtherance of which it is our duty to pray fervently, to work diligently, and to hope as bravely as we can.... For the earthly hope holds no promise even of its own imperfect fulfilment save as it refracts in the medium of the temporal the light of the hope that is eternal; so that the surest way to its disappointment would be that, in too much cherishing it, we should lose sight of that greater light which is its source. In proportion as a society relaxes its hold upon the eternal, it ensures the corruption of the temporal." All earthly civilizations are temporal and corruptible, even, surely (we shudder to remember), our own. Should a merciful God grant ours yet further continuance, and perhaps honor our efforts to honor Him and His laws, "it can only be in the strength of this more chastened estimate of its own majesty and this knowledge that 'here we have no continuing city' [Heb. 6:19]" (1945, 59).

What we mean, then (to return to the questions with which we began), by "Christian civilization" is a civilization, not necessarily of all genuinely converted men and women living in the grace and power of Christ—as that would be unlikely if not impossible under the most congenial of circumstances (think of the parable of the seed sown on various types of ground [Mark 4:3–8]). What we mean, rather, is a civilization "in which nearly all acknowledged the authority both of [Christian] truth and of [Christian] standards, accepting in their minds even what they delayed to take to heart, and trembling when they were farthest from obeying" (Baillie 1945, 45). We mean, in other words, a culture or civilization imbued with Christian ideas, if not informed by a Christian soul.

My experience suggests that our own culture is very far indeed from even an approximation to that ideal. That is why the attempt to inculcate a Christian worldview in the small minority of students such as we serve in Christian schools may be seen as a sort of rear-guard activity. Most of the population would probably not know what "Christian ideas" were! The point here is simply the meaning of "Christian civilization," not its imminent realization in practice. And if we are to make even the slightest dent in the national con-sciousness with regard to how men and women think—with regard to their worldview—we will have to accept, in schools anyway, where it is ideas that we are mostly about, that that is our task. We will also want to accept, as Baillie has forcefully reminded us, that the ideas will perdure only to the extent that they are grounded in genuine belief and worship. But, as we have acknowledged often enough, ours is a limited responsibility in but one corner of the Lord's vineyard. If we can get through on the matter of thinking Christianly with half (a quarter?) of our students, we will, I reckon, have done our job admirably well. For their conversion we must, as Baillie says, continue "to pray fervently, to work diligently, and to hope as bravely as we can" (1945, 59).

But, again, is a Christian society or culture such as we have described what we as Christians really want—a society in which Christian ideas to some extent govern but the lordship of Christ in individual hearts may or may not?

The answer is that in a sense we have no choice, for two reasons at least: (a) our Christian responsibilities, as we said, include those to society—its culture, its mores, its humanitarian concerns—because the way we think as Christians affects every area of our lives; and (b) perhaps more germane, we are, as Christian educators, already, in the nature of the case, invested in such things. By the very act of educating we are concerning ourselves with civilization, our civilization, its past, present, and future. It hardly makes sense to try to think about learning history, literature, philosophy, foreign language, even science and math, at the same time as we are trying to distance ourselves or shut ourselves off from civilization, however we define the term. Education *means*, in a sense, engagement with civilization.

Is "Christian civilization" therefore what Christian education should be about? I think we have already answered that question in a number of ways. Whether or not we ever achieve a Christian civilization in the sense of a culture permeated by Christian ways of thinking—and the prospect looks less and less likely, though not, may it please God, impossible—we in Christian schools will continue not only to press the importance of "the best which has been thought and said" in the Western tradition, but also attempt to show how it is still the wisest, the most sane and reasonable view of God, man, and the world—at the same time as we keep before us the truth that "here we have no continuing city."

Should Learning Be Fun?

Somewhere on the planet there is, surely, a computer pro-grammed to record the number of times in a day, in whatever language, it is said that learning should be fun—or words to that effect: "I never liked history until I had Mr. Smeegs; he makes it so fun," or "The reason our children aren't learning these days is that teachers don't make it fun," or ... You know what I mean. However many times such things are actually said, it is often. That learning should be fun is a given, in Christian education circles as elsewhere. This is the so-called "*Sesame Street* effect": if learning isn't fun it isn't any good (Bauerlein 2008, 106).

Well, then, should learning be fun? I suppose it should, all things being equal: as long as the purposes of education are being fulfilled, as long as the fun doesn't distract from the learning and is related to it, and so on. What's wrong with fun? Isn't it easier to do almost anything when it's fun?

Perhaps. But of course there are considerations. For a start, underlying most comments about the need for learning to be fun is the assumption that it isn't. A too-common view is that learning is a deadly boring exercise imposed by laws created by equally boring adults on already overcivilized children, an enormous hindrance to their freedom, not to mention their natural love of play, their more important need for physical exercise or social interaction. Learning, it is assumed, is *not* fun. To do it profitably therefore requires that we make it so, and those who are best at making it so, it follows, are the best teachers.

But how have we managed so thoroughly to convince nearly everyone, especially children, that their education, this thing we think so important that almost everywhere we mandate that they be improved by it—how did we manage to convince them that it was so uninteresting, so unpalatable, that, like broccoli or castor oil, it required subterfuge to choke it down? If we genuinely believe education important—essential to the survival of a democratic republic, for many an important ingredient in personal fulfillment, in the view of some the *summum bonum* of a civil society—why should it need so much sugar and artificial coloring, so much ingenuity and special training in devising play, puzzles, and prizes, just to get children through it? I thought education was a good thing, a desirable thing, a pearl of great price. Ought we not to believe that its inherent value, by itself, is reason enough to make it worth our best efforts? Why does it need to be, at almost any cost, made fun?

Second, isn't it possible that in this emphasis on making learning fun it will be the fun and not the learning that becomes the point—as it nearly always does? When we say that Mr. Smeegs is such a good history teacher because he makes history so fun, it is usually the fun we are remembering and not the history.

All education success has to be measured by its purposes. Does the student, as a result of our teaching, now know history, or English, or chemistry? That is the question—because that is the point of courses in history, English, and chemistry. That the subject is fun is relevant only to the degree that the fun contributes to the end for which it is being taught, namely, that it be learned. If it would be learned better by being taught in the absolute absence of fun, then the absence of fun ought to be the condition of its teaching—because, again, that is the point of teaching it. By the same token, if the class is a gigantic, whopping success of fun, but nothing is learned, then the entire exercise is a waste of everyone's time, educationally speaking anyway.

That is not to say that even in the important business of education we ought not occasionally to roll back, relax, drop what we're doing, and forget about our work long enough to be able better to take it up again. That is simply good sense, and an attempt to not take ourselves too seriously. But that is a very different thing from the requirement for subjects and their teaching always to be fun.

Third, why should fun be the index of success or failure in anything, unless it is having fun? Should we not be saying rather that Mr. Smeegs' history class is good because he makes the subject compelling, or thought provoking, or intellectually challenging, or simply rigorous? Are there not values more important than fun by which to judge an experience, especially perhaps in education? To a large extent the purpose of education is to lift up, to edify, to lead students into a profounder, more informed view of things than they now have, to demonstrate that a mature, a genuinely educated appreciation of the world, includes an understanding that the world is terrifying, tragic, confusing and mysterious, as well as beautiful and delightful; that it is much, much bigger and grander than anything that could be described merely as fun. If we teach in a way that emphasizes fun-ness, we may obscure the fact that fun-ness is a very minor aspect of the world's character. The means of our teaching sabotages one of our teaching's ends. Fun, after all, is a pretty insignificant consideration in the life of greatness, not to mention Christian greatness. Why make it a priority, not to say determinative, in our teaching?

What the teacher ought to be doing is spending his time coming to terms with his subject so thoroughly as to be able to draw out its inherent interest, demonstrating that the history or literature or math is important in and of itself, not because it can somehow be massaged or manipulated or otherwise rendered fun, as if it needed some special sauce or sizzle to make it worth studying.

To all such admonitions there is appended a down-to-earth reservation. Everyone knows that hard intellectual work, no matter how important or currently neglected, has to be approached with grace, humility, and a sensitivity to the age and ability of those we desire to be exercised by it. You can't require either the same seriousness or the same results from third graders as you do from college-bound seniors. Not even seniors need to be bludgeoned with the gravity of what they are doing. It is grave, of course, in the sense that they are obligated to do it well, but it is certainly not the most important thing any of us do, as Christians will be the first to acknowledge. To put what we are doing in its proper context, however, in a biblical and reasonable way, is not the same as believing that it all has to be fun, or that making it fun is the best means of fulfilling its purpose.

Neither am I saying, in attempting to take the shine off of the contemporary obsession with fun in the classroom, that teaching and learning ought therefore to be morose, soporific, or otherwise intentionally un-fun. If we are doing our work with the diligence, enthusiasm, and sense of high privilege, not to say humor, it deserves, then it ought to be enjoyable for our students as well as ourselves, but not in a way that is concocted, tacked on, unconnected to the subject itself. Teachers of English ought to think *The Divine Comedy* (or *The Love Song of J. Alfred Prufrock*) so profound or complex or ingenious—so interesting—that it is satisfying at least, maybe even, well, fun. That they once thought it so is probably why they became English teachers in the first place. It is now their responsibility and pleasure to stir a similar enthusiasm in their students—because the subject really is profound, ingenious, and complex, and therefore worth studying, whether or not it is fun in the usual sense. If the subject is neither profound nor complex nor ingenious, they have the challenge, and the fun, of trying to demonstrate why it isn't.

The greater thrill may come in having accomplished something decidedly not fun: the marathon completed, the mountain climbed, or storm survived. If the experience had been fun, all that made it what it was—gratifying, memorable, soul shaping—all those things would have been missed. It was good only because it was tough, terrifying, an adventure. Just as we ask students to prove themselves physically on court or field, why not allow them the opportunity to learn the thrill of accomplishing something difficult academically and intellectually: a poem understood, a calculus differential solved, a figure drawn well—not in every case fun, but that much sweeter therefore in its accomplishing. Or in its failing, because failure too has lessons that should not, must not, be missed if we are to be complete. It's the Christian virtue of perseverance (as well as pluck, courage, love of a challenge) we're after, and it is a lot more important than having fun; nor will it be learned if everything, all the time, is merely fun.

We require of our athletes, after all, that they run until they drop, with never an apology for its not being fun—because the training is secondary to and required for something else, the contest, where we want to prevail, and where it counts. I have never understood why we don't encourage the same approach to academic work—unless it is because we don't take academics with the same seriousness as we do athletics.

The contemporary world's obsession with fun ought, in any case, to alert us that from a Christian point of view something might be wrong with it, with too much emphasis on it anyway. You can be assured, besides, that it will not be long before the experts will be telling us, "We've emphasized fun too much. Our young people have been shortchanged by our doing so. It's time we got earnest." There is nothing as fickle as fad in education. Learning is learning. It is what it is. It is also an extraordinary privilege and an extraordinary luxury, one that children in some parts of the world walk miles through steaming jungles to obtain. Let's teach our students to value it for what it is—and along the way they will perhaps learn that there are thrills and delights in doing the hard thing, thrills and delights they can get no other way. You cannot enjoy the stunning panorama unless you climb the highest peak to see it.

If our goal is the highest peak, then whatever is required to get us there is what we will do: whatever is most effective, most thorough, whatever does best what we want done. If it is also fun, so much the better, but its being fun, as regards the results we desire, is irrelevant. Fun may be a pleasant by-product, but it is not a primary consideration, unless it can be demonstrated that fun will contribute to our accomplishing what we want to accomplish. There are some things that in the doing are simply *not* fun, and nothing we do will change that. The pleasure, the joy, the exhilaration of success comes at the finish, and it is of a richer, fuller sort than could be described as fun.

For Further Discussion

Chapter 1

1. Why do you think the author describes the purposes of education by the three Rs?
2. What does the author mean by "the transcendent aims of education"?
3. What is the point of the juxtaposition "school vs. education"?
4. In what ways did the medieval parish school represent "a new kind of education"?
5. Why does the writer say that "the important question" from a Christian point of view is "why schools at all?"

Chapter 2

1. Why does the author claim that "from a strictly biblical point of view" there may be a case for a Christian rejection of liberal learning?
2. On what grounds did the early Church adopt the classical scheme of education?
3. Why or why not in your understanding is "doing education" in terms of a Christian worldview not a violation of good scholarship?
4. What does the author mean by "attempting to get biblical instruction by classical means"?
5. What is the point of the author's distinction between Nature and Grace?

CHAPTER 3

1. The author claims that we are distracted in schools, in two ways. What are they? Do you agree? Why or why not?
2. What do you make of the author's use of C. S. Lewis' description of his schooldays routine? Is it relevant for our situation?
3. Do you agree with Bauerlein's critique of the effects of technology on education and citizenship? Why or why not?
4. How would you assess "the impact of technology" on education?
5. Do you think that, overall, the criticisms of education in chapter 3 are exaggerated? Why or why not?

CHAPTER 4

1. In your opinion, were Jefferson and Mann correct in their convictions about the relationship of education to democracy? Why or why not?
2. Given what you know about the sort of education Jefferson was advocating, how useful do you think it was/is?
3. In what sense is democracy a Christian thing?
4. Do you think the author's "qualifications" need to be made? Why or why not?
5. Do you agree that democracy has had deleterious effects on Christianity? Why or why not?

CHAPTER 5

1. Why, in your view, was leisure so important for the Greeks? Were they right?
2. In your opinion, do American students need more leisure? Why or why not?
3. What do you make of the attempt to apply "Be still and know that I am God" to Christian education?
4. What do you think of Pieper's understanding of leisure?
5. How might leisure be made more a part of the modern Christian school's life? Or should it be? Why or why not?

Chapter 6

1. What do you understand "the Socratic method" to be?
2. Do you agree that the greater responsibility for learning should be on the student rather than on the teacher? Why or why not?
3. The author maintains that the Socratic method "offers opportunities for the exercise of Christian charity." How so?
4. What do you make of the author's case for using the Socratic method in math and science classes?
5. Would you agree that a Socratic-style classroom does not require smart students?

Chapter 7

1. Has the author made his case that "the pedagogy of the Son of God" was not Socratic? Why or why not?
2. How would you describe Jesus' use of questions?
3. Was Jesus, in your view, a philosopher? Why or why not?
4. What do you make of the author's explication of Jesus' "interpersonal style"?
5. In your view, was Jesus in any sense "the model modern teacher"?

Chapter 8

1. Do you agree that there is too much emphasis on the need for education to be "useful"? Why or why not?
2. Do you agree that, as the author says, theory upholds practice; that is, "neglect or deny the theory and the practice expires"? Explain.
3. What does the author mean by "using the curriculum"? Do you agree that the practice should be avoided? Why or why not?
4. What do you make of the author's comparison of learning and worship?
5. How would you describe the proper role of education in the formation of citizenship or the formation of virtue? Or is there any role in either case?

CHAPTER 9

1. Do you agree that the liberal arts comprise subjects that "most students don't want to know"? Why or why not?
2. Do you agree with attempts to go back to ancient and medieval curriculums? Why or why not?
3. John Henry Newman said that "liberal education makes not the Christian, not the Catholic, but the gentleman." What did he mean? Do you agree? Why or why not?
4. What does it mean to say that liberal knowledge is "its own end"? Do you agree? Why or why not?
5. To what extent should we in Christian schools be prosecuting an education that is "useless" and "rooted in the past"?

CHAPTER 10

1. Do you agree that the question whether academic education is for everyone is our "most deeply practical and soul-searching" problem? Why or why not?
2. Do you think an academic education *is* for everyone? Why or why not?
3. In your view, is Christian education elite or elitist? Why or why not?
4. Do you agree that there are problems built into the attempt to give everyone an education? Explain.
5. How should Christians approach these problems? On what grounds?

WORKS CITED

Ansary, Tamim. Should college teach a trade? *Encarta*. http://encarta.
msn.com.

Antioch University. 2002–03. Horace Mann. http://www.phd.antioch.
edu/Pages/horacemann.

Aristotle. 1970. *The basic works of Aristotle*. Ed. Richard McKeon. New
York: Random House.

Arnold, Matthew. 1994. *Culture and anarchy*. Ed. Samuel Lipman. New
Haven, CT: Yale University Press.

Augustine. 1958. *The city of God*. Trans. Gerald G. Walsh, Demetrius
B. Zema, Grace Monahan, and Daniel J. Honan. Ed. Vernon J.
Bourke. Garden City, NY: Image Books.

Babbitt, Irving. 1908. *Literature and the American college: Essays in
defense of the humanities*. New edition with introd. by Russell Kirk.
Washington, DC: National Humanities Institute, 1986.

Baillie, John. 1945. *What is Christian civilization?* London: Oxford
University Press.

Barber, Benjamin R. 1999. Education and democracy: Summary and
content. In Gilreath 1999, 134–152.

Barclay, William. 1959. *Train up a child: Educational ideals in the ancient
world*. Philadelphia, PA: Westminster Press.

Barzun, Jacques. 1958. Science vs. the humanities: A truce to the nonsense on both sides. *Saturday Evening Post*, May 3.

———. 1991. *Begin here: The forgotten conditions of teaching and learning*.
Ed. Morris Philipson. Chicago, IL: University of Chicago Press.

———. 2000. *From dawn to decadence*. New York: HarperCollins.

Bauerlein, Mark. 2008. *The dumbest generation: How the digital age stupefies young Americans and jeopardizes our future (Or, don't trust anyone under 30)*. New York: Jeremy P. Tarcher/Penguin.

Bauman, Michael. 2004. The second death of Socrates. *Boundless Webzine*. http://www.boundless.org. Accessed 12/17/2007.

Blackburn, Simon. 1994. *The Oxford dictionary of philosophy*. Oxford, UK: Oxford University Press.

Boswell, James. n.d. *Life of Johnson*. London: Oxford University Press.

Bouchier, David. 1989. American higher education takes too long and fails to offer students what they want. *Chronicle of Higher Education*. April 26.

Butterfield, Herbert. 1962. *The universities and education today*. London: Routledge and Kegan Paul.

Channing, William Ellery. 1985. Self-culture. In *William Ellery Channing: Selected writings*. Ed. David Robinson. New York: Paulist Press.

Chesterton, G. K. 1953. *Selected essays*. London: Collins.

———. Bernard Shaw and America. 1960. In *The man who was Chesterton*, ed. Raymond T. Bond. Garden City, NY: Image Books.

Clark, Gordon H. 1946. *A Christian philosophy of education*. Grand Rapids, MI: Eerdmans.

Cohen, Patricia. 2009. In tough times, the humanities must justify their worth. *New York Times* (February 24). http://www.nytimes.com/2009/02/25/books/25human.html.

Confucius. 1997. *The analects of Confucius*. Trans. Simon Leys. New York: W. W. Norton.

Dahl, Robert A. 1989. *Democracy and its critics*. New Haven, CT: Yale University Press.

Davidson, F., ed. 1954. *The new Bible commentary*. 2nd ed. Grand Rapids, MI: Eerdmans.

Davis, Jeffry, and Leland Ryken. The future of Christian liberal arts at Wheaton: Drawing upon classical and Protestant foundations for direction. www.wheaton.edu/FandLpdf/DavisRyken.pdf. Article no longer available.

De Gruchy, John W. 1995. *Christianity and democracy: A theology for a just world order*. Cambridge, UK: Cambridge University Press

Dickson, Athol. 2003. *The gospel according to Moses: What my Jewish friends taught me about Jesus*. Grand Rapids, MI: Brazos Press.

Disraeli, Isaac. 1868. *The literary character; or, The history of men of genius*. New York: W. J. Widdleton.

Edmondson, Henry T., III. 2006. *John Dewey and the decline of American education*. Wilmington, DE: ISI Books.

Eliot, T. S. 1949. *Christianity and culture: The Idea of a Christian society and notes towards the definition of culture.* New York: Harcourt, Brace.

Fanton, Jonathan F. 2007. Do video games help kids learn? Introductory remarks given at Digital Media and Learning panel discussion, Chicago, IL, February 8.

Ferguson, Sinclair B., David F. Wright, and J. I. Packer, eds. 1988. *New dictionary of theology.* Downers Grove, IL: InterVarsity.

Freeman, Kenneth J. 1922. *Schools of Hellas: An essay on the practice and theory of ancient Greek education from 600 to 300 BC.* London: Macmillan.

Fuchs, Thomas, and Ludger Woessman. 2004. Computers and student learning: Bivariate and multivariate evidence on the availability and use of computers at home and at school. CESifo Working Paper 1321. Quoted in Bauerlein 2008, 120–21.

Gamble, Richard M., ed. 2007. *The great tradition: Classic readings on what it means to be an educated human being.* Wilmington, DE: ISI Books.

Gilreath, James, ed. 1999. *Thomas Jefferson and the education of a citizen.* Honolulu, HI: University Press of the Pacific.

Harrington, Norris Archer. 2000. What is the Socratic method? *Classical Homeschooling* (Summer).

Heclo, Hugh. 2007. *Christianity and American democracy.* With responses by Mary Jo Bane, Michael Kazin, and Alan Wolfe. Cambridge, MA: Harvard University Press.

Hirsch, E. D., Jr. 1996. *The schools we need and why we don't have them.* New York: Doubleday.

Honoré, Carl. 2008. *Under pressure: Rescuing our children from the culture of hyper-parenting.* New York: HarperOne.

Hu, Winnie. 2007. Seeing no progress, some schools drop laptops. *New York Times.* May 4. www.nytimes.com/2007/05/04/education/04laptop.html. Quoted in Bauerlein 2008, 124.

Hutchins, Robert M., 1952. *The great conversation: The substance of a liberal education.* The Great Books of the Western World, vol. 1. Chicago, IL: Encyclopaedia Britannica.

Iacocca, Lee. 2007. *Where have all the leaders gone?* With Catherine Whitney. New York: Scribner.

Jefferson, Thomas. 1904. *The writings of Thomas Jefferson.* 20 vols. Ed. Andrew A. Lipscomb and Albert Ellery Bergh. Washington, DC: Thomas Jefferson Memorial Association.

Jerome. 1954. Letter XXII, To Eustochium. Nicene and post-Nicene fathers, vol. 6. Ed. Philip Schaff and Henry Wace. Grand Rapids, MI: Eerdmans.

Johnson, Kirk. 2000. Do computers in the classroom boost academic achievement? www.heritage.org/research/education/CDA00-08cfm. Quoted in Bauerlein 2008, 120.

Johnson, Steven. 2005. *Everything bad is good for you: How today's popular culture is actually making us smarter.* New York: Riverhead Books.

Justin Martyr. 1908. The second apology. The ante-Nicene fathers, vol. 1. Ed. Alexander Roberts and James Donaldson. Grand Rapids, MI: Eerdmans.

Kelsey, Candice M. 2007. *Generation MySpace: Helping your teen survive online adolescence.* New York: Marlowe and Company.

Kierkegaard, Soren [Johannes Climacus, pseud.]. 1946. *Philosophical fragments.* Trans. David F. Swenson. Princeton, NJ: Princeton University Press.

Kimball, Bruce A. 1986. *Orators and philosophers: A history of the idea of liberal education.* New York: Teachers College Press.

Klein, Jacob. 1985. *Lectures and essays.* Ed. Robert B. Williamson and Elliott Zuckerman. Annapolis, MD: St. John's College Press.

Kralovec, Etta. 2003. *Schools that do too much: Wasting time and money in schools and what we can all do about it.* Boston, MA: Beacon 150.

Kreeft, Peter. 2002. *Socrates meets Jesus.* Downers Grove, IL: IVP Books.

———. 2007. *The philosophy of Jesus.* South Bend, IN: St. Augustine's Press.

Laertius, Diogenes. 1909. *The lives and opinions of eminent philosophers.* Trans. C. D. Yonge. London: George Bell and Sons.

Leithart, Peter J. 2008. The new classical schooling. *Intercollegiate Review* 43, no. 1 (Spring): 3–12.

Levine, Donald N. 2007. *Powers of the mind: The reinvention of liberal learning in America.* Chicago, IL: University of Chicago Press.

Lewis, C. S. 1939. Our English syllabus. In *Rehabilitations and other essays.* London: Oxford University Press.

———. 1949. Learning in war-time. In *The weight of glory and other addresses.* New York: Macmillan.

————. 1955. *Surprised by joy: The shape of my early life.* New York: Harcourt Brace Jovanovich.

————. 1961. *The Screwtape letters* and *Screwtape proposes a toast.* New York: Macmillan.

————. 1967. Christianity and literature. In *Christian reflections.* Ed. Walter Hooper. Grand Rapids, MI: Eerdmans.

————. 1986. Democratic education. In *Present concerns.* Ed. Walter Hooper. New York: Harcourt.

Lucian. 1961. *Anacharsis, or athletics,* vol. 4. Trans. A. M. Harmon. Cambridge, MA: Harvard University Press.

Mac Donald, Heather. 1998. Why Johnny's teacher can't teach. *City Journal* (Spring).

Maritain, Jacques. 1980. *Christianity and democracy.* Trans. Doris C. Anson. New York: Books for Libraries.

Marrou, H. I. 1956. *A history of education in antiquity.* Trans. George Lamb. Madison, WI: University of Wisconsin Press.

Merriam-Webster, Incorporated. 2003. *Merriam-Webster's Collegiate Dictionary.* 11th ed. Springfield, MA: Merriam-Webster, Incorporated.

Neuhaus, Richard John. 1981. *Christianity and democracy: A statement of the Institute on Religion and Democracy.* Washington, DC: Institute on Religion and Democracy.

Newman, John Henry. 1982. *The idea of a university.* Ed. Martin J. Svaglic. Notre Dame, IN: University of Notre Dame Press.

Newsome, David. 1961. *Godliness and good learning: Four studies on a Victorian ideal.* London: John Murray.

Padover, Saul K., ed. 1943. *The complete Jefferson.* New York: Duell, Sloan and Pearce.

Pater, Walter. 1905. *Plato and Platonism: A series of lectures.* London: Macmillan.

Pieper, Josef. 1998. *Leisure, the basis of culture.* Trans. Gerald Malsbary. South Bend, IN: St. Augustine's Press.

Plato. 1952. *The dialogues of Plato.* Trans. Benjamin Jowett. The Great Books. Chicago, IL: Encyclopaedia Britannica.

Plato. 1961. *The collected dialogues of Plato.* Ed. Edith Hamilton and Huntington Cairns. Bollinger Series LXXI. New York: Pantheon Books.

Princeton Review. 2007. Top 10 most popular majors. http://www.princestonreview.com. Article no longer available.

Quintilian. 1989. *The institutio oratoria of Quintilian*, vol. 1. Trans. H. E. Butler. The Loeb Classical Library, ed. G. P. Goold. London: Harvard University Press.

Random House, Inc. 1997. *Random House Webster's Unabridged Dictionary*. 2nd ed. New York: Random House.

Riesen, Richard A. 2002. *Piety and philosophy: A primer for Christian schools*. Phoenix, AZ: ACW Press.

——. 2007. *School and sports: A Christian critique*. Monrovia, CA: Grasshopper Books.

Rudolph, Frederick. 1990. *The American college and university: A history*. Athens, GA: University of Georgia Press.

Runes, Dagobert D., ed. 1972. *Dictionary of philosophy*. Totowa, NJ: Littlefield, Adams.

Sayers, Dorothy L. 1947. *The lost tools of learning*. http://www.gbt.org/text/Sayers.html.

——. 1949. The greatest drama ever staged. In *Creed or Chaos?* Manchester, NH: Sophia Institute Press.

Schall, James V. 2001. *On the unseriousness of human affairs: Teaching, writing, playing, believing, lecturing, philosophizing, singing, dancing*. Wilmington, DE: ISI Books.

——. 2006. *The life of the mind: On the joys and travails of thinking*. Wilmington, DE: ISI Books.

Shuppe, Edward P. The practical teaching methods of Jesus Christ. A paper presented at the Sunday School Teachers' Workshop of the South Atlantic District. http://www2.mlc-wels.edu/schone/jesusmasterteacher.pdf.

Snyder, Tamar. Liberal arts grads—Laughing all the way to the bank. http://uwf.edu.

Sowell, Thomas. 1993. *Inside American education: The decline, the deception, the dogmas*. New York: Free Press.

Spangler, Ann, and Lois Tverberg. 2009. *Sitting at the feet of Rabbi Jesus: How the Jewishness of Jesus can transform your faith*. Grand Rapids, MI: Zondervan.

Stein, Robert H. 1978. *The method and message of Jesus' teachings*. Philadelphia, PA: Westminster Press.

Svaglic, Martin J. 1982. Introd. to *The idea of a university*, by John Henry Newman. Notre Dame, IN: University of Notre Dame Press.

Taylor, Vincent. 1949. *The formation of the gospel tradition*. London: Macmillan.

Tertullian. 1980. On prescription against heretics. The ante-nicene fathers, vol. 3. Ed. Alexander Roberts and James Donaldson. Grand Rapids, MI: Eerdmans.

Tocqueville, Alexis de. 1966. *Democracy in America.* Trans. George Lawrence. Ed. J. P. Mayer and Max Lerner. New York: Harper and Row.

Tolbert, La Verne. 2000. *Teaching like Jesus: A practical guide to Christian education in your church.* Grand Rapids, MI: Zondervan.

Wagoner, Jennings L., Jr. 1999. "The knowledge that is most useful to us": Thomas Jefferson's concept of utility in the education of republican citizens. In Gilreath 1999, 115–133.

Waugh, Evelyn. 1998. Scott-King's modern Europe. In *The complete stories of Evelyn Waugh.* Boston: Little, Brown.

Weaver, Richard M. 1984. *Ideas have consequences.* Chicago, IL: University of Chicago Press.

Wells, H. G. 1961. *The outline of history.* Rev. by Raymond Postgate. Garden City, NY: Garden City Books.

Welsh, Patrick. 2008. A school that's too high on gizmos. *washingtonpost. com.* February 10.

Wilson, Douglas L. 1999. Jefferson and literacy. In Gilreath 1999, 79–90.

Wilson, Marvin R. 1989. *Our father Abraham: Jewish roots of the Christian faith.* Grand Rapids, MI: Eerdmans.

Wolfe, Alan. 2007. Whose Christianity? Whose Democracy? In Heclo 2007, 185–208.

INDEX OF BIBLE REFERENCES

Name and Subject Index